# SIDEMAN

# SIDEMAN

## THE LONG GIG OF W. O. SMITH

### A MEMOIR

RUTLEDGE HILL PRESS

NASHVILLE, TENNESSEE

Published in Nashville, Tennessee, by Rutledge Hill Press, Inc.,
513 Third Avenue South, Nashville, Tennessee 37210

Typography by Bailey Typography, Nashville, Tennessee
Design by Harriette Bateman, Studio Six

**Library of Congress Cataloging-in-Publication Data**

Smith, W. O. (William Oscar), 1917-1991
    Sideman, the long gig of W. O. Smith : a memoir.
      p.    cm.
    Includes index.
    ISBN 1-55853-132-7
    1. Smith, W. O. (William Oscar), 1917-1991.   2. Jazz musicians—
    United States—Biography.   3. Afro-American musicians—Biography.
    I.  Title
    ML419.S64A3   1991
    787.5'165'092—dc20                                           91-25226
    [B]                                                          CIP MN

Printed in the United States of America
1 2 3 4 5 6—96 95 94 93 92 91

## For Kitty

*Without her love, faith, sacrifice, and
nagging, there would have been no
doctorate, no career at Tennessee State
University, no Community Music School,
no book. The rest is unthinkable. As it is, I
am happy and grateful.*

# FANFARE

**W**hen I left the little town of Cheraw, South Carolina, for the big city of Philadelphia in 1935, I had to learn fast how to be cool and street-wise, and how to stay out of harm's way. Those were big lessons. I was eighteen, and maybe a little bit scared—but not much—and I didn't want my country ways to show. I got by with a lot of luck and a little help from my friends.

Down the street and around the corner from where we lived, W. O. Smith had a poolroom. He also had a son, Oscar, who was my age. They had come up from Georgia long before me and my family. Oscar was in high school, and he played bass fiddle. We started out in music together. For more than a year—until I left for New York in 1937—we were members of the Frankie Fairfax Band. For such a little fellow, Oscar could make a mighty big sound thumping that bass. It was about twice as big as he was, but he sure knew how to handle it.

In 1943 our paths crossed again in Philly. I had a quartet playing at the Downbeat Club there, and Oscar played with us for a little while before he went into the service. Then, after the war, we both ended up back in New York. I used to see him at a musicians' hangout called the White Rose Bar in midtown Manhattan. I was about to take my band out on the road, and I asked Oscar to go with us; but he had a wife and baby by then, and he was in school at NYU. So he couldn't do it. Instead, he introduced me to Ray Brown. "This cat is one of the best," Oscar said. He didn't lie.

Once or twice in later years, I ran into Oscar in places like

Houston and Nashville, or back in Philly. He was always the kind of guy who went out of his way to be nice. I remember playing with the Nashville Symphony one year when he was a member of the orchestra and going home with him afterward to meet his wife and kids and others who came and went as we sat around the kitchen table talking. Those things—the family, the food, the friends, the music—pretty much told you about the man. He was basic and unpretentious. What you saw was what you got.

That's the way he has always approached music, too. Oscar played what I would call big-band bass—he was the rhythm section for about a dozen other guys. I always thought he had the ability to go solo, to explore the outer limits, but he chose to harmonize instead. I think his choice reflected his personality. He was always a team player, concerned about his companions and eager to make them look good. Sideman extraordinaire—that's Oscar.

Of all the musicians I've had the pleasure of associating with, I can say that Oscar Smith was among the most gifted. His timing and resolution were almost perfect. He helped me discover my own sense of harmony and rhythm. I learned a lot from him in my early career, and I also found in him a friend for life.

Anyone who is seriously interested in a historical account of the early days of jazz will find a lot to learn and a lot to like in this book. It's the story of a great sideman—my main man, Oscar Smith. If you know the music, you'll love the words.

Be-boppingly yours,

Dizzy Gillespie

# Warmup
## WITHOUT NOTES

**I** am a witness, an anonymous witness. If I had realized all that was happening, I would have kept notes. Instead, I have to rely on memory, which fortunately is still quite good in this, my eighth decade of life. I can't remember everything, of course, so some stories may tend to be a little romanticized, but my wish and intent are to be as objective and accurate as I possibly can.

A lot has happened to me and to the world since I was born in rural Georgia in 1917. Through war and peace, depression and inflation, social and technological revolutions, and unending cultural cycles, most of us have stumbled along like so many sleepwalkers. But I have always tried to keep one eye open, hoping to see what's really going on. I consider myself lucky to have survived the perils of an adventurous life and to still be here, alive and well, in the waning years of the twentieth century.

In my formative years I was a witness to life among black folk in the inner-city ghettos of Philadelphia and New York. For most people in those circumstances, the daily grind held occasional moments of triumph and joy sandwiched between long hours of defeat and desperation. The casualty rate was shamefully, damnably high. Survival was mostly a matter of luck, but there could be other factors. In my case three things saved me: a God-fearing family, a superior high-school education, and a consuming passion for music.

My parents and grandparents, aunts and uncles, siblings, cousins, and other *de facto* kinfolks showed many of the enduring strengths of the black family and few of the weaknesses. They kept me pointed toward my goals in life. Others helped out along the way—a Sunday school teacher, a family doctor, several high-school and college mentors, and many giants of the jazz world, from Frank Fairfax and Coleman Hawkins to Duke Ellington and Dizzy Gillespie.

Out of this background, I developed an abiding faith in black talent and competency—call it black pride and confidence—and also a respect for the abilities and skills of many white people I have known. One paramount lesson has been indelibly stamped in my mind: people are people, regardless of race or any other identifying feature, and the only way to deal with them is out front, one by one, with no preconceived notions of individual worth or value.

I have been a witness to the birth and growth of jazz as an American art form. The connection between the early New Orleans jazzmen and modern jazz took place right before my eyes, and I watched in awe and even participated in some of it. It was, to say the least, an exhilarating experience. Meeting and knowing such masters of the art as Ellington, Gillespie, Hawkins, Bessie Smith, Fats Waller, and Nat "King" Cole was a privilege I will always cherish. Being a sideman with the likes of Hawkins and other great band leaders of the 1930s and '40s gave me a bird's-eye view of the jazz world. I only wish now that I had been far-sighted enough to keep a record.

Later on, when I was a college teacher of music, I was also a witness to the unfolding drama of the civil rights movement; and though I have been spared many of the harsher manifestations of civil wrongs, I rejoice in the victory of black Americans over racism and bigotry. It is not yet a complete victory, but it is substantial and continuing. I am, by nature, an optimist about the future.

It has been a long and interesting gig for me. I have played with abandon, giving myself to the music and to the life it opened up to me. I embrace it all, body and soul. I live, I hope. I am still a witness.

William Oscar Smith
Nashville, Tennessee

# ACKNOWLEDGMENTS

**M**ore people than I can count have encouraged me to write these memoirs, and many of them have actually helped me, in large ways and small, to see the project through. Kitty is first, followed by Jackie, Jay, and Joel. I could never name all the others, but a baker's dozen of them must be recognized.

I give public thanks to five who typed—and typed and typed. Pat Burton and Tammy Petty Brewer started, Ellen Ballinger and Dawn Bohannon finished, and Maxine Caruth carried the lion's share in between. And two who edited: Adele Mills Schweid and Natilee Duning. Not only did they do it well, they did it on short notice and on a very tight deadline. And one who gave a thousand favors: Juanita Dean.

Three others—Del Sawyer, Frank Sutherland, and Ken Wendrich—breathed life and permanence into the idea of a storefront music school for kids, and I owe them my deepest thanks and gratitude.

And two more: Richard Schweid and John Egerton. They coordinated this project, drove me unmercifully to get the writing done, led me to Larry Stone and Rutledge Hill Press when it was time to find a publisher, and promised me I'd be rich and famous as soon as the book came out. I can't wait.

Not only did all these people help me, they exemplified the best of Nashville, a caring, loving community. They're my kind of people, and this is my kind of town. I only wish I could give them and it as much as they've given me.

# CONTENTS

## THIRD SET: THE NASHVILLE YEARS

# SIDEMAN

*W. O. Smith, 1990* [Photo: Robin Hood]

# THE PHILADELPHIA-NEW YORK YEARS

# CHAPTER 1

# OUT OF GEORGIA

My story begins in the late spring of 1917 in Bartow, Georgia, where I was born. What followed soon after that event was unusual, to say the least. (I think of it that way, although blacks in the South at that time would not have considered it so.) My father, William Oscar Smith, was run out of town by the Ku Klux Klan. He had opened a grocery store next to a white business. They gave him twenty-four hours to clear out.

Leaving my mother and three of us children behind to stay with relatives, Dad made it to Philadelphia with seventy-five cents in his pocket. He rented a pushcart for a quarter and bought fifty cents' worth of cabbage. This investment he parlayed into enough money to buy some more cabbage to sell the next day. A store owner on South Street allowed him to set up a fruit stand in front of the business, and he was on his way. By the time he sent for us a few weeks later, he had gained a toehold in the heart of what most blacks idealized as the Promised Land.

Eventually he bought that store on South Street, and still later he converted it into a neighborhood poolroom. This establishment became well known and featured occasional tournaments with pool- and billiard-playing greats of the day, among them Greenleaf Rudolph and a cue master named Ponzi. My dad also acted as a paralegal counsel in the magistrate's court for many of his customers and for people of the neighborhood who could not afford a lawyer. He accomplished this with a fourth-grade education.

My mother, Ida Beatrice Smith, was one of those strong, farm-

*W. O. Smith, age eleven,*
*with sister Alma, age ten,*
*and their mother, Ida Smith,*
*in a city park in*
*Philadelphia, 1928.*

reared ladies with a queenly bearing. She had followed Dad to Philadelphia in that late spring of 1917, taking with her a nine-year-old son,
Charles Spencer (called C. S. by one and all), an eight-year-old daughter, Willie Mae, and a screaming infant. I have often wondered how
she managed such a difficult journey, spending two or three days and
nights in a succession of sooty train stations and Jim Crow day
coaches from Augusta through the Carolinas and Virginia to Washington, Baltimore, and finally Philly. The Chickenbone Special, they
called it—no diners, no beds, no Traveler's Aid Society, no rest for the
weary.

    She had a fifth-grade education, but you never would have
known it from her cultural interests. She believed in education so
strongly that my sister and I had to be practically dead before she
would let us stay home from school. After our demonstrations of
coughing and sneezing, she would say, "Get out of here and let the
school nurse send you home with a note." We had no choice because
in those days they had real truant officers who gave whoever they

*W. O. Smith, Sr.,*
*Philadelphia, about 1927*

caught a physical "workout" and who were thanked (not sued) by the parents. In all fairness, if we were actually sent home with a note, my mother gave us all the love and attention necessary. But she dealt with any disrespect to elders or sass immediately and on the spot.

My mother was also a psychologist. When a whipping was in order (thankfully, there weren't many), she sent us upstairs to wait. Then she proceeded with her normal business—telephone calls and the like—for what seemed an eternity. You had time to think! After the execution she would tearfully pray with you to remove this evil from your life. I got the message.

In those days black women could not try on clothes in the downtown department stores. Mother developed the talent of looking at a particular dress, then buying the material and making an exact duplicate. She later parlayed these skills into a dressmaking school. One day she sent me to Frank and Seder, a local department store, to pay a weekly bill. I stopped at a friend's house, and we put the money in a pot to buy some gin. (I must have been all of thirteen.) Needless to say, it ended badly. We all passed out, and my friend Leon Allen's mother arranged us across Leon's bed. When I got home the next morning, my mother did not say a word—that psychology again. I was so shaken that I proceeded to do the unthinkable: I got a job. With my newspaper route, I paid off that department store bill.

Her main legacy to me was her determination and motivation for me to get a college education. Her last orders to me when I took off for New York in 1938 were, "While you're there playing around, go to school." I registered at New York University because of this advice. After my father's death in 1936 during the Great Depression, she was unable to help me financially. She gave me more, though, for I could not have gone as far without her love and determination. Thank God she lived to see some of the results.

I was less than thirty days old when we went North in 1917, so I grew up knowing nothing of Georgia and considered Philadelphia my home. Also, in keeping with the black culture of the period and led by the glamour of Harlem and Chicago's Southside, I kept my southern origins secret. In my later years I have become increasingly aware of my heritage and my roots. I am proud to say now that I am a native of Georgia. Returning South in 1946 and witnessing since then the tremendous changes in race relations and opportunity, I now consider myself a Southerner, a Nashvillian, and a gentleman.

# CHAPTER 2

# BROWN STREET

**W**e lived throughout my childhood at 1306 Brown Street, just eight blocks from City Hall. The neighborhood was an authentic inner-city ghetto in North Philadelphia, with narrow, three-story row houses long since turned into multifamily units. Therein lay the problem: too many people sardined into too small a space. My father bought the house in about 1918 for six hundred dollars—I think he paid fifty dollars down. He almost lost it in the depression.

A census at 1306 Brown during my high-school years, 1931 to 1934, would have shown my mother Ida and father W. O., Sr., as heads of a household that was often a haven for our southern relatives entering the Philadelphia scene. There were usually four or more of us in the immediate family, but there were others as well almost all the time. C. S. was usually away on his frequent excursions throughout the United States as a hobo, visiting with us for a few days between trips. Willie Mae married before she was sixteen and lived with her husband in a house farther uptown on Mole Street, not far from Baker Field, home of the Philadelphia Phillies. We saw them only occasionally.

My younger sister Alma and I were the constants, along with my maternal grandmother, Rosie Wright (another exiled Georgian, of course). A stern and assertive person, she effectively ruled the household—ruled Alma and me, at least. Then there was Uncle Charlie, Grandmother's youngest son, a longshoreman, who introduced me to and developed my taste for good bourbon whiskey. The very idea of that was anathema to Grandmother, a holy and sanctified woman if there ever was one. She had the heart and soul of a crusading, temperance-minded feminist, and she would smash any bottle of liquor she could find hidden in the house. Uncle Charlie and I had to devise clever means of hiding booze from her. We managed to outwit her most of the time. We couldn't cuss around her, though. She simply wouldn't tolerate it, and Charlie found it the better part of wisdom to watch his tongue.

Another person who lived there a lot was my cousin, John Harmon, who was a year or so younger than I. We were friendly rivals and constant companions. I think of him as my brother. He's now the only one in this cast of characters besides me who's still living. We're the survivors.

Nothing much happens on a street like this—unless you count the police raids, the drunks, and the numbers writers with their Cadillacs. Also, you know all the members of the neighborhood gang. There is a sort of security in learning how to deal with this in your daily life.

Our gang was the Forty Thieves, led by Ali Baba, and they were a fact of life for me. There were the senior members (some of these guys were in their middle twenties) and the younger guys who were initiated. I was one of the neophytes at about age thirteen. I had mixed feelings about all this, but living in that neighborhood, it was judicious to associate for protection, especially if you went into another gang's turf. Their favorite practice upon catching an unfortunate transgressor was to stomp the individual. Stomping was exactly what it sounds like. Take about fifteen or more guys stomping one guy, and he'd be in pretty bad shape by the time the police arrived. So for that reason, and even though I knew better, I maintained a reluctant association with the formidable Forty.

There was a price to be paid for membership. I had to steal something to maintain credibility. My specialty was car radiator emblems, such as a small figure of "Winged Victory." Two or three of these a week were enough to keep the brothers off my case. I received about fifty cents for each emblem delivered. I didn't feel good about it, though, because some of these emblems sold new for up to thirty or forty dollars (especially Cadillac emblems). I didn't try anything heavier by way of stealing, because I didn't want to be there at all anyway. It went against my nature and upbringing.

I managed to miss all of the rumbles with warring gangs, using any excuse I could find. When later I became a sideman in one of Philadelphia's most popular bands, the excuses were easier (rehearsal, a gig, or something like that). The Forty Thieves threatened me with initiation (that is, full membership) along about my senior year at Central High School. I dreaded the initiation—it called for sex with a female gang moll witnessed by the gang and also blood mixing with Ali Baba and his key lieutenants. Blood mixing consisted of cutting a vein in your wrist and holding it against another cut wrist. The oath and the ritual followed.

The event that finally turned me off from the gang was the afternoon we went to Blatt's Grocery on the corner of Thirteenth and Brown. About fifteen or twenty guys would saturate the place, knowing that Mr. Blatt couldn't keep tabs on everybody. The store was relieved of groceries, edibles, and cigarettes. I stayed for a while in the rear, crouching so Mr. Blatt wouldn't see me. Mr. Blatt was a Jewish store owner who not only lived on the premises but carried many of the poorer families on the books. He knew me and my family, and if word got to 1306 Brown Street that I was in the latest hit on his store, I knew I'd be skinned alive. After a brief struggle with my conscience, I sneaked out so that the guys wouldn't miss me. I gradually disassociated myself from the gang, and they no longer made any demands on me.

Although we were all poor, most of us didn't realize it. We were happy with a whole lot less in terms of material things. Actually, the neighborhood was safe, especially to the residents who knew everybody. Our door was never locked. I never had a key until I was in college. One reason was that, in the absence of television and air conditioning, the chief entertainment for the unemployed and housewives was patrolling the front window, people-watching. They saw everything. It was impossible for a youngster to be in the wrong place or trying something unprescribed without its being immediately reported.

I found Brown Street a good place to grow up. There in the central city, close to City Hall, the main library was within easy walking distance, as were the museums, the academy of music, and other cultural offerings. Central Philly was great, but Brown Street was greater because we did not have poverty of spirit.

As I grew up, our dining room (really an all-purpose room) became a gathering place for the young black jazz musicians. Dizzy Gillespie and Jimmy Hamilton (clarinetist with Duke Ellington) would discuss and argue matters of music construction, form, and aesthetics as they pertain to jazz. A young West Philadelphia pianist, Calvin Jackson (later to challenge Art Tatum for keyboard supremacy) was also a member of the round table. There were many others. Through these exchanges I learned that music was not all play and self-indulgence, but some study, listening, and work.

My first instrument was a clarinet. It was an old battered Albert system clarinet given to me by Kaiser, a World War I vet who frequented my father's poolroom. I'm a little vague about this, but I must have been in about the third grade. I had no teacher or even an instruction book, so I had to learn by trial and error. This process drove my grandmother crazy, so I was subsequently banned from the interior of the house. Our back yard became my practice studio. The arrangement was satisfactory for me, but not for the neighbors, especially after five o'clock when they returned home from work. Also, my trial-and-error (mostly error) system did not reveal to me the mysteries of accidentals (sharps and flats). The usual children's tunes sounded unusual as they took on a Schoenberg, Hindemith, and Bartokian flavor.

I was selected to play third clarinet for the U.N.I.A. (United Negro Improvement Association) children's band, led by Marcus Garvey. Actually, they took in any kid who had an instrument. I was emotionally attached to the rather simple uniform of a satin shirt emblazoned with U.N.I.A. on the front. I was in deep bliss whenever we had a parade, usually down Ridge Avenue. Even though my skills were limited, I learned to play my part and the usual oom-pah-pah parts with the right notes at the right time. Our main piece was "Stony Point March." I had no understanding of Marcus Garvey's Back-to-Africa movement, nor was it important to me. At nine years of age, I was caught up in peer activities, in being part of something. Besides, my mother would have had to kill me to keep me from wearing the uniform and marching down Ridge Avenue.

Next in my musical life was a real teacher, Fred Tindley, whose father was the Reverend Tindley, founder of Tindley Temple and a historic figure in the evolution of black gospel music. Mr. Tindley— Fred—was basically a trumpet player, but he taught everything from piano to piccolo. This is not to imply that he knew all instruments; but in all fairness, he had good music sense, if not technique, and the ability to teach it. He started me on a violin and taught my sister piano. We had an old nineteenth-century piano—basically a box on four legs. Every home had a piano in those days, and in the absence of television, most young people entertained themselves with musical parties. A surprising amount of musical talent could be heard. Although I did not get the necessary technique for the violin, Mr. Tindley instilled in me an enthusiasm and curiosity about good music.

As to fingering, hand position, and bowing on the violin, I was basically on my own. Needless to say, I got it mostly wrong, but the enthusiasm and curiosity held up. I was to be that way the rest of my life. It was the catalyst for my going into music education and musicology. I had to figure out things like positions, double stops, and vibrato, not to mention a satisfactory tone. I was hooked on baroque composers like Corelli, Vivaldi, and Tartini, and would check the music out of the Philadelphia Library and agonize over problems of how to read and play the music. To be truthful, there were no rave notices, but in an amateur situation where extra violins were needed, somebody would recommend "this guy I know in north Philly who has a violin . . ."

There was a Settlement Music School in South Philadelphia at the time, which could have solved my problem, but it was located in the Italian enclave. I preferred to remain alive, so I did not pursue this option.

I did take on the First African Baptist Church's Sunday school orchestra. We played primarily church music and some extremely light classics. The attraction was its leader and violinist, Archie Durham. He was the first black person I had ever heard actually play pieces like Brahms' Hungarian Rhapsody No. 5 to the standards associated with the great white violinists like Fritz Kreisler and Albert Spalding, whom I occasionally heard on radio. I was flabbergasted, and even though there was not time for him to teach the group, his example opened up a world of possibility.

There was also, during the thirties, a Negro symphony orchestra that rehearsed at the Y.M.C.A. It was not the Philadelphia Orchestra, but I still was not good enough to play with them.

# CHAPTER 3

# CENTRAL AND MASTBAUM

*I*n 1984 I attended the fiftieth anniversary of my Central High School class, and that was a trip. It reminded me of Philadelphia in the thirties, the depression years, my real formative years.

Central High was an elitist school, with boys being selected from all over the city. Needless to say, there weren't many blacks, maybe twenty-five out of twenty-five hundred. It was not a fun school. The academic program was rigorous. I received a bachelor of science degree from Central and was admitted to all the colleges I applied for. The trouble was that it was the depression, and I couldn't afford Cornell, Dartmouth, Brown, or Northwestern. There weren't any "black" or "poor" scholarships in those days.

After graduation, with no employment, some of us were counseled into the first vocational music class at Mastbaum Vocational School. This was a great gift from the city of Philadelphia, and in retrospect it was to become my conservatory. Meyer Levin was the director. He was completely color-blind. Any miscreant would be chewed out immediately, regardless of race, color, or creed. He had exacting standards and high expectations, although there were not enough teachers (only three) to carry this out on an individual basis. We were still expected to sound like the Philadelphia Orchestra, the Edwin Franko Goldman Band, or the Budapest Quartet.

Mastbaum was located in Frankford, a section of Philadelphia that formed the upper limits of the "greater Northeast." The whole area was referred to by blacks as Johannesburg. At certain times we had to form groups in order to negotiate the two blocks from the building to the trolley stop. There is safety in numbers. Since we were on some white gang's turf, we waited until there were enough guys, especially if we had to walk the three or more miles home.

Mastbaum provided many opportunities for us to try different instruments. The school had an orchestra, a band, and various chamber groups. The main library of Philadelphia was rich in chamber music literature, so we would form congenial parties and play (or try to play) a Mozart trio or a Haydn quartet. Standard practice then was for a dispensable violinist to substitute for a missing viola. Having been relegated to the third violin part on many occasions, I had plenty of viola experience. Consequently, I seized this opportunity to do the real thing. I took up the viola on my own, wrestled with the baffling mysteries of the alto clef, and was eventually invited to fill out many a quartet, trio, or other group. I thank Mr. Levin and Mastbaum School for this experience. Anybody who has tried to play chamber music knows that there is no place to hide. You are on your own, and you have to listen in order to coordinate. For me, it was the ultimate school for musicianship.

I spent a couple of years at Mastbaum learning theory, music history, and orchestration and experiencing the orchestra, the band, and various chamber music groups. It was here that Mr. Levin created an instant bass section by waving off the last-stand fiddlers and telling us to check out basses, an instruction book, and come up with the bass part of the Mozart Symphony No. 40 by the next rehearsal. I was introduced to the tuba by Ross Wyre, one of the instructors.

To own your own instrument is the dream of every aspiring musician. Consequently, my parents set up a dollar-for-dollar program for me to buy a bass fiddle. The magic day came when I had saved up about $30. My father, a member of the South Street Merchants Association, took me to Sutphin's, a music store near the poolroom. The first thing he did on arrival was to put $75 on the cash register (he knew the owner). For about an hour we looked at and tried several instruments. Of course nothing under $125 was satisfactory. At the end of this frustrating experience, Dad said, "Let's go to another music store." With this remark he reached for the $75 on the register, but that was as far as he got. We left with the $125 King blond plywood bass durable enough to be the one advertised with a 300-pound man standing on it.

Mastbaum Vocational School was an incubator for many jazz musicians who made contributions through arrangements or performance. There I saw the money the students who were gigging spent in the lunchroom and made up my mind to study music and become a musician. The sharp band uniforms they wore didn't hurt either.

Being given the opportunity of two extra high-school years was like being red-shirted in football. The difference was that you had a chance to play all the way through. It was like becoming a six-year senior. I was sixteen when I graduated from Central. The two extra years at Mastbaum contributed to my maturity and self-reliance as a musician. I say self-reliance because of the lack of individual instruction and the competitive level of the students. Most, like me, were high-school graduates.

My crowning experience was being selected for the all-Philadelphia high-school orchestra. I was picked three years running and on three different instruments (viola, bass viol, and tuba). Some may quibble that I had two extra years to do it, but for me the satisfaction was enough. I was accepted by my peers and teachers as a contributing musician. It placed girls further down my list of priorities. That does not mean that I didn't notice a shapely leg or a pretty face, but music was first.

As important as music was, I was also learning about black history from Eustace Gay, editor of the *Philadelphia Tribune*. As our Sunday school teacher at Zion Baptist Church, he saw to it that we got information not available in the public schools. I had self-reliance from my parents, I was nurtured by the public schools, and I was developing a realization of my heritage. How could I lose?

Dad was a great guy and contributed in a very supportive way to my interest in music. He was not in any way a musician. I never heard him sing, not even in church. He did buy tickets for me to hear the Philadelphia Orchestra, especially when "Stock-oh-whiskey" (Stokowski) was conducting. He and I would make the long trolley trip to Willow Grove, Pennsylvania, to hear John Philip Sousa's band. That was his favorite group, and I think I was his favorite companion. He worked six days a week until midnight, and Sunday was his only day off. Several churches that we visited would ask him to sit in the pulpit, thinking that he was a visiting dignitary. I would carry out my part, and they evidently never suspected he was a poolroom operator. In those days people in the "Toasty" black churches sat according to color, with the near white on one side and the brown and black on the other. My father was light in color and I am brown, so we thoroughly enjoyed the deception. My wife and some other friends have noted the inherent impish qualities that I occasionally impart. It is because I learned from my father not to take myself too seriously.

Probably Dad's most traumatic experience after his Ku Klux Klan episode was the 1932 presidential election. Being born of parents who had experienced slavery, he was a lifelong Lincoln Republican. Because of the depression, he could not vote for Hoover, but his experience in Georgia would not allow him to vote for Franklin Roosevelt. Our whole family agonized with him. We watched a man who took his civic responsibilities very seriously wrestle with his soul as he stayed away from the polls for the first time since he was able to vote. He was spared a repeat of this terrible dilemma by his death before the election in 1936.

The year 1936 was a good one for me, except for that sad event. The death of W. O., Sr., was fairly sudden and unexpected. He was in his early fifties. It was so traumatic for me that to this day I do not remember a single thing about the funeral. It's as if I have a psychological block, a jolt of amnesia blotting it from my memory.

Dad's work schedule left us with very little time to be together, except for Sundays. What time we had, though, I would have to call quality time, to use a contemporary phrase, because he influenced me profoundly in several ways. He never used profane language, and now I rarely utter anything stronger than an occasional damn.

Another way he influenced me was in his interaction with the white community. He did business with them, and I sensed that there was mutual respect. He was the only black member of the South Street Merchants Association. I've always said that if I could produce with my Ph.D. on the scale he did with his fourth-grade education, I'd be a millionaire. Within our little circle I was known as "Little Oscar," and I didn't assume the title of W. O. until decades later. I couldn't do it earlier, simply because of my respect for the man. He was a real father who took his responsibilities seriously, and I have always tried to do the same.

In the four years between my graduation from Central High and my departure for New York, many fateful events took place in my life, but I was too young to appreciate them fully at the time. For example, my first gig was with Bessie Smith, the famous blues singer. I later found out that she was the first black woman to make commercial recordings. At the time I didn't know of her importance and place in history.

My experience came about because Jack Gee, who later was to

marry my widowed mother, had been married to Bessie Smith. Since she was to us a member of the older generation, we called her Aunt Bessie. I had been trying to learn bass violin for about three weeks when Mr. Gee asked me, "Son, do you want a bass job?" Since I was not yet a player, I grabbed at the chance, but I was also frightened at the prospect of this first gig.

The club was a very familiar place in Lawnside, New Jersey, an all-black town right across the Delaware River. I don't remember the name of the club, but while it was not of the chitterling-circuit variety, it was also clearly not the Waldorf. Bessie must have been down on her luck—why else would they want to hire me? I came cheap enough, something like two dollars a night. I asked the piano player, "Do you have the music?" He told me, "Don't worry. You'll know what to play." He was partially right, because with my black church and gospel background, the blues presented few problems concerning what bass notes to play. My problem was where to find them on a bass fiddle. I watched the piano player's left hand and tried to find corresponding finger positions on the string bass. The problem with this is that when the pianist hits a bass note, it's already too late to make the connection. I had to anticipate, or, in other words, hear where he was going. Somehow I lasted the first night and on through to the end of a four-week session.

What kind of person was Bessie Smith? She certainly knew a wide variety of blues, a lot of which were suggestive or even explicit. She sang these with a gruff and almost masculine raw power. I remember that she drank a lot of whiskey but would never offer me any. I guess she thought that at seventeen I was too young to drink. Little did she know! Anyway, she was nice to me, and when I visited her she would point to a dresser drawer loaded with all kinds of folding money. She would then say, "Son, get you some money." I never took a lot, five to ten dollars at the most. You have to remember that ten to twelve dollars was a weekly salary for most people at the time. The whole experience was a good one, and it focused my attention on listening to music in order to play.

The mid-thirties musical picture in Philly as far as black musicians were concerned included about four major groups. Doc Hyder and Jimmy Gorham had the two prestige big bands—twelve to fourteen pieces—and they played the major dances and the large dance halls. Harry Monroe had a smaller eight-piece, so-called "society" band. His group played primarily for the black bourgeoisie, which meant that they played less but got paid more. They played show tunes, the tango, the waltz, and things like that. Most of the sidemen had good jobs at the post office or in the city civil service. They were good-to-excellent musicians. Like the Jimmy Gorham and Doc Hyder groups, they were the older and established musicians. Monroe's band paid eight to ten dollars a night. The Gorham and Hyder groups paid four to five dollars. The younger groups got a percentage of the house, maybe, or two to three dollars—maybe.

None of the younger musicians would play for Monroe, even for the extra money, because of the sedate music. There was another band of Dixieland led by George Baquet from New Orleans. Most of us knew little about this group because they played the white hotel and club circuit. They probably paid the most. The younger arriving musicians like Dizzy Gillespie, Charlie Shavers, and Jimmy Hamilton were less concerned with how much they were paid than with not compromising on the quality of pure jazz. The two dollars, or more likely a percentage share of the attendance, was satisfaction enough for being able to play our standard of music. I wish the younger musicians of today would take note.

# CHAPTER 4

# PHILLY'S BIG BANDS

*T*he mid-thirties were exciting times for aspiring jazz musicians. There were plenty of role models, partly because the top players were so competitive. Just take your pick, say, among bassists Israel Crosby, Milton Hinton, and Walter Page to idolize and imitate. I did precisely that, much to my grandmother's dismay. We had a generational gap on how loud the phonograph or radio should be. Playing along with these artists and their great groups taught me a lot about bass lines and chordal strategies. There were lots of opportunities to see and hear our favorite bands, either at the theatres or even better at a dance hall. We didn't come to the dance hall to dance, and as a result I'm still a klutz in social dancing. We came to crowd the bandstand, observe, and make mental notes on the masters of the instruments. At the theatre we had to observe from a little farther out, but with a bit of luck we could meet our stars at the stage door and get into a little seminar on the art of playing. My immutable rule is: the greater the star, the more gracious he is apt to be about giving tips to aspiring players. I still say that if you don't know what you're doing, find somebody who is doing it and copy him to the best of your ability. At least it's a good start.

Right after my stint with Bessie Smith, I was asked by Shep Shepherd to bring my bass to a Jimmy Gorham rehearsal. Shep was a classmate of mine at Mastbaum School, and this was tantamount to my being considered as their next bassist. I was on clouds and notified all friends and family members of this impending honor. The Gorham orchestra was one of the most prestigious groups in Philadelphia in the eyes of younger musicians. I floated up to that first rehearsal at a private home in North Philadelphia awash in the glow of impending recognition and respect.

Shep was the drummer with Gorham and guided me through the intricacies of the famed Gorham book. Since this was a first-time experience, I had some problems, but I left with the feeling that I had it made. An announcement had been made concerning the time and date of the next rehearsal. I didn't pay any attention to the location, as everybody knew where the top bands rehearsed. Still in the clouds and awash with glory, I floated up to the next rehearsal complete with bass and pride.

What followed was the most traumatic experience of my life. I didn't hear any horns as I approached the house. I was still not apprehensive when I rang the bell. After an eternity, in utter disbelief I realized nobody was there! Rather than tell me that I didn't make it, they simply changed the location of the rehearsal. I was crushed. I returned home with that terminal feeling of ignominy and defeat. I couldn't tell my peers, family, or friends about the experience. I just had to deal with it alone, hurt, and feeling rejected. It was many years before I overcame the grudge, and then only after stints with some name bands had rebuilt my confidence.

Many other bands besides Jimmy Gorham's and Doc Hyder's were striving to make it in Philly in the mid-thirties. Most notable were the groups led by Charlie Gaines, Hot Lips Page, Madame Keene, and Bert Hall. No doubt this scene was duplicated in the black ghettos of many cities throughout the country. The whole scene was a natural outgrowth of our religious music, the depression, and decades of discrimination. Most of our role models were jazz musicians, plus a few athletes, like Joe Louis and Jesse Owens, of international athletic fame. In music we had the likes of Earl Hines, Fletcher Henderson, Duke Ellington, and later Count Basie. Everybody in the community knew the broadcast times and theatre dates. These were the main and most exciting events in our somewhat limited lives.

One result of this competitive state of affairs was the organization of some younger groups. The ones led by Frankie Fairfax and Bill Doggett were outstanding. They slugged it out in the mid-thirties for supremacy in the Philadelphia area. Both had brilliant young personnel, some of whom were later to make names for themselves on a national and even international scale. Dizzy Gillespie, Charlie Shavers, Jimmy Hamilton of Fairfax's group, Bill Doggett (later to be an arranger for Count Basie), and drummer Shadow Wilson were probably the best known.

There were also the West Philadelphia Dukes, a group of no-names who came from almost nowhere to achieve a top spot in popularity. The West Philadelphia Dukes were actually a social club, the euphemism for a gang that had turned to positive purpose. I was one of the group. We had guys who ranged from beginner to intermediate in musical ability, and we had guys who did not participate in music at all. Most were still in high school in 1936. We were fortunate to have Mr. Thompson as a counselor. He was highly motivated because he had three sons in the group. Since most of our rehearsals were at his house, he was usually present. We were rank amateurs who worked hard at playing the popular stock arrangements of the day. You could buy these arrangements of what we now call "Top Forty" tunes, especially the ones of Benny Goodman, Duke Ellington, and Count Basie. Eventually we were sought for dances, especially by the teen-age social clubs of the black community. After I finally got the orchestration right, we played a song entitled "Lamentations," my first creative effort. We had guys who developed into locally respected musicians. One of our pianists, Calvin Jackson, achieved international recognition.

We reached a pinnacle of sorts when we were booked to play a jazz battle with none other than Count Basie in the Strand Ballroom. We had mixed feelings about this, as we considered it an honor even to be considered, but we would have preferred to battle someone of lesser stature. In other words, we were scared. As a band, we were at the top of our game, playing the popular favorites just as they sounded on the juke box, but terror struck when we got ready to open the festivities with our first set. In confusion, we couldn't decide what we should play. We had made our reputation on the juke box hits of Ellington, Goodman, and Basie. Somebody said, "Let's play what got us here." With that encouragement, we lit right into Basie's "One O'Clock Jump" and followed with other Basie hits, which were our best numbers. I made like Walter Page. Joe Woods imitated Basie on piano. Vince Butler made like Lester Young. Our loyal fans loved it and egged us on. We were just like the record. We got off the stand feeling triumphant and inspired. We didn't notice the Count leaning back and nodding a slow "uh-huh."

What followed as the Basie entourage took the stand was awesome. We received a good old-fashioned blues lesson—something like a boxing lesson that a veteran professional boxer administers to a novice. Instead of playing "One O'Clock Jump" in the three-minute format of the record, they played it as if they were in a Kansas City dance hall. Basie pulled out all stops. The embarrassment went on for about fifteen minutes, and then they followed with other numbers we had played. Much chastened, we avoided all Basie tunes for the rest of the gig.

After I left the Dukes, I got to be the bassist with the newly formed Frankie Fairfax Orchestra with its home base at the Strand Ballroom in South Philadelphia. It turned out to be my most significant conservatory of music. The band was just right in its blend of older experienced musicians and young lions. The older guys included Whitey Grove (who was probably the darkest guy in the band) and Pete Brown, a dead ringer for Joe Louis, on trumpets; Tasso Richardson and Nelson Wapler, saxophones; Fairfax and Bert Claggett, trombones. Those were the veterans. John Berry, tenor sax, and Bert Hall, drums, were intermediate characters. Most of the young guys, ranging in age from the late teens to about twenty-three, were later to become famous. I didn't know this at the time, but I was aware of the electricity in this environment.

Rehearsals were a joy. Everybody was there at least an hour ahead of time. We were discovering each other, and, best of all, we were discovering music. We learned to play hard tunes with difficult chord changes. We played these challenging tunes starting in the original key and proceeding a half step up each chorus until we returned to the original key. Imagine playing tunes like "Body and Soul," "Sweet and Lovely," and "Smoke Gets in Your Eyes" in this fashion. If nothing else, a few weeks of this would give you control of your ax (your horn, or whatever you were playing). A year of this with frequent rehearsals and gigs would put anybody at the top of his game. This band did not play stock arrangements; we played only our own written or "head arrangements." With head or ear arrangements, we built up a repertoire in which no written music would be in sight.

Can you imagine a situation like this? Somebody starts off a riff (straight out of the black church or a blues pattern) and goes not more than couple of bars when he is picked up by the rest of the members in his section—we'll say it's the saxophone section—and within the space of two bars or less, the riff is harmonized with each saxophonist instinctively grabbing his part, usually with the correct notes. Then the trumpet section, at the correct instant, plays a counter riff, something like the call and response pattern of the black church. This, too,

*Frankie Fairfax and his orchestra, Philadelphia, 1935. Among those pictured are Fairfax, holding sheet music; trumpeter Dizzy Gillespie, to Fairfax's left; and W. O. Smith, holding bass violin.* [Photograph courtesy of Mrs. Kathryn Fairfax]

is instantly harmonized in three or four parts, depending on the number of trumpets. Mind you, everybody has different but effective notes. The trombone section, not to be outdone, then plays a counterpoint to the whole arrangement. From the very beginning, the rhythm section realizes harmonic patterns or chord changes implied by the first riff, and the result is a new addition to the repertoire. Mix all of this with appropriate solos by the most dynamic soloists accompanied by the appropriate section and the appropriate riff. What we usually got was a crowd-pleaser.

We gave them titles like "The Uptown Breakaway," "The Broadway Stomp," or "The Ridge Avenue Shuffle." This was the incubator for Count Basie's "One O'Clock Jump" and really the basis of the famous Basie style. Duke Ellington's band also used this procedure, and that's one reason there were problems in transcribing the famous Ellington book: a lot of it was not on paper. Professional arrangers from Fletcher Henderson on have transcribed or arranged this music until today I doubt that you could find a fourteen-piece group that could instinctively and harmonically make these "head" arrangements correctly. It was the genius of black music and the art and skill, not to mention ears, of the musicians of that period that provided the basis of much of what we hear today, whether it be rock, rhythm and blues, or jazz.

That was how the Fairfax band played. Ably led by the elders, the younger guys reaped the benefits by going on to make names for themselves, not only in Philadelphia but in New York, Chicago, and later the West Coast. They were Dizzy Gillespie, Charlie Shavers, Johnny Lynch, Bama Warwick, and Palmer Davis on trumpets; Harold Reed, John Brown, and Shorty Cawthon on saxophones; Calvin Jackson and Ernie Washington on piano; and Norman Dibble and Shadow Wilson on drums. I had the great good fortune to play bass with the likes of these.

Along with Fairfax the leader, guitarist Sam Sadler and I were the constants through the various personnel changes that came about because somebody was "sent for." Being sent for was every musician's dream; it was recognition and status. Usually it meant New York with a nationally known outfit. It came in the form of a telegram and a bus or train ticket to meet somebody, sometime, somewhere on the road. We were traumatized when we lost Dizzy Gillespie to Teddy Hill's band in New York. The trauma pointed up everybody's desire to get better and hope somebody would notice. New York was the end of the rainbow.

I first met John Birks Gillespie at a rehearsal of the Fairfax organization. He was one of our new trumpet players. My first impression was that he was one of those walk-loud, talk-loud characters. Certainly, he was brash, forthright, and mercilessly honest, but I found out eventually that despite the nickname "Dizzy" he was anything but dumb. Beneath that sometimes humorous exterior was a cool, calculating, and analytical mind. The world found this out when he extended the boundaries of jazz to bop and beyond. When he first came into the band, his trumpet solos were imitations of Louis Armstrong. He and Charlie Shavers then took up the style of another favorite knowledgeable musician, Roy ("Little Jazz") Eldridge. That style improved their technique, and both Dizzy and Charlie proceeded to their own inimitable styles.

Since Gillespie and his family lived near my father's poolroom, we met often. He came to 1306 Brown many times, and over the din-

*Dizzy Gillespie at the Smith kitchen table in Nashville in the late 1970s with Jackie Smith* (left) *and her brother Jay.*

ing table we discussed music issues. We had Jimmy Hamilton on occasion to intellectualize the discussion. I'll talk about Hamilton later, but on one occasion we discussed alternatives to the standard song form (AABA) used in popular songs. I had just learned about the rondo form (ABACA), which has two contrasting middle sections, so I brought it up in the conversation. Dizzy's response showed perception and insight.

Dizzy always had an acute sense of harmony. He would change the chordal background of a stock or standard tune until it fit his higher harmonic sense. To play with Dizzy was an aesthetic experience in that we basically had to relearn a standard tune like "Body and Soul" to conform to his musical requirements. His reaction to a mistake was immediate. He would yell out his correction at the danger spot even while soloing. I was in fast company here, and the experience greatly increased my confidence. Dizzy once told me, "Oscar, you ought to play solo." I was flattered that he thought I had the potential to do so.

Jimmy Hamilton was another breed of cat. He was quiet and introspective. He, too, was mercilessly honest. Beneath a taciturn exterior was a scholar of all phases of music. Few people will remember that he came to the Fairfax organization as a very credible trumpeter. We actually called him "Joe Trump." Because of illness, he resigned from the band for a short time. Then he shocked everybody, including me, by re-auditioning as an alto saxophonist and clarinetist.

The rest is history; the world knows about his eventual exploits with the Duke Ellington Orchestra. The versatile Mr. Hamilton excelled in another area not usually associated with jazz musicians. He loved and knew classical music, especially as it related to the clarinet. Years later, whenever Ellington's band came to wherever I was living, Jimmy and I got together on a chamber music project, usually a Mozart trio. It's frightening to think of what he could have accomplished had he had the college or conservatory experience.

As a bassist, I was most involved with whoever was the pianist in our rhythm section. Ernie Washington was a perfectionist for chord changes. He believed there was only one natural sequence of harmonies regardless of what the sheet music said. In other words, he fiddled around for hours until he had improved on the composer—and he was right just about every time. We never played a standard tune with the published chord changes. Ernie's chord progressions were more tasty and sophisticated. Most of the musicians associated with Ernie followed suit. Listen to Dizzy Gillespie's playing and arrangements of standard tunes even today, and you will hear a more musicianly version of the harmonic background. For myself, I had to learn to rely more on listening than reading.

Another pianist who played with us was the brilliant and explosive Calvin Jackson, my boyhood friend. Jackson was basically a concert pianist who later received a scholarship to Juilliard. We went to New York together in 1938 and were roommates for most of my undergraduate years. At the time he was one of the very few pianists who had the technical equipment and temerity to do battle with the mighty Art Tatum. Cal was a jazz and a classical pianist with prodigious facility in both. Our rhythm section with Calvin at the piano was so frisky and frenetic that our exasperated leader, Fairfax, said at one rehearsal, "Let's let the horns play four-four (basic rhythm) and have the rhythm section play all of the solos."

Charlie Shavers, our other trumpet soloist along with Dizzy, was a neat little jewel. He was natty and precise, probably because of his Bordentown Military Institute background. A small person with sharp facial features, he played the way he looked—with mute, but cutting, intensity. He, too, took inspiration from Little Jazz Eldridge. Charlie's formidable technique extended the dimension. He wound up playing with Tommy Dorsey and later with John Kirby at the Waldorf in New York. He always referred to me as "Professor Smith." I guess the direction I was headed was evident even then.

Our two tenor saxophonists at the time were John Berry and

Shorty Cawthon. John looked like John Barrymore with "straight" black hair. Needless to say, he was a ladies' man and scored on nearly every gig. Ironically, he turned down being "sent for" by Duke Ellington. He wanted to stay in Philly to raise his teenage daughter!

After every number and set we played, John wrote on music paper. He started on the first alto or first trumpet part and then filled in the remaining parts on separate pieces of paper. After the gig, he would respectfully ask if we would take a few minutes and run down what he wrote. Most of the time it was a swinging masterpiece. What was unusual is that there was no score; all of it came out of his head. In spite of my doctorate in music, his ability to keep track of the individual parts without a score remains a mystery to me.

Shorty Cawthon was called "Mr. House" because with two or three wading into a solo, he would bring the whole house down into a frenzy. Reading was not his greatest talent, but he made up for this with ears that could hear around a corner. He demonstrated his uncanny hearing when Shorty auditioned for a spot in the Jay McShann Band at the Savoy Ballroom in New York. He would excuse himself for some reason whenever a new number was passed out. He would stay gone long enough to hear the rest of the band give the arrangement a tentative run-through. Thus fortified, he would take his place and, with eyes glued to the music, wade through with only a few mistakes. The arranger-conductor would correct the mistake by singing the offending part. That was all that it took—that and a phenomenal musical memory. I think that I was the only person in the Savoy, other than Shorty, who knew the secret.

As important as pianists to the development of bass players were the drummers. We had a succession of four team players who tended to blend, as against the "total percussion" domination of today's percussionists. To this teenager's ears, Norman Dibble was a very mature and seasoned drummer. He had blue eyes and was light enough that we could send him or trumpeter Bama Warwick into the segregated food places to buy food for the band. Strangely enough, these two guys were blacker than the rest of us in attitude. At thirty, Bert Hall was the senior citizen who had had his own band, the Jungle Band, prior to joining Fairfax. A consummate rhythmicist, he set our rhythmic style. He also got me so drunk on sloe gin that I slept through a show at the Nixon Grand Theatre—and I was on stage.

Shadow Wilson, who was a regular drummer with Bill Doggett's band, made several appearances with us. Later to play with Count Basie, he was one of the three or four swingingest drummers I have ever heard. Martin Mackay, an ex-Basie drummer, was a human metronome, famed for his ability to play shows in exact tempo from memory. As he was my guru in many ways, there will be more about him later.

The Strand Ballroom on Broad Street in South Philly was the home of the Fairfax band. Since we were the house band, we were provided with regular employment and a place to rehearse. Usually there was a public dance on Saturday nights and holidays, and unless there was a featured name band, this was our gig. We were not on salaries, but we worked on a percentage basis. The pay ranged from as little as thirty-five cents to a holiday jackpot of five or six bucks. The average was closer to two dollars. You can see that this had an effect on how we put out to maintain our popularity. We were aware of public fickleness. Nobody ever got sick or didn't feel like playing. We all pulled with a common oar to get the "house."

One social note of the times was that youngsters from the old Philadelphia families, and those of middle class pretensions, were usually not allowed to attend. My sister Alma was allowed to attend only if a social club was sponsoring the dance. Perhaps this ingredient led to the demise of the big band. It was an unfair rap on the Strand Ballroom, which was well run.

The Fairfax band made occasional forays into the hinterlands, and this was to be my introduction to the "road." Usually we packed all fourteen of us (with instruments) into two ancient Packards. Getting there was always problematical, much less making it on time. Most of the time we made it, largely through the efforts of our ad hoc committee of back-yard mechanics. These guys could come up with brilliant and ingenious solutions, often involving chewing gum, rubber bands, or safety pins. I enjoyed every minute of it since I was not involved in the solution. Most of our trips took us to places like Wilmington, Delaware; Trenton, New Jersey; Reading, Pennsylvania; and Hagerstown, Maryland.

On a trip passing Hagerstown to some place in West Virginia we had an experience symbolic of the times. Fortunately, on this trip we used a Greyhound bus. As it turned out, that was what saved our necks. We arrived in the metropolis of Hagerstown about eight o'clock in the evening. One of our guys wanted to stop at a drugstore and get some cigarettes and aspirin. Our white bus driver would not leave the highway but mentioned that there was a drugstore one block away on a parallel street. My unfortunate colleague left the bus for the drugstore. After about half an hour, we sent another colleague to see what was happening. After about twenty minutes, we sent still a third to find out what was the situation with both. After about ten more minutes, we dispatched a fourth member. The situation became baffling to the four people still on the bus. We were now about two hours into this charade. The impatient bus driver finally decided to investigate. He returned a few minutes later with everybody in tow and escorted by the local sheriff who wanted to be sure that everybody got back on the bus. It turned out that there was a curfew. Negroes seen on the streets after 8:00 P.M. were immediately jailed, no questions asked.

# CHAPTER 5

# ON THE ROAD

Somewhere around late 1936 or early 1937, the Fairfax band was transformed by pen strokes into the Tiny Bradshaw Orchestra. This meant that we were to be booked by a New York agency with the famous Moe Gale as our promoter. The primary target for our engagements was to be the Theatre Owners' Booking Association (TOBA) black theatres. We soon came to agree with the other hands on the TOBA circuit that the real name of that organization should have been "Tough on Black Asses." We were upgraded to a permanent Greyhound bus, with *Tiny Bradshaw's Orchestra* and *New York* painted on both sides of the bus. We also had a road manager, Norman ("Jonesy") Jones, and a band valet. This was big-time stuff. We performed our one-week stint at the Royal Theatre in Baltimore without much mishap. The same thing was true at the Howard Theatre in Washington, D.C. Then our bookings started to fall through, and the real fun began.

By the time we reached Richmond, Virginia, we were transformed from name-band big shots into road survivors. On the days when we didn't have a hotel, the bus was our hotel. When the motor wasn't running, there was no heat. I used the cover from my bass as a sleeping bag. There was a daily collection of assets so that we could have food. I was generally trusted as the treasurer and purchasing agent. You would be surprised at what two loaves of bread and about eight to ten cans of sardines, all for about $1.25, could do to appease (more like stave off) fourteen hungry musicians. When we were lucky enough to make a P.C. (percentage of the gate) gig, we could rent two

47

rooms in a hotel. The fourteen of us often had to sleep in shifts with three or four in the bed crosswise. For me, coming from a protected family, this was pure fun. When my father sent me a money order for thirty dollars for me to come home (unbeknownst to the band), I quietly returned the money with a note that said, "Everything is great!" I didn't tell the guys. They would have killed me.

After the first week in Richmond, which was covered by a theatre gig, we were temporarily stranded. By the end of the second week, the manager of Miller's Hotel would not let any of us leave the premises with instruments or luggage until our bill was paid. I guess the management would have confiscated the instruments as partial payment. By the end of the third week, the situation was intolerable. Not only was the bill getting bigger, but we couldn't rehearse except at the hotel and then only at specified hours. We couldn't even take a gig if it was off the premises. Jonesy, the road manager, told us one afternoon that a gig was awaiting in Charlotte, North Carolina. He then laid out the strategy for our great escape. At nightfall we went into action. We had guys sitting in the lobby, and from time to time they would either go out or return to the rooms in a business-as-usual manner. The rest of us made ropes out of bed sheets. We then lowered the instruments one by one out of the window of a second-floor room overlooking the back alley. Our closest call came with the drums and their attendant cymbals. These instruments were greeted by waiting arms and rushed around the corner to our waiting Greyhound. With all of the instruments and luggage secured, we left one by one or in pairs, sauntering nonchalantly through the lobby and out the front door. It was an Academy-Award performance. We breathed sighs of relief and sped toward the North Carolina line.

The Charlotte gig was in a supper club for whites at the downtown intersection of Trade and Tryon. Our contract was unusual in that it was basically a P.C. gig, but we would take our meals at the club, and they would pay our room rent. The whole arrangement worked very well except for what happened after New Year's Eve. The management had advertised a special turkey dinner and the musical attraction of the famous Tiny Bradshaw Orchestra from New York for the occasion. With a special cover charge and our programs on local radio, we expected to make a killing. However, it was not to be. For the first time in fifteen years it snowed, and by opening time the temperature dropped below freezing. This was definitely not the "sunny South." Nobody showed but the management, the employees, and the band. We celebrated the New Year with the special turkey dinner, not realizing what would follow. For about a week our meals consisted of some form of turkey. On consecutive days we had turkey à-la-king, turkey salad, turkey hash, turkey soup, turkey sandwiches, and whatever else the mad-genius chef could come up with. It was too much of a good thing.

Many of the customs of the Old South had to do with race. For example, if whites booked a black band into a club or dance hall, they roped off a space for blacks. This was reversed when blacks booked the dance. If the band was popular enough, it would be booked for two consecutive nights in the same place. Usually the first night would be sponsored by the whites, with tickets sold to blacks in the roped-off area. This would be reversed on the black night. In any event, the custom meant extra gigs for us. The night that stands out in my memory was at a Durham, North Carolina, dance in a tobacco warehouse. Now these are some big places! The usual arrangement prevailed as the majority—white fans—stood around watching the blacks dance. After all, we were a black band and we catered more to black tastes. The black dancers reflected that in their dynamic dancing. There were no protests, and everybody got along amiably. The thing that burns this in my mind is the recollection of how cold it was. There was no heat, and in that huge area it seemed colder inside than out. Everybody wore overcoats. We, the band, had another problem: It's hard to play an instrument with gloves on and still make any semblance of the music the fans expect.

Another custom of the road was the audition. The itinerary would call for us to be in the new town by about 2:30 P.M. and set up to play by four. There would be a large crowd of people by that time in the dance hall, and there was no admission charge. This meant that, given our percentage arrangement, we had to sell our band to the crowd. We had to prove we could do the job they required. If we flubbed our half-hour arrangement, it would have an impact on our wallets. I was always surprised that so many people could be there during a working day until I found out that it was customary for business establishments and private homes to let their workers and domestic servants off for a short time on these occasions.

We all pulled together. There were no excuses, no prima donnas, no self-excusing hangovers. We played the audition as if it were the final and deciding game of the World Series. Sometimes I think we played better for that half-hour than when we played the regular gig at night for paying fans. To show you what I mean, I have myself played on rare occasions with a cold, a headache, or even a hangover, but that never affected me for the audition. I wouldn't dare, nor would anybody else. We produced, or at least we gave it our best shot—because we had to.

On an unscheduled bus break somewhere in South Carolina, I had to put my ego in perspective. We stopped at a country store on the highway, one of those stores that sold everything. This was a routine rest negotiated with the bus driver for the purpose of taking a break and buying some cigarettes and other supplies. Sam Sadler went in with me. The first thing I saw was a pair of black musicians with a guitar and bass violin standing near the entrance. They were dressed in overalls and looked like local laborers or farmers' helpers. The bass that the guy had was very beat up and had holes in it. There was nothing to suggest any sophistication in anything but maybe country blues. Here we were with our Greyhound and big-name band status. So what did I do but arrogantly toss them a quarter and tell them to play something. Maybe it wasn't arrogance. Maybe it was pride in our assumed status and support for any black musicians trying to do it. Anyway, the two musicians struck up on "Lady Be Good" and demonstrated their virtuosity for everybody in the store. That guy played as much bass as I had ever heard. When the dazzling exhibition was finished, Sadler said, "W. O., I have another quarter. Would you like to hear it again?" With that remark he tossed the coin, and the two musicians—particularly the bassist—proceeded to embarrass me in front of my colleagues. His bass lines were highly inventive, and his sense of rhythm was impeccable. I had visions of being replaced in the band with this guy and being left in South Carolina. Fortunately, that did not happen, and we proceeded back to Philadelphia a little older and possibly wiser, but no richer.

We could tell who did what by where they sat in the bus. The pot smokers held down the rear seats, while the lushheads sat in the front. The neutrals provided a buffer zone in the middle because the smokers and the drinkers never spoke civilly to each other. The neutrals were the go-betweens. Being under twenty-one and not legally able to buy liquor, I was a reluctant neutral. The band was about evenly divided, with four or five guys in each group. I was able to keep friendly relations with both active groups and provided messenger service between them. I believe the pot smokers were the most arrogant. Their condescension toward their drinking colleagues was naturally returned in kind by the drinkers. The interesting thing is that very little of this affected their professionalism. We played most gigs with surprisingly few problems. One of the pot smokers, the section leader of the reeds, would call to me, "Hey, Professor, would you tell that bubble-head drunk up front that we'd like to have a section rehearsal at four o'clock?" I would transmit the message and bring back the reply, which was usually affirmative but unprintable.

One of the things we found out on our way back home was that Greyhound was a business—not one wheel would turn until they got their money. With our spotty record, they had no intention of becoming a credit institution. No ride-now-pay-later for us. The bus driver wouldn't even turn the motor on for brief periods of heat. Jonesy, our road manager, was up to the challenge and booked us into a P.C. gig in Goldsboro, North Carolina. We were tipped off when we arrived to keep our eyes on "Jake," the promoter of the dance. I don't remember who warned us, but slightly before the intermission we found out why. While we were playing, Jonesy stayed in the box office to check on our share. When it looked as if we had just about got all the customers likely to show, Jonesy walked back to the bandstand to give us a report. He was about halfway to the stand when I happened to look up in time to see Jake bolt out of the box and begin running down the street with a bag in his hand. I yelled, and Jonesy reversed himself and took off after Jake. The whole band, leaving instruments on the stage, immediately bolted after Jake and Jonesy. We were about a block behind when the sheriff drove up and arrested Jake. By the time we got to the spot, the sheriff had sent Jake off to jail. He then waved all of us toward him where he promptly placed all of us under arrest. This was not funny, as all of us had visions of southern justice. The sheriff, without letting us explain anything, put the whole band in the cell with Jake. The ensuing fracas took about twenty minutes. Jake still had the money bag with him! There was not much of a confrontation—we outnumbered him fourteen to one. We got our money plus some punitive damages. The more I think about it, the more I had the feeling that the sheriff must have been through this scenario before. We returned, found our instruments still there, and finished the dance. Greyhound got its money, and we happily proceeded back across the border—the Mason-Dixon line.

# CHAPTER 6

# PHILADELPHIA FADEOUT

**W**e got back to Philadelphia and immediately turned back into the Frankie Fairfax Orchestra. Our brush with the big time was over, for we were again in fierce competition with the very good local groups.

One of the first things that came up was the organization of a musicians' union for blacks. Without one we could not play downtown in the various big white clubs, the theatres, or the hotels. The union opened an entire new dimension for the expansion and recognition of our art. I was one of the charter members of Local 274, American Federation of Musicians. Little did I realize the impact that membership would have on the rest of my life. We got a job at the Warwick Hotel rooftop club, a gig that in those days seemed inconceivable for black musicians. When we went to the club, we were met by a chick we knew. She was going by the name of Tandalayo (or something like that). She told us not to recognize her because she was passing for white. I didn't see how she could get away with it, since she was only about two shades lighter than I am, and I am dark, coffee brown with very little cream. But she succeeded, and we maintained this strange relationship although she was very well-known in our community. I guess a lot of powder (she looked like a ghost) and make-up got her over, although she would have fooled no black that I knew.

Martin Mackay, our drummer during this period, was my mentor—my guru, if you will. He was in his thirties while I was just turning twenty. He was a loyal friend and a knowledgeable, experienced musician who had been Count Basie's drummer in Kansas City. He was also educated, with a bachelor's degree in English from the University of Illinois. At a time when college-educated blacks were all but unknown, I attribute his constant talking about college to my eventually being pushed in that direction. I am the first of my immediate family to graduate from a college. Mac and Fax were the only college people in our band. It simply was not in the realm of our environment and experience. Mac lived near me on Fairmont Avenue and was a constant companion, whether on the gig or other escapades. He could and would talk about anything from philosophy to street sociology. He said that he was attracted to my intellectual capacity. That was the first time that I heard there was such a thing.

Mac's ability as a drummer was a primary reason that we got the job as house band at the Nixon Grand Theatre. When the featured bands could not play the show with the chorus line and tap dancers, we were called in—sometimes at midnight. If an act—dancer or singer—complained about our accompaniment being too fast or too slow, the management would dismiss it by saying, "That's what you gave Mac during the rehearsal."

Mac was also my romantic advisor, although I think he went too far on one occasion when he sent a young lady some flowers and signed my name to the card. It was effective because that young lady was all over me until we both found out what happened. He fixed me up one time with the girlfriend of the number two light heavyweight boxing contender, a dude who was the rage of Philadelphia sports fans. I had misgivings about the deal all the way, in spite of Mac's support. Even though the lady in question was cooperative, I chickened out. I realized that I could not count on the fighter's professionalism and understanding.

Mac's eventual demise came about because of demon rum. He could drink more than anybody I have ever known, and he often didn't know how drunk he was. He once played an entire show at the Nixon Grand so drunk that he collapsed through the drums, crashing the cymbals, at the end of the show. Meanwhile, he didn't miss a beat or a tempo. Everything was in order during the show, but I could see his glazed eyes. He contemptuously dismissed beer and white wine as being merely water. It must have taken about a half-gallon of some really hard stuff to put him in this shape. In later years he spent some time in alcoholic rehabilitation in various hospitals. He died sometime in the late seventies while working for the *St. Louis Argus* newspaper as a typesetter. I miss Mac, even now. Who else would come by the house with a contribution toward a fifth of good bourbon and sit down head to head and discuss anything from Shakespeare or Kant to how to deal with the opposite sex? It was as simple as this: He was a master and I was a novice.

The Nixon Grand Theatre was a hand-me-down from whites, a result of black expansion farther up into North Philadelphia. The largest theatre we had, it was in the grand old style, with chandeliers in the lobby and a huge stage. It could easily have been an opera house like the ones you see in the movies. In 1937 they featured first-run movies and three stage shows a day. The Fairfax Orchestra was the house band. The good thing about it was that, although we had to be on hand, we did not have to play whenever bands like Jimmie Lunceford or Duke Ellington were featured.

The pay, if I remember correctly, was forty-five dollars a week, which we sometimes earned without playing a note. Aside from the notoriety and prestige in black Philadelphia, it gave us the opportunity to meet and hear most of the leading bands of the time. It gave us close and personal contact with the likes of Fats Waller, Earl Hines, Bill Robinson the dancer, Cab Calloway, and their accompanying musicians. These musicians were usually local like ourselves. Somebody in our group knew somebody in the visiting group, and that led to drinking sessions, card games, and teasing the chorus girls (what a hardhearted bunch!).

We were part of a national fraternity, the black jazz musicians. This sometimes paid off when you got to New York; you were not completely unknown. Sometimes you were even "sent for," recommended by these same visiting musicians. Often there was a jam session with all of the above-mentioned musicians at some club in South Philly. Every local musician's dream was that somebody would remember his contribution to the session. That's what happened to several members of our band, most notably Dizzy Gillespie, our star trumpet soloist. He was sent for by Teddy Hill's band to join them on a trip to Europe. Losing one of our leading attractions traumatized us, but life went on and we proceeded to the most improbable of happenings at the Grand.

I didn't realize it at the time, but being members of a union was to have an immediate impact on our lives in the future. Being a member of a labor union was not a common experience for blacks in those days. In fact, most of the unions that we knew were anti-black. It turned out that the white stage hands and projectionists went out on strike. Local 274 was called out in a sympathy strike. This was a break for us, as I had thought we were out of a job since the theatre was closed anyway. It meant that the American Federation of Musicians would pay our salaries. We had to report to the theatre every day. We also had to stay there for our normal working hours, and we filled in the time with card games and rehearsals. I got to be pretty good at pinochle and whist, but, more importantly, the rehearsals sharpened my musical skills. Since the strike went on for over six months, I was able to amass a good stake for the future.

After the theatre strike, I played with some other local groups and finally with the dynamic Fats Waller. First was George Baquet, who had a "society gig" in an exclusive club on Market Street. He was a historical figure because he was from New Orleans and had the first black group to play downtown. His basic style was Dixieland, which most of the young blacks disdained. I had my eyes opened on this gig to the conventions of that style. The tailgate trombone and the accidental counterpoint with right notes required real musicianship, understanding, teamwork, and creative freedom. The rambunctious, alternating with the soulful, soon taught me that there was no holding back, no half-hearted playing. We went all out on everything. This was harder work, physically and mentally, than playing with an organized big band. I think size had something to do with it. There were enough guys in a big band so a player could coast from time to time and come on strong when his turn came. In a typical Dixieland group, everybody is on a solo line all the time. All the guys in Baquet's group were at least fifty years old or older, and I was twenty at the time. If nothing else, I got lessons in stamina and inter-team playing.

The next gig was with Charlie Gaines, trumpet star, who was what I would call the absentee band leader. Charlie was so popular that he would book three or four engagements on the same night. He would send combos to the various locations (without the trumpet star, of course). I was in one of these combos. One night we were sent to a club in Frankford, to which I have earlier referred as Johannesburg. Charlie's name was emblazoned on the marquee. From the moment we arrived we had problems with the crowd. They didn't come to hear any pickup group. They wanted to hear Charlie Gaines of the records they had purchased. We did our best to hold the fort, but that was not good enough. They bugged us with "Where is Charlie?" We tried excuses like "He had a late record session," but to no avail. Just before midnight, when the tension was about to snap, Charlie made his grand entrance with a plump blonde white chick on one arm and the trumpet on the other. Considering that this was "Johannesburg," Pennsylvania, the combo and I were terrified. Somehow we finished the engagement, but we must have set a world record for leaving the premises.

I have fond memories of the really fine trumpet player Hot Lips Page. With his Kansas City background it was natural that he specialized in the blues. Page educated me in many ways besides music on our numerous one-night stands. He drank considerably on the gig, and it was all right for his sidemen to do so. It was *de rigueur* to have a pint of favorite beverage just inside my stand, out of view of the customers. This would be there all night if I paced myself. Guys would take an intermission and leave the bottle right there. They trusted one another. One night, the trust was broken; various members complained that liquid levels were not where they had left them. Who was the thief? Page organized us quietly to gather all the bottles but one. This bottle was then three-quarters filled with urine. Everybody left the band stand at intermission, but kept a furtive eye on the stage. In a few minutes we heard some coughing and sneezing, mixed with choice profanities. We also saw our favorite trombonist (who shall remain nameless) rush off the stage. The problem was solved forever.

When Fats Waller, the "harmful little armful," came to the Nixon Grand Theatre in Philly, only two of the musicians who had recorded with him, Gene Sedrick, tenor sax, and Al Casey, guitar, accompanied him. The group had to be filled out with local musicians. Fairfax, our regular band leader, was now secretary to the musicians' union. Fortunately, he sent me and Mac Mackay, drummer, and Johnny Lynch, trumpet, to fill out the Waller band. That week at the Grand was one of the most fascinating of my life. To play with Al Casey, a name guitarist, was a treat.

Make no mistake: Fats Waller, for all of his clowning, was a serious, style-setting jazz musician. At the rehearsal, Fats had a case of whiskey brought up and placed under the grand piano. He then ceremoniously presented each one of us with a quart (fifths were unknown in those days). He then said, "Now everybody's got a bottle, so don't anybody ask me for a drink." I took my bottle home, but I swear he drank a whole quart during our two-hour rehearsal. After each number we rehearsed, he took a healthy swig. I never noticed any diminution of his constant humorous repartee or his dynamic playing. He played a crowd pleaser like "Your Feet's Too Big," balancing it with a sensitive, soulful tune like the "Blues Waltz." The local jazz establishment buzzed: a jazz tune in three-quarter time! He was a couple of decades ahead of Dave Brubeck! I have heard few piano players with his depth and virtuosity. He stayed in his dressing room and drank, so I got little chance to talk with him. However, I had ears enough to know that Fats was a serious jazz musician, one to be studied and analyzed.

Studying and analyzing had taught me a lot. I was twenty years old now, and I had my little stash. I was ready to move on to the hub of the action.

The evening before my departure for New York in the fall of 1938, I sat down at the dinner table and made my announcement. Nobody was upset. Nobody tried to dissuade me. My mother, in her calm and reserved fashion, admonished me not to waste my time just hanging around jazz orchestras but to go to college. We had never had a college person in our family. Out of the Philadelphia branch of the family, I was the first high-school graduate. My father had died two years previously. I was leaving behind my mother, my grandmother and my Uncle Charlie, and not one of them was impressed by names like Calloway, Ellington, or Basie.

I did have some second thoughts, but I also had stars in my eyes. I didn't want to be a bandleader. I just wanted to play, to be part of the scene. I would go to college as a part of the price of getting to New York. With that concession, the characteristically unemotional Smith family proceeded with the dinner as if nothing of importance was about to happen. I made a phone call to Calvin Jackson for last-minute arrangements about train schedules and the living plan, and then I retired and slept peacefully, unconcerned about what the future would bring.

# CHAPTER 7

# SUGAR HILL

*T*he next day, a bright September morning in 1938, I took off on the Pennsylvania Railroad for New York. I was accompanied by my friend Calvin Jackson, the brilliant young piano virtuoso. He was going to Juilliard on scholarship. I was going into the unknown. Fortified with about five hundred dollars from the theatre strike, my plan was to stay for a year and see what happened. Remembering my mother's admonition about going to school and not wasting time, I formulated my battle plan on the train ride. The very next day I would go down to New York University and talk to somebody.

Calvin had arranged for us to stay at Lenny and Edna Foreman's apartment at 940 St. Nicholas Avenue. We were delighted. This was in the Sugar Hill neighborhood of Harlem. The subway stop at 155th Street was only two short blocks away. The Foremans were to become our "parents" and New York counselors.

The counselor part was sorely needed. Compared to New York, Philly was just an overgrown country town. We had a lot to learn about managing a fast-moving city. No extended family here. I never did know about the people living in the adjacent apartments, nor did they care about us. At twenty-one years of age, I was a not-so-big kid. Calvin was a year younger. We knew nobody except a few Philadelphia expatriates. We were ignorant of subway intricacies; to this day Brooklyn remains *terra incognito* to me. Insecure, if not outright terrified, we had cut the umbilical cord from the Quaker City; we were on our own, sink or swim.

With instructions from Mr. Foreman, I went to New York University's admissions office. The whole journey was fascinating. The express train from 125th to 59th Street blew my mind. The Village, and the walk through Washington Square, turned me on in terms of excitement and anticipation. I had gone to the registrar for exploratory talks, so he surprised me when he told me I was admitted and could attend a class that day as soon as I had cleared the music department office. I asked him, "Don't you want to see my transcript?" He said, "If you graduated from Central High in Philly, that's enough for me. You're in." I did as he told me and went to the eighth floor of the education building.

Sure enough, just as he had said, I was in a college class on my second day in New York. What I saw shocked me. All the students there had their textbooks, and they were answering questions as if it were mid-season. I wasn't prepared at all for this, so I asked the guy next to me, "Where do you find out all of this?" This was the first meeting of that class! He told me that there was a list of required texts on the bulletin board in the front of the music office. Admitted at nine o'clock, counseled at eleven, fees paid by twelve, and in class by one is what I call fast action.

It turned out that in the examinations I had tested out of most of the freshman courses, courtesy of the beefed-up curriculum at Central High. I would be able to take almost a year's worth of electives to get the required number of semester hours to graduate. Also, I noted that once I had declared an instrumental major, I had no further control over what music courses I would take, or their times. Consequently, I had a lot of eight or nine o'clock classes. This would prove something of a problem for a musician whose club gigs were usually from ten at night to four in the morning.

I spent the next few days discovering the delights of New York, the subway system, the architecture. I was in love with New York. I made the most of the museums, the Forty-Second Street Library, and the main parks. I even thought that New York women's legs were better shaped because of all the walking they had to do between subway stops, not to mention the walk-up apartments. The streets were not crowded with cars as they are today. Therefore, walking was not as dangerous. New York was a much safer place then; muggings and the like were still infrequent. It was a walking city, and as Frank Sinatra was to sing, "The best things in life are free." That was the size and the privilege of New York City in 1938.

There were several obstacles for new musicians in New York. One was trying to get known so that somebody would call for a gig.

The musicians' union, Local 802, had two main procedures to keep that from happening. The first was their jam session rule: There should never be more musicians on the bandstand than there were under contract. Jam sessions were advertised when no regular group was employed. Since jam sessions were very popular, the club owners used this scheme to get free music. The business agents of Local 802 patrolled this situation vigilantly. Word soon got around about how merciless the union would be to any miscreant who broke the rule. Newcomers had to keep in mind whether or not they could take the chance. All were welcome to a jam session until somebody proved that he couldn't play. Calvin and I would walk, both of us carrying the bass, funeral style, from 157th and St. Nick to 86th and Columbus Avenue looking for a session. A club on Columbus Avenue featured Lionel Hampton, a known favorite for sessionists. If a player was lucky, after many nights and many clubs, word would get around that he was in town, capable, and available.

The second procedure the union employed to stifle new musicians was the six-month probation period. A newcomer could not take a steady job, and no more than one gig a week with the business agent's permission. To ensure compliance, the agent would police all places of possible activity and call upon the newcomer unannounced. He was even supposed to leave information saying where he would be, if absent from the apartment. This meant that the agent could knock on the door of your ladyfriend's house. To me, it was downright undignified that somebody, not my parents, would know every move I made. To get around this, and because of economic necessity, some guys would cross the river to Jersey, figuring that the agent wouldn't go that far.

Some nights we would go on the prowl for a house-rent party instead of a jam session. Neither paid off financially, but a musician who would play could get free food and drinks at the party. These were not publicized, but were advertised by word of mouth. The house-rent party was a Harlem institution. Calvin and I would take the bass to the general area and start looking. We could tell the location by smell, sight, and sound. First there was the open door, followed by the sound of a boogie-woogie or stride piano, and then the smell of chitterlings and barbecue. When you got in, you found a crush of humans doing the slow drag with only the light from the kitchen illuminating the darkness. Smoke was always thick enough to chop with an ax. My bass was an open invitation for me and would soon be followed by barbecue and bourbon. We would play until the lights went on, sometime in the wee hours when the hosts had enough to pay the rent. We didn't even know their names, nor did it matter, because all of this was potluck.

The year 1938 held a lot of firsts for me—my first choir rehearsal, for one. I was a reluctant choir member. My interest and talents were in instrumental music. Unfortunately, choral experience was required for freshman and sophomore music majors. We had a choir of about three hundred voices. A surprise to anyone who has heard me talk (in a low, unrich baritone) since I passed forty is the fact that I was classified as a first tenor back then and could make sounds up to high C.

Attendance was taken by seat position. There were only about six black kids in the choir, so our absence was readily spotted. Mr. Goodhart, the director, would walk in at the beginning, take a quick glance, and immediately yell, "Where is Smith?" He was as adamant as I was reluctant, and on one occasion he left the stage and came around to the students' building where he caught me in the middle of a Ping-Pong game. He marched me right back to the rehearsal.

Singing was by no means my strong point, as was demonstrated to me when I was in the Fairfax orchestra in the Strand Ballroom. I had written an arrangement on Don Redmond's tune, "If It's True," and a good arrangement it was. There was one fly in the ointment: I wrote it for me as the singer. I had noticed the attention that the other guys in the band had gotten from the ladies for singing. On that fateful night, "If It's True," with me caressing the microphone, got its first and last performance. For some reason they never called that number again.

As if choir were not enough, Mr. Goodhart invited me to try out for the Men's Glee Club. He told me the time and place. "Mr. Goodhart," I said, "that's ridiculous. We both know that my singing is horrible."

He ignored the remark. "Be there," he commanded. Since I had two classes under him, I thought it prudent to obey.

A dozen guys were in front of his office when I got there. You could hear the piano chord followed by the vocal arpeggio: "Ah-hah-hah-hah-hah-hah-hah-hah-hah." Some of the singers sounded like Caruso or Ezio Pinza to me, but not to Mr. Goodhart. Periodically, the door would open and the master would advise Caruso, "We may have an opening next semester." You can guess what I felt like. These guys were voice majors. The NYU Men's Glee Club was an elite, constantly-traveling group. They gave concerts at Yale, Rutgers, and Steinway Hall.

The door opened, and it was my turn. "Mr. Goodhart," I said. "Is this trip necessary?"

He answered me by hitting the first chord. Resigned, I squeaked up and down the vocal arpeggios. When the session was mercifully over, I said, "You don't need to tell me. . . ." I started for the door.

What he said was, "The first rehearsal will be at the student building, Tuesday at 3:00 P.M. Be there."

The guys lined up outside looked at me in amazement. "Jeez, you made it."

For many years I reflected on this. All I could come up with was that Mr. Goodhart wanted somebody black in the organization. The Women's Glee Club was lily-white, although the two best singers in the school were two lovely but very dark females. When the Women's Glee Club finally integrated, you would hardly have known it by looking. The two colored girls who made it were not our best singers but had that Lena Horne look and color. Maybe Mr. Goodhart really liked me as a person, although I couldn't exactly say the same for him. He was the one responsible for everyone calling me "Willie," which I hated. I never heard what he actually thought of my voice, which may be just as well. As much as I disliked it at the time, I now consider the choral experience a significant footnote in my development as a musician.

In 1938 Sugar Hill was really a nice place. It was home to the Negro bourgeoisie. It actually was a hill, beginning at 145th Street and rising to the boundary of 163rd Street. I say boundary because north of 163rd, being black meant being in trouble. The eastern boundary was Edgecombe Avenue, which was sort of a cliffside where we could look down on the rest of Harlem—Lenox Avenue and all. In other cities, it would be called the Gold Coast. Duke Ellington and other employed famous musicians, as well as entertainers, writers, and professionals, lived on Sugar Hill. The neighborhood had recently changed; its ambience was new to black people. Coming from a row house, I found it especially attractive. The house at 940 St. Nicholas had no roaches, no rats—and it had an elevator. The standard of living was beyond anything I had known.

Mr. Bailey, a West Indian Negro, owned the building. Black ownership was an extreme rarity at that time, and we were all proud of him. However, looking at Mr. Bailey in his overalls, you would have thought he was the handyman. The superintendent, an American Negro, dressed impeccably and drove a late-model Cadillac, in contrast to Mr. Bailey's tin lizzie, which was so beaten up that Calvin and I refused his offers of a ride. To all outward appearance, the super played the role of the owner. I heard that Mr. Bailey had paid $200 thousand cash for the building. That meant our sharp super was just an employee (earning about eighty-five dollars a month), who did nothing but arrogantly collect the rent. Things are not always what they seem.

I didn't see much of my roommate, Calvin, in the apartment since there was no piano. He practiced at Juilliard until about dinner time. My situation was different because my tuba and string bass were parked in the living room. I practiced in the afternoon as soon as I got uptown from class. The Foremans were out working, so I had a free run of practice until they were home. The main thing wrong with this setup was that in September it was still warm outside. Air conditioning was unknown in those days except for movie theatres, where we froze. The windows of all apartments were open from about noon on. My practicing the tuba was not the most enjoyable thing for my neighbors, some of whom had night jobs. I have to admit that the heavy growls and grunts of the tuba are a bit much for someone trying to sleep in the afternoon. After several complaints were registered with the super, a meeting was called. I explained that I had to practice in order to do well at school. The compromise was permission to practice one hour between four and five daily.

I wound up my freshman year in good shape, except for finances. After two semesters' tuition, Local 802's initiation fee, and a year's room and board, my five-hundred-dollar stash was gone. I had economized as best I could. The director of instrumental music at NYU was an organist, so I saved money by passing up that fee for private instruction. As for practice-room fees, I simply sneaked into unused practice rooms and worked until expelled either by the custodian or the student who had paid the fee for the room. This served as my *modus operandi* for my entire undergraduate career.

NYU did not give credit for any applied music until the student took the exam and performed a recital in the senior year. The music department did supply a repertory list for the year. In a way this was a trap that waylaid the students who failed to realize that they were on their own and that four years of development could not be compressed into the few months before hoped-for graduation. Despite my omission of the applied music fee, I was advised graciously and helpfully by the music staff.

Singing in the choir and the glee club, playing in the orchestra and the band (both football and concert), filling in with the informal quartet or quintet chamber groups formed by students, I was in an atmosphere conducive to exploring good music. I finished up the year with a B+ average. I was fresh out of funds, but I realized that I was hooked. In any event, I did not have it in my mind to leave New York. I had done what my mother had asked me to do, and I would try all means possible to stay in school.

The summer of 1939 was the prelude to an eventful year. War clouds were looming in Europe. The depression that had encompassed our lives was beginning to wane, and people seemed happier, freer. There were prospects and promises of jobs, even for two unknown, young, draft-age musicians. Calvin and I were making social progress. Our Sunday afternoons with a group of young ladies made New York seem like the Promised Land.

I had an unusual arrangement with Miss Ophelia Devore, who at the time was a Hunter College student. She would later found the Ophelia Devore Charm School, where her graduates would include beautiful black women like Diahann Carroll. Ophelia was secretly married to a New York City fireman but was living at home with her immediate family. I believe she wanted to finish college before announcing the marriage. We had an agreement that, in effect, I would be her boyfriend or, really, her escort. For me it was like being asked to escort Miss America. I got quite a bit of prestige in our social circle for this bit of serendipity. My fame spread in this group of young people, and I was no longer an unknown hick from Philly. Ophelia made the whole thing more realistic by planting a kiss or a hug in strategic situations. I played my role happily with only the regret that it couldn't be for real. We went "Dutch" on all pay occasions. Ophelia was a beautiful person, not only in appearance but with poise and charm. She had a formidable mind, and just being with her was stimulating. The performance was so successful that it canceled out my chances with other attractive possibilities. I didn't mind. For that matter, I'd do it again; it was nasty work, but somebody had to do it.

Calvin and I had an occasional gig, but we were still doing all we could think of to become better known. We spent hours at the Rhythm Club and even visited the Clef Club. The latter was a famous place where past generations of black musicians visited and rehearsed. The Rhythm Club was entirely different—a cafeteria, if you will, of food and of musicians; an emporium with benches where the hopeful waited for a gig. Many last-minute replacements originated there. Some guys came in the morning and camped all day, dressed in dark clothes (the uniform) with the sax or the trombone parked under the seat. At intervals somebody might walk through the front door and say, "I need a tenor sax." Immediately two or three cats would stand up and say, "I'll take it." Somehow situations resolved, and the employer and the triumphant employee would leave after a brief discussion of the gig. Local 802 down on Sixth Avenue had a similar arrangement, but the black musicians considered that primarily for whites.

# CHAPTER 8

# 393

Sometime in the summer of 1939, Mr. Foreman's two daughters from Philly, by a previous wife, came to live with him. Both were teenagers, so Calvin and I had to move. Calvin, who had made our original arrangement with the Foremans, promptly came up with another miraculous and timely connection. In playing around Sugar Hill, he had become known to a Mr. William Willis, who was the building super at 393 Edgecombe Avenue. Bill and Emma Willis were lovers of classical music with Cadillac tastes on a Chevrolet budget. The arrangement was that we would get free room and board in exchange for assisting with the work around the apartments. My job was to pull the garbage in the evening, put out the trash on collection days, and occasionally stoke the furnace. Did you ever try to shovel coal into a bathroom-sized furnace without throwing your guts in? The secret, taught to me by Mrs. Willis, is to suddenly drop the shovel, allowing the coal to fly to the inner reaches. Calvin and I alternated in mopping down the steps and lobbies of the six-floor building. It was not my favorite gig, but considering what we got in return, it was a bargain. We were very grateful.

Bill Willis, the consummate music lover, had developed a living room from the various cubicles of an apartment house basement. The room was apart, separated from the living quarters by about forty feet. Bill enclosed the area with maroon velvet drapes. We also had a top-of-the-line Capehart phonograph with the largest collection of classical music records outside of Steinway Hall. My tuba became a lamp with a bulb in it. A Beethoven death mask under a spotlight

67

became a point of interest. (Some of our guests speculated that Beethoven had Negroid features). Weekly programs of classical music drew Harlem intelligentsia, artists, and some Harlem Renaissance figures. These affairs featured mimeographed programs and guest appearances (at intermission) by such stars as Jonathan and Carol Brice, Marian Anderson, and Paul Robeson. It was the best that Harlem had to offer in this area of culture. I eventually became the master of ceremonies, or commentator, at these Sunday afternoon events. I had to read and do research in order to keep up with the level of our audiences.

There was, however, one leveling point. My bed was a mattress underneath the Steinway grand piano. I had to wait until everybody left to be able to go to sleep. Sometimes the action was still going on when I had to leave for school. I was eventually assigned a sleeping place in the library.

Bill Willis was a remarkable cat. He had played football and run track for the University of Pennsylvania for one year, and his knowledge of music was phenomenal. Give him a few bars of anything, and he could tell you who wrote it. He was on a program with radio station WQXR, one of those "guess the composer" panels. He guessed everything, no matter how obscure. The radio station soon diplomatically removed him from the panel. His record collection had multiple recordings of his favorites. If, for example, you requested Beethoven's Seventh Symphony, he would ask, "Who do you want, Stokowski, Toscanini, or Klemperer?" If he had known anything about the mechanics of music, he could have been an excellent conductor. As it was, his criticism was sacred to me. He was a community leader in the arts, and the artists knew it. They gravitated to him. Most of the black concert artists, ballet performers, writers, and visual artists sooner or later got to 393 Edgecombe. Willis's business headquarters was an artists' colony. To hear music with Bill was a very serious business. He would brook no interference—no noise— and would countenance only total concentration. It gave me another dimension, and I soon learned to be his favorite listening partner. We argued points of criticism, and let me tell you that I had to be keenly perceptive to stay in the game.

Three-ninety-three became a safe haven for any artist or intellectual who was temporarily down and out. The nucleus of residents was at all times prepared for anything or anybody. At different times, we had black school principals and superintendents who were temporarily out of work. They were all intellectually stimulating. We even

*William Willis of 393
Edgecombe Avenue, Harlem,
1940s*

had a classmate of F. D. R.'s, who received an invitation to the White
House for a Roosevelt birthday party. We were all thrilled because—
number one—none of us ever got that close to the power circuits of
this country, and—number two—this made me aware of another
world: There really was an F. D. R., and he was a human being who
lived in my time. Unfortunately, our invited friend (who had a doctorate from Harvard) didn't have a quarter to his name. Not up to the
more demanding physical chores, he took over the daily dishwashing.

My best remembered and most beloved character was Tina. I
call her Tina because I don't remember her real name. Tina fits as a
name because she was tiny—say, about four feet, eleven inches—and
weighed in at about ninety-five pounds. She was fearless and tough;
she talked tough, looked tough, and was all rawbone and whipcord. In
her own way, she was attractive, but most of all she was experienced.
She had traveled the world in her job as personal maid to Tallulah
Bankhead. Tina had fascinating stories to tell about the experience.

Three-ninety-three was her home residence for a while, and I answered the phone to the famous Miss Bankhead on many occasions.

One evening when we were listening to some music, we heard a terrible commotion in the alley to the rear of 393. All the available manpower went out to see what was going on. The alley between Edgecombe and St. Nicholas Place was often the scene of petty crime. We got out there and found Tina, a whirling dervish, completely surrounding a would-be mugger. She was so fast in her kicking, pounding, slapping, and screaming that the best this unfortunate mugger could do was cover his head, keeping his back to the wall. When we got there, he broke and ran. I guess he was grateful to be rescued from complete destruction. But don't get me wrong—Tina was kind and considerate with everybody she knew. Even so, we all knew better than to mess with her.

There were never fewer than ten people or more than sixteen staying at 393 in a constantly shifting arrangement. The Willises, Calvin, and I were the only constants. Whoever had a job at any time supplied the food and other necessities for everybody. Willis, at the time, had a salary of seventy-five dollars a month. With that he enriched us all intellectually and culturally by keeping up with the latest books and records. Money was no object to him; he met his own high standards of taste regardless of costs. Witness our nine-foot Steinway grand, which later turned out to be Art Tatum's favorite instrument.

Being a scholarship student at Juilliard and practicing six to eight hours a day, Calvin was not in a position to take many of the 10:00 P.M. to 4:00 A.M. gigs. Therefore, from about August 1939 through the subsequent winter, I was the main food and beverage supplier for this motley commune because I happened to be the one who was picking up the most gigs. Despite the shortage of funds, we were a happy share-and-share-alike crowd. We celebrated often with beer and bourbon in our impromptu parties. We even celebrated F. D. R.'s birthday, the one that our Harvard Ph.D. could not use his personal invitation to because of his lack of funds. So we managed to salvage some measure of pleasure from the event.

When school started in September, I received a call from Clark Monroe, whom I didn't know but had heard of. He was an entrepreneur and promoter, and he owned Monroe's Uproar House, an after-hours house located, I believe, on 133rd Street near Seventh Avenue. The place did not open until one in the morning and closed at 8:00 A.M. Actually, nothing went on until about 4:00 A.M., the closing hour of the regular clubs. Clark had heard me play in a jam session and wanted me to make the gig. He already had Clarence Williams on piano and Jimmy Shirley, who was acknowledged by many to be the finest jazz guitarist in the city. The gig eventually became known as the "guitar battle." Charlie Christian, Floyd Smith, and Tiny Grimes often came by to challenge Jimmy. The heat was intense with the flying tempos and dazzling displays of technical virtuosity as they tried to outdo one another. This left me in the middle because any number we played, no matter how fast, had to be a dozen or more choruses long in order to accommodate everybody. Often I was the only bass player, but the level and the musicianship of these fine guitarists made it all easy and interesting.

Only one thing spoiled this dream: my nine o'clock music theory class. Fortunately, I was able to use the time from one in the morning until the actual four o'clock start to do my homework. Sleep was a different problem. Usually, I came in from NYU at about three in the afternoon. However, all my life I have had trouble sleeping in the daytime. I always want to participate in the activity going on around me. Also, there was my social life. I received calls from the time I got home until about ten or eleven o'clock at night. Mrs. Willis policed the situation and tried to get me to bed by six. Millie from Bermuda, who was about to be my main girlfriend, used to call as soon as I got to sleep. I am sure I didn't make much sense to her, which may be why we broke up so soon.

Monroe's Uproar House was an unusual place—two places in fact—basement clubs in adjacent brownstone buildings. They were connected with a single door with a warning red light. When the red light went on, my orders were to take my bass, go through the trap door (disguised by a covering drape), and await instructions. What kind of place *was* this? I soon discovered that it was a precaution against the weekly unannounced police raid. The sale of alcoholic beverages after 4:00 A.M. was illegal in New York. So the raids were usually after that hour and when the bulk of our customers were there. During an intermission I was outside and saw several police squad cars congregating with the spotlights blazing. The doorman said, "You better get your fiddle and take it next door." When I got in, the red light was on. The drape was removed, and the exodus began.

Next door we were in a club almost like the one we left. Although it didn't take long, I always wondered how they held up the police until everybody passed through the door. There was a small look-through like the ones on apartment front doors. We could observe the progress of the raid while the rearguard crew cleared tables and put chairs on top of them. Two of them would be mopping the floor. Policemen with flashlights peered into every corner. After about half an hour, the charade would end. We continued for the rest of the night in the other club.

I've thought about this many times since, and the best I can figure is that the raid was staged. First, I can't believe the other club was soundproof. Second, the police must have noticed the many "un-Harlem" type cars parked on that quiet residential street. I suspect that suave and dapper Mr. Monroe was paying off somebody and that the raid was an inconvenience to satisfy a complainant that the police were doing their jobs. After the second raid, I stayed at the club for several weeks with complete peace of mind.

I had relatives in Harlem and in Newark, but they had problems housing their own families in those little three- or four-room apartments in the core of the ghetto. Of course, Aunt Kate, my father's sister, would find a bed or mattress for me somewhere, but the situation was tight. I would have had to alternate with somebody for sleeping privileges. The welcome mat was always out for me, and I used it later whenever my money was light. My relatives were always good for a real home-cooked meal, regardless of their own financial situation.

Calvin had a major weakness. He could not drink alcoholic beverages. One tablespoonful of good bourbon would render him silly for hours. I was the direct opposite. I could drink a fifth over a period of a few hours and still take care of business. Calvin didn't need a drink in order to make himself known to some unknown females. Somebody said that Calvin was born high and didn't require alcohol to become supercharged. He fostered what little social life I had by introducing me to practically all of the females I knew, including Ophelia Devore. His popularity and outgoing personality, not to mention his prodigious piano playing, were the main reasons we were invited to live with Bill and Emma Willis.

Calvin was also really girl-crazy, again the direct opposite of my style. I was shy, reserved, introspective, and quiet. We were a package of opposites, and were to become known throughout Sugar Hill as "Oscar and Calvin." We complemented each other in just about every way, including music.

One afternoon Calvin came running into the apartment gasping that Sy Oliver wanted to see me! See *me*? Everybody knew who Sy Oliver was, but hardly anybody knew me, I thought. What did he want to see me for? It turned out that he lived in the neighborhood and was aware of the musically active kids at 393 Edgecombe. Of course, everybody was aware of Calvin, the young piano prodigy, and I got some of the reflected glory, such as, "Who was that guy with Calvin?" What Sy wanted was some information on how to write for the viola. Since I was at NYU and had taken a course in orchestration, I was the nearest available instructor.

Sy had achieved fame as the arranger for Jimmie Lunceford's band; he was the creator of the swinging Lunceford style. When that fame was at its height, Sy left the band and became an independent arranger for several white bands like Tommy Dorsey's. Most black arrangers' backgrounds never included writing for string instruments, but they were experts at writing for horns (brass and reed) and rhythm sections. They knew every aspect of instruments like the alto saxophone or the trumpet, but nothing at all about the cello or the viola.

The Oliver encounter turned out to be a social as well as an educational occasion for all of us. I took my orchestration textbook and explained the alto clef (as against the bass and treble clef). I talked about the range of the viola, which is the alto member of the violin family of instruments. I showed him sample passages, bowings, and general ideas of technique. Actually, all he really needed was the transposition—where and how you write for the viola. He already knew what he wanted by way of sound; he just needed the trick of writing for the instrument.

He got the idea in a few minutes. Oliver said his present arranging gig involved a string section session. He invited me and asked that I bring along my bass, which I did. He had us play through some sketches of what he was working on and then proceeded to give me a lesson on how to make the bass more incisive in sound. He actually took the bass and stroked through a few patterns to demonstrate. Receiving this invaluable lesson from someone of his great experience and fame, I almost swooned.

Sy lived about three buildings from us, so we had occasion to see him often. Sy was sophisticated and articulate, as was the whole Lunceford organization. The musicians of the Lunceford group were mostly college types and were different from most of the musicians of the other bands in manners and conversation. They were acknowledged as gentlemen in contrast with the image of the hard-drinking, chick-chasing, foul-mouthed black jazz musicians who were my cronies.

# CHAPTER 9

# BODY AND SOUL

**B**y the time we were ensconced on Edgecombe Avenue, it was the fall of 1939 and time for school again. I didn't have enough money to pay the full tuition. I went through all the motions of registering except for the final stop at the bursar's window. I asked all my instructors for permission to attend classes until I was officially enrolled. They all cooperated. The dean of the School of Education took my case personally. He asked me how much money I had. It wasn't enough, so he took what I had with me and told me, "Bring the rest of what you have to me, and let's try to get straight by midterm."

He then went to the bursar's office and brought me back my official "paid" registration. Even though I was extremely grateful, I still had an uneasy feeling because gigs were not a certainty. However, the whole thing progressed smoothly.

The year 1939 was a magic, if unsettling, year. The news from Europe was not good at all. I didn't concentrate on it, but negative thoughts were always there. The World's Fair was in New York that year, and, in spite of the war clouds, it was a ray of sunshine before the deluge, a happy dose of make-believe in the face of developing stark reality.

During the summer of 1939, Calvin and I had met Mercer Ellington (Duke Ellington's son), Luther Henderson, Richard Cunningham, and other members of the Cavaliers, a club of young blacks about our age. We were soon to be invited to become members of that club. The whole process opened up our social lives. Some Sundays we met at an ice-cream parlor on Seventh Avenue. That's where the girls were. Mercer would point out various older black musicians of note. He showed me Willie ("the Lion") Smith, who certainly looked the part strutting down St. Nick. The Lion was a famous old-timer who had much to do with the development of jazz piano playing. We occasionally ran across members of the Ellington band, and Mercer would introduce us. Harry Caroney (baritone sax) and Sonny Greer (drums) came to recognize us.

On other occasions, we stopped by the various clubs, primarily the ones on Seventh Avenue. We made a special trip to Small's Paradise to hear Earl Bostic, who was then considered to be the king of the alto sax players. There were bigger names, but the young musicians felt that he was the best. This was before he went commercial. There was also a Philadelphia reason for going to Small's. We knew the two trumpeters, Gabe Bowman and Palmer Davis; we had worked with them in Philly. This enabled us to go in the club, past the outer bar, and hear the music as friends of the specified musicians. Occasionally, Calvin and I got a chance to sit in with the band, but this was very chancey with an orchestra that had an organized repertoire book.

Downtown, meaning the Village (the area below Fourteenth Street in Manhattan), was open territory for cruising black musicians. In contrast with both up and down, the midtown clubs were mostly for white customers, and blacks were not welcomed unless they knew somebody. It wasn't mean or vicious. It was, as they put it, strictly business. We couldn't get past the doorman in those clubs unless we knew one of the musicians, and it would help if he or she were the featured attraction. Even then, the musician would sometimes have to come out and escort us in. Another trumpeter, Frankie Newton, who had played in Philly, was our main target in the Village. We thought a lot of Frankie's playing but felt that his career was limited because of his predilection for white women, who were prevalent wherever he worked. The Village tolerated this, primarily because of its political climate, so most of the clubs were more open to cruising black musicians.

There was some unrest in Harlem during this period. The depression was winding down, which meant that the unemployment situation was improving gradually, but not enough to appease those without jobs. This situation was exacerbated by the various businesses in Harlem that didn't employ any blacks. This was especially noticeable on 125th Street, which had the larger establishments. At the time, 125th Street was Harlem's business street. It had the clothing and furniture stores, and it had the main black hotel, the Theresa, at the corner of Seventh Avenue. For blacks, that corner was like Forty-second and Broadway. This was the downtown of the Negro capital of the New World.

The disturbance that took place in 1939 was small potatoes compared to the riots that would erupt in Harlem and Detroit in 1943, but it was the tip of the iceberg, a precursor of things to come. Black ownership of businesses or commercial real estate was practically nil. There was an occasional mom-and-pop business like a drugstore owned, most likely, by a West Indian or a southern black. Because there was no overt segregation, native or long-time Harlemites looked down on southern blacks, which is ironic because black-owned and -operated businesses could be found in all the main citadels of segregation in the South.

The disturbance was short-lived and consisted mostly of breaking windows and appropriating some radios and other desirables. One Chinese store owner had painted on his storefront window, "Me Colored, too," hoping to prevent damage to his shop. We read about the disturbance in *The New York Times* because most of the people on Sugar Hill stayed away. As I remember it, Mayor LaGuardia merited high marks for his restraint and sympathy for the plaintiffs. Right after that, I began to notice a black employee or two behind counters. The whole event made me aware of Harlem as a community and as a home. I had no intention at that point of returning to Philly. I had learned some of the basic survival techniques in the big city, and New York was home, even though my family ties in Philly remained.

Back at school I worked on my part of the tuition settlement—with a broom and a mop. I had several classrooms to clean as my obligation for the fifteen dollars a month from NYU. The white kids on the same program got desk, clerical, or lab-assistant jobs. I didn't resent this because I needed the money to stay in school. Also, it gave me a closer connection with NYU's black janitorial and service staff, a connection that would pay off mightily in my junior year. A more immediate payoff was the enhancement of my relationship with the black female students. In their quest for husband material, they viewed me with the attitude: "At least he will work." This was not obvious with my black colleagues, especially those whose parents paid the freight.

Mac Mackay, my guru, had come to New York as a kept man. He had married DeLoyd Mackay, a former star of the Blackbirds of 1929. She was featured at the Hickory House as a jazz singer. Their apartment was near Juilliard and City College of New York. Mac suggested to DeLoyd that the apartment needed painting. He said he knew a painter who would do it for a good price. Since I needed the money for my tuition settlement, I took the job. It went well except for the living room, where I started painting from the entrance and painted myself into the proverbial corner. I eventually extricated myself from this dilemma and, with Mac as my agent, proceeded to get more business in the neighborhood.

Other than riding down to the Hickory House with DeLoyd in a cab, Mac had nothing else to do but drink and associate. I looked forward to the nightly or daily cab ride, and DeLoyd, who was very jealous, was happy that Mac was with me. We always rode back on the subway. He would accompany me on the various painting jobs and supplied the beverage and the conversation, but never any painting. That was all right with me since I got to keep all the proceeds.

Having nothing else to do, Mac spent his days at the Willises. He saw me off to class and was there on my return. He helped me pull garbage in the evening and took charge of all salvageable materials and deposit bottles. These were collected and deposited with Bootsie, the janitorial assistant at 401 Edgecombe. What we had was an informal association which we called the Basement Rogues. It included the janitorial assistants of the eight buildings contiguous to 393. Our back alley also served St. Nicholas Place and became our business headquarters. Bootsie sold the collected materials to a local junk dealer. The amount we collected from these few buildings was surprising. Mac had the responsibility of purchasing the wine—or even bourbon if the money was long enough. We had business meetings, usually on Saturday afternoons, and consumed the proceeds. Those meetings lasted all afternoon or until Mrs. Willis got tired of it and called me in to do some chores. While the conversations did little for my academic pursuits, they did expand my awareness of life in black America. Mac, the philosopher with the common touch, was a master at this. He had provided the idea and the leadership, yet he was the only one in the group who did not have even a part-time hustle. Mac was an organizer, especially when it came to the socialization of alcohol. I wonder how far he would have gone if he had turned his talents to politics.

Autumn in New York is very nice. Since this was my second year, I had the mind-set to enjoy it. Walking out on the street (St. Nicholas or Seventh Avenue), I could meet and talk with the most interesting people. We met Billy Still coming out of the 155th Street subway station. I didn't realize who he was at the time. It had to be explained to me that he was the arranger for Paul Whiteman, who was Mr. Big in jazz in 1939. We had an unmemorable conversation, so I can't quote any significant statements. William Grant Still became acknowledged as the dean of American black composers. He dealt in another world, the alien world of classical music. He was more than a black arranger of jazz. He wrote pieces for the New York Philharmonic, something I had never imagined possible. He enlarged the dimension of my possibilities long before I had any notion of performing with a symphony orchestra.

Another sight to see was Big Sid Cathett strolling down St. Nick with his entourage of young musicians. He was a different drummer and a master of the wire brush technique. He used wire brushes in lieu of drumsticks in a sensitive and sensuous way. With that technique, he could fire up a rhythm section and, in consequence, a band or a soloist.

He was always playing out his role as father-confessor to jazz aspirants. I was surprised that he knew our names and probably our capabilities, but he was readily accessible for advice and encouragement. Since he was at the height of his fame, we considered it an honor that he would take time to counsel us. What he had to say would have been perceptive and valuable to any young musician with sense enough to listen.

His main theme was that you didn't have to play loud but that you needed intensity to get the listener's attention. This turned out to be the greatest of all lessons in how and what to play. In contrast to today's rock and roll percussionists, Big Sid demonstrated playing at a level where everybody else could be heard. The remarkable thing was that this blend was accomplished without the electronic amplifiers of today. Big Sid was always good for an invitation to hear him and his colleagues play. And what colleagues! The names read like a *Who's Who* of jazz.

Cozy Cole, the famous drummer, was next. Mac came by the house one evening and asked if I would like to visit Cole at home. From his previous experience in Kansas City with Count Basie, Mac was connected to a network of really good black jazz musicians who shared a kind of bond—no matter what a musician's fortune was at any given time, he was known and respected by the brotherhood. So Mac took me to see his friend Cozy Cole, who was playing with John Kirby's group at such dreamed-of places as the Waldorf and Cafe Society. His wife let us in and directed us back to the bedroom. There we saw the very dark Mr. Cole receiving a pedicure from a very white young lady. I was shocked. This kind of lifestyle was completely beyond my experience or comprehension. In fact, two things in that operation shook up my vision of the affluent lifestyles of successful black musicians. The first was the pedicure, which I had never heard of or even considered as a necessity. When you have your shoes on, who's going to see your toes? The second was the white woman as the pedicurist. Growing up in a black ghetto, I never imagined white people in a service capacity. Mac and I watched the whole process while we exchanged pleasantries with Mr. Cole. I didn't learn as much music from him as I did from Big Sid, but I got a different view of what was involved in making it to the top.

Before class work became really serious at midterm, Calvin and I made a couple of pilgrimages to black musicians who were not connected with the jazz world. We first went to see Carl Diton, who lived just two buildings from 393. He was a very fine organist and composer from Philadelphia, and we responded to suggestions from home that we contact him. We had a nice conversation, but as our lines of endeavor were so different, he had very little to offer but encouragement to stay in school. We next went to see Edward Margetson, a prolific composer who gave annual concerts of his own works. What was intriguing to me was that he was a graduate of the Royal College of Music in England. This was another new dimension for me. Black people were international. Black music was international! We need to remember both Diton and Margetson and to revive some of their works.

Langston Hughes was a frequent visitor, and we all were delighted by his storytelling. He brought to us a dimension of Negro life that was important to all of us in sophisticated and chic Sugar Hill. He reminded us who we were and where we came from. The Willises' at 393 was the "in" place for black intelligentsia. Almost anyone in Harlem with pretensions to or achievements in culture would sooner or later wind up at 393. We met a lot of the Harlem Renaissance figures. I must confess I didn't know who most of them were. However, everybody knew Langston Hughes, even I. Zora Neale Hurston was not well known, even among her own people, and when she came by sometimes with Langston Hughes, I was not aware of her presence. I was appalled by her story about being down on her luck and working as a domestic for some midtown white literati. She was serving at a party in high society when somebody recognized her as the writer of a short story for the prestigious *Saturday Evening Post*. The incident was indicative of the fact that black artists' efforts in culture were in the main unrecognized—not only by whites, but by their own people as well.

Dan Burley of the *Amsterdam News* came by frequently and gave us demonstrations of old-time, boogie-woogie piano. I still have a love for authentic blues of this genre. Dan was not really a pianist, but he would have made many a house-rent party happy with his simple but effective renditions of old-time blues. Ted Poston came by on another matter. He was the only black journalist on a major newspaper, the *New York Post*. He probably was the first in the nation. He participated in our various cultural soirées, but his primary interest was in Miriam, a young lady who lived at the house. They later married.

Then came the event that was to change my life. A cat named Jerry, whom I had known in Philly as a band valet and who was now working in New York, came by the house and told me to bring my bass down to Kelly's Stable and audition for a new band being formed for Coleman Hawkins.

Coleman Hawkins, the premier tenor saxophonist of the time, was a person I had heard very little about. He had been an expatriate living and working in Denmark who had returned to the United States because of the racist climate in the brewing storm, courtesy of Adolph Hitler. I read now of his fabulous exploits with the Fletcher Henderson band of the 1920s. A pioneer of jazz, he opened possibilities with his sophisticated improvisation and set tenor saxophone standards for many years to come. He was, as I was to find out, the ultimate standard. Also, through the years he was capable of change from the classical jazz style of the twenties to the very best of the boppers of the fifties. I was pleased to learn that he had begun his musical life as a cellist. Perhaps that explains his lyrical and logical way with the tenor. He was a private person, so his sidemen did not know him well. However, he was an educator who could tell his musicians what and how to play.

His standards were high, and that, combined with his experience, made everybody else reach. Guys hung around the bandstand in hopes of stealing his mouthpiece. I guess they thought his famous sound was the result of some special gimmick. As far as I could see, he used a saxophone that could be purchased at any reputable music store. It was just that his concept of playing was superior to everybody else's at the time. I had never been associated with a world-class musician before, so this was an awesome experience for me.

Coleman was a bandleader musician, which meant that he was

not built into most of the arrangements. He made spot appearances as a featured soloist while the band played the remaining portions of the set. We would set the stage for him with one or two pieces that featured other soloists in the band. Almost every night his performance climaxed with a rendition of "Body and Soul," and it became so well known that the record session was inevitable. I will say here and now that the recording, famous as it was, was not nearly as effective as those nightly performances. Every performance was an adventure. He could pull out stops and ideas that had his supporting cast wondering what he would do next. To hear a musician of this caliber was a rare privilege; to perform with him was a turning point in my life.

Most of the guys in the band were older, established sidemen in New York. They didn't know me, and I didn't know them except for my immediate associates in the rhythm section. Joe Guy, the trumpet player, was the youngest musician, and I was the next to youngest at twenty-two, so we got along fairly well. Joe was fresh from Alabama and at age nineteen or twenty was not prepared to fend off the pitfalls of the New York scene. He fell to the blandishments of narcotics. It was a shame, because he had so much ability so early. He was not a Dizzy Gillespie, but at that age he could have been on his way. He survived long enough to marry Billie Holiday in what evidently was a union of two lost souls. I hope I'm not passing judgment, but history has revealed both of their tragic endings. I was deeply distressed to hear that Joe wound up in prison in Alabama and died very young. What a waste! He could play, and he had such a promising future.

Gene Rodgers, the pianist, was my closest associate in the band. He was a huge guy, about six-feet, four inches tall and 240 pounds, yet he was gentle, sensitive, and humorous. He was our chief prankster and agitator. Having never heard of him, I was surprised that he could play jazz so well. He had just returned from Australia, and that in itself was intriguing. My knowledge of Australia came from reading that black people were not allowed to get off the boat. It came through to me that Australia was very racist. Evidently, entertainers and musicians with contracted jobs were exceptions to this policy. So I listened to everything Gene had to say about his experience, with a rapture derived from my curiosity about the unknown.

Gene could break up a pinochle game with his humor. He actually relieved the tension of the very serious pinochle games or dirty hearts that the guys would play during intermission. The games were too serious. The penalty for the queen of hearts was that the loser had to drink a quart of water. The penalty was enforced unmercifully.

Have you ever tried drinking two or three quarts of water in a single half-hour period? Gene's moderating influence was welcome.

Arthur Herbert, the drummer, was our no-nonsense drill sergeant. He was a time machine with all of the technique known to percussionists. I had not heard of him prior to my coming into the band, but evidently he had a following of percussionists who respected his ability. He was well versed and practiced in the rudiments of percussion. He used these basic skills in all of his playing and therefore had a different sound as compared to the drummers who knew only rhythm and banging. He reminded me of military band drummers with their precision. Art was not what was considered the jazz musician type. Rather, he was a family man from Brooklyn who came across more as a businessman. But he did not let his academic approach to drumming get in the way of his swinging.

During my tenure with Coleman Hawkins, I took up with our female vocalist, Thelma Carpenter. Aside from Joe Guy, I was the member of the band closest to her age. She was seventeen at the time, but a sophisticated and hep seventeen. This to me was part of the excitement. She knew the musicians and even at that age was experienced with night clubs. This was new to me—a female who did not play the usual male-female games but who stood on her own two feet and met me halfway as an equal partner. That is what we became, equal partners in exploring New York's nightclubs and bars. She did not exploit me, nor I her; we were two kindred souls who were bent on discovery of New York's delights, within our budget. In short, we were buddies, and sex, as such, was not important to our relationship. We shared our money and times with each other. We took care of each other and could sense changes of mood. I even thought of the possibility of marriage after graduation. As it turned out, she never married, and I suspect that I was as close as she ever got to marriage with a male.

One evening, Thelma asked me to come with her to a place I had heard about but never had a reason to visit. It was the apartment of the celebrated Countess Fustendam (not her real name), a white groupie of black jazz musicians. The apartment was on the second floor of a building about two doors east of the Spotlight on Fifty-second Street. Certain musicians took their intermissions there in order to light up. It was a haven for the tea smokers. History records that Charlie Parker died there on his last tea session. I balked at the prospect of even experimenting with marijuana, but Thelma prevailed and we went on our journey.

The rather large living room was filled with people sitting on the floor around the four walls. No furniture was available. Most of the people were musicians working on the street. I knew some of them, names that are part and parcel of jazz history. Conversation was at a minimum. Thelma consoled and encouraged me, saying that it would be all right. My philosophy was that alcohol was enough of a monster, and I didn't need two. The joint was passed around, and everybody took a drag or two. When it got to me it was about an inch long. I imitated what I saw and took two tokes with what I hoped was the same reaction as the other people. I got no satisfaction or even pleasure and passed the joint on to Thelma, who took her puffs. To me, it was like smoking smoke, but I carried on so that Thelma would not be disappointed. It was my first and last encounter with narcotics. I probably did not inhale or do what the veteran smokers habitually do, so it may not have been a fair test.

I was glad to get away intact and return to my old faithful whiskey. Thelma was unable to get me to go back; I always came up with an excuse. I never did find out what I was supposed to get out of it.

Thelma Carpenter was a pretty, brown-skinned young lady with a dynamite shape. She was short but still was able to display the gowns she wore to advantage. Some say she was wild, but that was not my impression. I will say that she was assertive and adventurous, but that did not add up to wild. Most of my friends were surprised that since I was mild-mannered and quiet, we could be such close and intimate associates. She didn't graduate from high school, but was an intelligent and perceptive observer. To me, she was a warm, vibrant, and loving person. She was my girlfriend. She went on to make several record albums and sing with other leading bands of the day, including Benny Goodman's. It was her tour of Europe with Benny Goodman that terminated our togetherness. I have not seen her since 1940, though I did talk with her on the phone decades later. I often wonder what might have been if Brother Goodman had not intervened. To me, a lot of strong and assertive women have been labeled lesbians after the accuser failed to make out. I prefer to think that the rumors about Thelma were unfounded.

While at Kelly's Stables with Coleman Hawkins, we had a trio from California as our relief band. We played our sets on the half hour, and the trio played on the hour until we came on. The custom of the musicians was to run to the nearby clubs to catch other groups doing their thing. That whole area around Fifty-second Street and Sixth Avenue was really the world capital of jazz. We could hear Stuff Smith,

Errol Garner, or Count Basie and the like in the half hour we had off. Despite the temptation of these available delights, I seldom left the club, simply because I was enchanted with our own relief trio. The piano player especially intrigued me. He was a poetic and lyrical version of Earl Hines. This guy had rhythm, technique, and original ideas. I was fortunate enough to catch him before he became commercially successful as a singer. His name was Nat ("King") Cole. At the time, his trio was purely instrumental. I was stunned to hear him a year or so later as a vocal recording star. I don't think that the jazz world realized how much piano he played. His recording format featured his singing and limited him to maybe eight bars of pianistic exploits. This was to me a tease, but not the real thing that I heard during the intermissions at Kelly's Stable in 1939.

My encounter with King Cole consisted not only of listening to him play piano, but of coming to know him as a person. He knew I was a student at NYU. He also knew I had a 10:00 A.M. class and that there was a 4:06 A.M. train at the Fiftieth Street station. He came to me one night and said, "Oscar, let's catch that train."

He finished his stint at three-thirty, but he offered to wait for me to finish at four. I demurred, feeling that I couldn't negotiate that four-block run in about three minutes and would settle for the half-hour wait for the next train.

"Not so," said Nat Cole. "We'll do it. Just follow me." At exactly four o'clock, with the last chord still echoing in the place, we flew out of the front door. We sprinted, I do mean sprinted, all the way—like Olympic champions. Nat was in good shape. He must have done this in high school; also, he didn't drink and smoked very little. I was not at all prepared for this kind of athletics. However, we made it every night (really, morning) flying down two or three flights of stairs with the sound of the arriving train assaulting our ears. We usually made it as the doors were closing. We got off at 155th Street, and Nat would go into his brownstone house at 156th. He would say, "Let's try it again tomorrow!"

Thank you, Nat, wherever you are. I needed that half-hour extra sleep to perform well in that ten o'clock class. Thanks to you, I didn't have to withdraw.

It was the nightly excursions with Thelma Carpenter that finally endangered my studies at NYU. I missed some of those morning classes, or I arrived very sleepy and not at my most alert. Considering that we got off work at four and enjoyed partying until seven or eight in the morning, a ten o'clock harmony class became a very chancy occasion. The truth of the matter was that at midterm I was failing. On occasions when I made the class I got up at about midway (ten-thirty) and walked out to make my way to Thelma's home in Brooklyn. This used to shock my classmates. Consequently, I was invited to attend the academic dean's scholarship meeting, a scene in which students in this condition met with their teachers, dean, and counselors to discuss why they should remain in school.

An appointment for my meeting was issued. Everyone knew what this meant. I knew former students who had been asked to leave! Miss Sanford, a professor who was a Southerner from Missouri, saved me when she said to the council, "Willie has a lot of ability, and I would like to give him another chance, since his people have so few chances."

This from a woman whom I had mentally classified as a cracker. The rest of the council was not so nice, but Miss Sanford carried the day and saved my butt. It was that close.

When we were free from the Nat ("King") Cole attraction, we would depart Kelly's for Fifty-second Street proper to catch some of the musical action. Most of the black musicians skipped the Hickory House and opted for the Famous Door, the Three Deuces, or the clubs on Fifty-second Street between Sixth and Seventh Avenues. They would let us in if we were very unobtrusive and were there solely for the purpose of listening to our peers. Sitting at a customer table was taboo.

It was on such an occasion that we caught the opening night of the increasingly famous Count Basie band. We had heard them many times broadcasting from dance halls. Therein was the rub; they were not used to playing in small clubs, most of which were less than two thousand square feet. The clubs were all situated in the basement or the first floor of a single brownstone row house. When they opened up with the blast characteristic of the big band that they were, the customers moved to rear tables. We could hear Basie's band half a block away. After one week we had to get inside the front door to realize that they were playing. They had learned to substitute intensity for loudness. I think it is this quality that makes Basie's recordings so successful.

Stuff Smith's gig was one of the favorite spots to stop. His violin playing was ingenious and clever. I had never heard anything like this before, including Joe Venuti with Paul Whiteman. Stuff Smith's playing was less classical and more soul and blues. I had heard Eddie South, the black angel of the violin, who was a great virtuoso, but he betrayed his classical training. Smith's playing was unpredictable and displayed a lot of wit. Jazz violin was very unusual in the late thirties and early forties. Yet pictures of black bands of the twenties often displayed a violin or two. The big band period practically did away with the violin or the string section. Jazz violin was primarily for the cognoscenti, as it was not a drawing card in black establishments. It was a shame, too. If more people had heard Stuff Smith, the instrument would be established among the masses.

After about seven weeks at Kelly's Stables, the Coleman Hawkins band moved downtown to the famous Roseland Ballroom. Part of the glamour of this gig was the periodic network broadcast. I had heard these broadcasts since I was in high school, and there we were, in this huge place with the opportunity of being heard nationally! There were two adjacent bandstands, and we were the featured band. The house band was white, and we never came into contact with them. We even had separate dressing rooms. Contributing to the noncontact was the policy of continuous music. There was a curtain between the two stands so that each group could take its place on hearing the sign-off of the other. This was known as a taxi dance. The hosts and hostesses were all white, so the Roseland was taboo for black would-be customers. After all, blacks had their own ballroom, the equally famous Savoy.

The management carefully explained the house policy of nonfraternization with the hostesses. From what I saw, this policy did not apply to the white group. However, it turned out to be our undoing. The white hostesses were the aggressors; the discipline suggested by our leader soon broke down. Coleman Hawkins even suggested that the guys who were the main culprits try to be cool and meet the various hostesses out of view of the management, that is, uptown. He claimed that Lunceford's guys did that, with nobody but the people of Harlem any the wiser.

Our separate (but equal) dressing room had telephones and furniture, and we could order food and drinks at the employee's discount. We could entertain there, provided we were not with white women. Between the aggression of some of the hostesses and the weakness of some of our guys, the policy broke down. One evening a trumpet player and a hostess walked across the dance floor arm in arm and in full view of everybody. The ax fell. Our engagement was shortened.

One unusual event happened before the demise. We rehearsed at the ballroom in the afternoons. One day Don Byas came to the audition for a spot in the band. Don Byas was a well-known young tenor saxophonist, in my estimate one rung down from the king himself, Coleman Hawkins. Hawkins was content to let Byas read the book without taking a solo. The younger guys in the band agitated to get Coleman to let Byas take a solo. His reputation was tremendous. He was not nationally recognized nor recorded, but we knew of his ability. Coleman finally let him take a few solos. What playing! This guy was amazing; he was challenging Coleman. That night we heard another dimension of Coleman's playing. It was as though he were answering the challenge for his own band. Actually it was unnecessary, for we were all believers.

I read somewhere that the recording of "Body and Soul" took place on October 13, 1939. In my memory it was an unpromising day and a date uncertain. We had worked the previous night at Kelly's Stables until 4:00 A.M. Since I had to take my bass home in order to use it for the session, I obviously missed that 4:06 train. I got in bed about 5:30 and slept for a couple of hours. The session was to begin between 9:30 and 10:00 in the morning. I would not permit myself to be late for my first record session. All of us band members were on time, except for Hawkins himself. We were all sleepy. Some had opted to stay up all night. The edgy feeling in the studio offered little prospect for our best playing. And it didn't help when Coleman himself showed up almost an hour late with a giggling young blonde on his arm. Almost everybody was quietly furious, and I would have bet that the session would be a flop.

The RCA studio was very simple, in contrast to the studios of today. It was a medium-sized room with just two microphones and a piano. The usual glass windows and a very simple control room were in evidence. The control board for the engineers looked like a home set compared with the boards used by the rock bands of today.

The engineers usually recorded symphony orchestras or society groups like Eddie Duchin. Consequently, they wanted to put a damper on the "noise" coming from a black group. I'm sure they thought this recording would be a primitive experience. According to the philosophy of RCA in those days, no black groups were permitted on their Red Seal label. Not even Duke Ellington was considered musical enough for such an honor. Most of the major record companies had race records divisions with markets targeted in the South or black neighborhoods.

Arthur Herbert, the drummer, got into an argument when the engineers started trying to put him in the next studio. When that did not succeed, they tried to put some blankets over the drums. Herbert finally told them, "Don't tell me how to play."

The engineers had a lot of power in those days and were intimidating to most black groups, especially the ones who didn't get many opportunities to record with major record labels. It would have been all right if the engineers had been more experienced with jazz and had respected it. After Herbert's encounter, all of us, including Hawkins, stood up for our artistic principles and got the engineers off our backs. None of this helped the prevailing mood or atmosphere. Everybody was tired. There was none of the relaxation we would have had at the club. Most record sessions are like that since they are contrived affairs. However, being the professionals that we were, we pushed on and gave it our, by then, limited best.

We had played "Body and Soul" at least a hundred times, and many nights two or three times by special request. We had no written arrangement, as each performance by Hawkins was different. He would go from unbelievable to impossible on successive renditions. But what should we do for a record?

There was a brief discussion, and Coleman instructed me to play 2/4 bass as against playing a note for all four beats of the bar. I think it was Joe Guy, our trumpet player, who improvised the trumpet background. Considering that none of this was written down, it was a minor miracle that the trumpet players all grabbed the right notes throughout. As I remember it, there were only about two or three tries before we had a "take." I felt that the engineers and the session director just gave up in order to complete the three or four numbers in the allotted time. I thought the trumpet background was crude and the only redeeming feature after Hawkins' always-brilliant playing was the piano opening by Gene Rodgers. However, I notice that the 2/4 bass idea has prevailed on most of the subsequent recordings by others that I have heard.

I left the session with mixed feelings. Nothing we recorded sounded as good as I had heard it done at Kelly's Stables. Most of us left the studio quietly, almost with a feeling of failure. I think the majority thought that "Fine Dinner" (on the reverse side of "Body and Soul") was our best effort and was at least representative. It had a written arrangement, and we had played it enough not to mess it up even in our fatigue. Little did I realize on the way home and back to sleep that what was done that day would have an impact on the rest of my life.

In 1964 I received a twenty-fifth-anniversary copy of one of the first million-sellers, "Body and Soul," compliments of RCA. I guess they found me through the musicians' union. I had no idea that the recording would be so successful. I am extremely grateful for the lucky accident that placed me in association with Coleman Hawkins. Not only was it providential in terms of my education as a musician, but also for the fame it gave me in the world of jazz.

# CHAPTER 10

# MY OWN BAND

**J**ust before I registered in January for the 1940 spring term at NYU, Coleman Hawkins presented me with a terrible dilemma. He announced that the band was going on the road. If I hadn't had anything else to do, it would have been great, but there was the matter of NYU and my promise to my mother.

The decision was agonizing. I would have given my right arm to continue with this organization. We were just coming into our own, and the guys accepted me and respected my playing. The musicians of Harlem recognized me uptown and downtown as Coleman Hawkins' bassist. This was what I had come to New York for.

However, NYU was not so perceptive. The policy there was: no class, no credit. Registration was upon me, and I had to decide immediately. My mother's concern surfaced in the boiling cauldron within me. It was a very unhappy young man who reluctantly handed in his two-weeks' notice to the band.

As it turned out, fate was not unkind. Kelly's Stables hired me as a sort of house bassist, and that gave me the opportunity to play with Sabby Lewis's band from Boston. At least it was work, income, and a semblance of tuition money. Also, Coleman's road tour was unsuccessful, and the band broke up shortly after their return to New York. Looking back, I can see that things worked out for the best for me. At the time I didn't understand why fate had dealt me such a cruel blow, but now I can see and give thanks to the guiding forces that moved me reluctantly and apprehensively onward.

I had just enough money to register for the spring semester. I would have had more but for my nocturnal exploits with Thelma Carpenter, and the fact that I was almost the only person working in our little commune at 393 Edgecombe. I had purchased food and clothes for just about everybody there, as well as medical services; in one case, I paid for an operation. My only solace was that even if my cash reserves were very light after paying tuition, I would be taken care of by the commune. Having looked after everybody else during their hard winter, I was in a privileged position. Some would even do my chores out of gratitude. This was not a "what have you done for us lately" situation. It was a situation in which whoever had it put out for the benefit of all. For me it was family as close as any blood relatives I ever had. I felt that I had received more than I had given. It made the uncertain year of 1940 happy and secure.

My mother complained that I didn't come home to Philadelphia often enough, but with either seven-day-a-week gigs or lightness of cash reserves, I had to make my visits few and far between—something like once a year. She visited the commune one weekend and was treated like royalty. I took her up the street and ran into Mercer Ellington outside 409 Edgecombe. By the time we got there, Duke himself drove up and got into our conversation. Duke was a ladies' man and soon had charmed my mother into accepting an invitation to come up to the apartment for coffee. Mother, an attractive widow for almost five years, was practically speechless. Duke, a perfect gentleman, acted as if he had known us all for years. Although he had only seen me once or twice in his son's company, he knew that I was a college music student.

Duke was a very gracious host. His sister Ruth, the lady of the apartment, treated Mother so well that she talked about it for years. For Mother and me, this was our first foray into black high society. Their large apartment at 409 Edgecombe was probably the most prestigious address in Sugar Hill. Duke and Ruth chatted mostly about black current events and a little about music and Duke's travels. Ruth gave the conversation an international flavor by mentioning her recent sojourn in Paris while she attended the Sorbonne.

Duke told my mother to let him know the next time she was in New York, as he wanted her to hear the band. You have to picture the Duke—very dapper, suave, and sensitive—to imagine how all this made my mother feel. She never forgot it.

Classes went on uneventfully while my cash reserves dwindled to nothing. Just about the time they reached zero, I received a call from the guy who owned Kelly's Stable. He told me to bring my bass to the club and play bass for Sabby Lewis, the band from Boston. This was a mixed blessing in that their bassist, Milt Hinton, had union troubles with Local 802 and could not make the gig. I was drafted on opening night to take his place. Hinton, respectfully and affectionately known as "Mr. Time," was, in my mind, one of the half-dozen greatest jazz bassists who ever lived. No matter how well I played, I was second-best to Mr. Hinton. I went apprehensively to the rehearsal that afternoon and I was able to fulfill the gig perfunctorily, except for Mr. Time's great moments. Evidently he had many. I was never able to be one of the guys.

Sabby Lewis had a strange band in that he had a white saxophonist who overplayed the part of being in a black band. A person of differing color was unusual with any band at the time. This cat was extremely profane. I have never considered profanity a black cultural asset. Traditionally, it never was a black attribute. Only those who bought into the "uninhibited nature of savages" theory or who put down any sign of intellectual ability in blacks considered profanity to be characteristic. It was not true, but the white saxophonist bought it, and he was one of the most foul-mouthed cats I ever heard. It turned me off, and we never got close.

Like many, Lewis's band did not have all written arrangements. However, this did not present much of a problem for me except for the solos or breaks of Mr. Time himself. I got as close as my stage of development would allow, but to the band members I was not Milt Hinton. This made it difficult because I would never be Milt Hinton. But I tried with all of my ability to get as close as possible. It was not good enough. Not that I failed; I simply was not the superstar that he was. It was an unhappy experience, and I finished out the four-week session with very little satisfaction.

Sometime early in the spring, probably around Easter, the Cavaliers, a club of which I was a member, had a social affair. Each member was supposed to invite enough people for a table of six, that is, his girlfriend and two other couples. Each member supplied drinks. Food was furnished by the club.

The location for the party was at a place called the "something" Palace. I only remember the Palace part because that was what it most certainly was not. Barn, maybe. It was somewhere east of Seventh Avenue on 146th or 147th Street. Richard Cunningham brought the seventeen-year-old Carmen MacRae who was beginning to earn a reputation as a jazz singer. Ophelia Devore was my date, and I had invited two other couples. The only problem with them was that nobody drank alcoholic beverages. I was stuck with almost a full gallon of port wine.

I say "almost" because I had started partying as soon as I bought the wine that morning. I took care of my host duties but added a little extra. I exuded my charm over all of the other tables and, of course, had to toast the host. This was all right except that each table had something different. Mercer Ellington had Scotch at his table, and so on down according to the affluence of each participating member. I sampled them all, as well as taking up the slack for my invited guests. By midnight, I had finished my gallon of wine almost unassisted.

Ophelia and Calvin got me home to 393, walking "uphill" all the way. A historic hangover followed. For several days even a drink of water brought back the sickness of that fatal night. Worse was the fact that I had pulled Bill Willis out of bed with several complaints that might have been tolerated if he'd known my condition. But I threatened (or promised) to move out as soon as my hangover permitted. I carried out my threat three days later and became the resident "phantom" of New York University.

All of the elevator operators, janitors, and porters at New York University's Washington Square campus were black. What this meant for me was that as soon as I had acquired their friendship, I was a member of the underground world of this distinguished university. I had a place to hide and take a drink or a shower. It also meant that I had a pipeline to some choice campus gossip. I was shocked to find a thriving numbers game running, with the faculty as customers. I'd always thought the numbers racket was exclusive to inner-city black ghettos.

In this windup of my sophomore year, when I had no funds and no place to stay, these maintenance men took care of me. They took such care that none of my classmates could even guess what was going on. Only my two closest friends knew that I had no address. A Washington Square park bench was my bedroom, and my washroom was in the student union building. Food, mostly soup, was compliments of the elevator operators, who had an electric burner in their basement headquarters. My limited laundry was a problem, but we took care of it on the premises. All this sounds pretty sad, but actually I thrived. I got some of my highest grades during this period. And, truth be told, it didn't last all that long anyway. Within a couple of weeks, the goodhearted Bill Willis had found me and coaxed me back to 393. It didn't take much coaxing.

By the first of May, I was unemployed and nearly exhausted. My grade point average fell below the requirements of keeping the scholarship. All of the extracurricular activities had taken their toll on my academic efforts. And I had another excuse: The daily flow of information about the war in Europe contributed to a sort of general malaise. Germany invaded Denmark, Norway, Belgium, and The Netherlands that spring, and it seemed only a matter of time before our guys—maybe even me—would be going to the rescue.

One sunny afternoon in May, I ran into Nat Rudnick on Broadway. Nat was the chairman of the NYU School of Education student council. He had recommended me for several small combo gigs on campus but had something different on his mind this time. Nat had rented a club on Broadway and was playing the role of entrepreneur. He had gotten a wage-scale concession from the musicians' union and with the help of some partners and, of course, a liquor license, was about to open the Keynote Club for business. He knew me as a student from NYU, but also as the former bassist with Coleman Hawkins. He was a frequent customer at Kelly's Stables. Nat said, "Oscar, how about you forming a five-piece combo, and we'll start with one night a week?"

I said, "Fine," although I was not sure about who would play with me for the less-than-scale wage. I had to find musicians who were between gigs or who were in the six-month probation period. I called the group Oscar Smith and the Keynoters, and what a group it was!

We started with my old roommate Calvin Jackson at the piano. He was his usual fabulous self. From time to time we alternated two drummers, Shep Shepherd and Shadow Wilson, depending on who didn't have a better-paying gig or wasn't with his regular group. Both were fine, swinging drummers, and we were lucky to have them. My biggest catch was Jimmy Hamilton on alto sax. It turned out that Duke Ellington was in a slack period, and Jimmy was available for all those Saturday night sessions; our old Philadelphia connection helped me recruit him. I had asked Dizzy to make the gig, and he would have had he not been already engaged. He did the next best thing and introduced me to Freddie Webster, a trumpet player on his six-month probation period with the union. He was the only guy in our group who did not connect with Philly. I got permission from the union to use him, and we started on a one-night-a-week basis. Hardly anybody knew who Freddie Webster was, but we all soon found out. From what I heard, I'd say Freddie was the equal of Dizzy Gillespie, Charlie

Shavers, and trumpeters of that stripe. I'm glad we got to hear him. He died a year or so later, and there are very few extant records to confirm what a prodigious performer he was. I have often wondered what would have happened if fate had allowed me to keep that group together.

Each Saturday session was a delight. Every number was exhilarating. Every set was discovery, serendipity. We heard things from each other that inspired other things. Shadow or Shep would swing us right out of the building. Jimmy Hamilton, away from the confines of the Ellington repertoire book, showed his inventive side. Calvin Jackson anchored the group with his explosive Art Tatum technique. Freddie would make original and unconventional riffs. How I wish we could have had today's tape recorders. We played standards, made up new stuff as we went along. We had no rehearsals. Every chorus was innovative. The solos were all inspired, inspiring. As for me, I did my best just to keep up. Actually I played beyond myself, pumped up with this music all around me.

But fate did *not* allow me to keep this band. The Keynote Club couldn't turn a profit. After about six weeks, Nat Rudnick told me, "I'm afraid this is the last night." I was disappointed but grateful for the experience of having covered this extremely talented group of musicians with my name. It was a true privilege, and I wish sometimes that I could roll back the calendar and stop right there.

It was mid-June by then, and I was still low on cash and badly in need of a gig. Once again, Nat Rudnick came up with a life-saving idea. A resourceful and well connected cat, Rudnick made a few calls and then unveiled his plan. He urged me to form a five-piece band and be ready to leave the following week for a summer-long gig, all the way into September, at Camp Lakeland, near Hopewell Junction, New York. The camp was a recreational and cultural experience primarily for Jewish youngsters, but with facilities for parents and other guests. I think it was sponsored by the International Ladies' Garment Workers Union. Their political philosophy was a little left of center. I had no idea what to expect, as this was my first gig in residence. Most of the guys that I had worked with previously were unavailable for an entire summer or didn't want to leave the city. The pay was not great, unless we factored in room, board, and recreational facilities. As it turned out, it was to be one of the most pleasant summers of my entire life.

I found Teddy Thompson, a young pharmacy student at Brooklyn College, an alto sax player. He was not a member of the union and had never played a gig. I had to get special permission from the local to use him. He was a jolly fat man who could play reasonably well in spite of just three years' experience on the instrument. The trumpet player for that first year at Lakeland was my New York friend Mercer Ellington. Mercer had been allowed to sit in his father's band and was not totally without experience. I think that this was Mercer's first gig for pay. Calvin Jackson was the pianist. We built most of our musical arrangements around him because of the inexperience of our horn players. I don't remember how I met our drummer, Leroy ("Boots") Battle, but it was sheer good luck. We were destined to be together at Lakeland and later in Baltimore for years to come. He was not a professional musician at that time, but had all the tools necessary for a successful career as a jazz drummer.

Lakeland was a cultural shock to all of us. Our clientele, young and old, were primarily Jewish with roots in Europe. We had to learn to play Russian waltzes, polkas, *troikas,* and the like. Actually we played more of those than we played jazz. We were coached in the nuances and traditions of performance by the well-known dance teacher and poet Edith Segal. We thought she was kidding when she made us take this stuff seriously. She did her job so well that we became the champs of the other bands around Lake Sylvan who tried the same thing. It was something to see and hear an all-black band handle this European material with conviction and panache.

We got another cultural shock, a culinary one. At first most of us didn't trust the food and waited for the canteen to open so we could buy hamburgers. But slowly we filtered in such items as gefilte fish, bagels and lox, cheese blintzes, borscht, and so on. By the end of the summer, I was a complete central European in all but color and language. It was not that I didn't try the languages. I did learn enough Russian words to order a meal. I also studied Hebrew with the kids, but soon gave that up in favor of some street Yiddish.

Camp Lakeland was really two camps—one for the counselors, workers, and adult guests, who were usually related to the kids, and the other for the kids themselves. The latter was known as Camp Kinderland and was the primary reason for the existence of the entire complex. Here was another cultural revelation; the place was crawling with bright, intelligent, and informed youngsters. I made many friends among these children and was impressed with their level of conversation; their knowledge of languages, culture, and politics; and their skill at intellectual games. While I could beat them at Ping-Pong, I didn't stand a chance at chess or checkers. It's tough to be beaten by some grinning adolescent, especially if you are a college junior.

Most of our social life was spent with the counselors, who were all white and mostly Jewish, except for one black female. We made some romantic, or quasi-romantic, alliances with the female counselors. We ate together, attended programs together, or did things like hiking or rowing. This was perceived by the surrounding community as improper, if not downright un-American. The sight of a young black male and a young white female participating in social activity was too much for this rural, racist community, and on one occasion we were shocked to witness a cross burning. I'm sure they imagined the worst. Fortunately, it never got worse than that. What they didn't know was that what they saw was about as far as the social activity went.

Lakeland was an easy gig. Usually there was a featured guest artist. Names like Paul Robeson, Pearl Primus, Pete Seeger, and Victor Borge were featured in weekly engagements. With the casino opening at eight in the evening and the show lasting until about ten, we didn't get to start playing until after ten o'clock. At that time our folk-dance mentor Edith Segal took over, and there would be an eastern European hoe-down until about eleven. Then we started our jazz program and played until about midnight, when the casino closed. We were so starved for jazz performance that we closed the curtains on stage and played for our friends until one. This was our free contribution, since our contract called for an eight-to-twelve performance schedule. Victor Borge, when he came to Lakeland, was just off the boat and practically unknown. However, most of us predicted his inevitable stardom after cracking up over his hilarious routines. Paul Robeson was quite an imposing character, with a voice that boomed even as he spoke. Since I was part of the "help" at Lakeland, I could not get as close to him as I would have liked.

Not only was it an easy gig, it was fun and educational, even though that period was marred by the fall of France to the Nazis. We agonized over the German advances for the rest of the summer, wondering how long it would be before the United States entered the war.

My constant female companion during this magical summer was a thirty-four-year-old counselor at Kinderland. She was Mrs. Body Fitness USA personified. Besides being the tennis coach, she was a perpetual motion machine—always in some kind of sports activity. Our little "affair" involved no physical intimacy; she often brought her son with her. I would have been embarrassed by the relationship if she hadn't been so pretty and well built as to be irresistible.

At least my band members accepted her as "my lady" and didn't realize that what they saw was all there was to it.

I'll call her Myrna for purposes of this memoir. She was a card-carrying Communist who would practically undress to show me her machine-gun wound from the Russian revolution. She was from the city of Kniepropretrovsk in the Ukraine. We had all our meals together and attended the nightly shows in the casino. Whenever she made an appearance during our jazz session, I stopped the band and played "I Love You Much Too Much." Just about everybody in camp knew the significance of this action. For all my outward behavior, though, I was uncomfortable with the relationship; my religious and cultural background could not encompass a liberated white woman—and a married one at that. I certainly valued the friendship, the companionship, and the intellectual parity, but I had to acknowledge a sense of relief when we parted company after Labor Day.

When the camp was over, the band members and I returned to New York. The city was the same as we had left it—up to and including the increasing threat of war. This was not a good time for anyone of potential draft age. Even though I had miserable vision, I suspected that I would still be available meat for the army. It was cause to worry.

There was a difference at the Willises'. They had an after-hours club in the big living room. Our regular customers included Art Tatum, the premier pianist, Benny Goodman and members of his band (including Teddy Wilson), the John Kirby band, and their various female consorts. We had a variety of alcoholic drinks, including beer. I was the part-time or relief bartender-waiter, depending on what was needed.

One Saturday a cold rain made the streets very slick, so we had no Sunday morning customers. This was disastrous because there was no food in the house for our commune of about a dozen people. Mrs. Willis promptly presented each of us with a quart of our unsold beer for Sunday breakfast. Nobody complained, but have you ever tried cold beer on an empty stomach? It has a different (possibly more potent) taste. It is a tradition that I have carried on into my more economically secure days.

On other occasions, when the larder was depleted and there was little money, we trekked over to Father Divine's Palace. As I remember it, Father Divine's complex ran from about 145th to 150th Street on Seventh Avenue. This was a little city in itself, complete with second-hand clothing and furniture shops, a restaurant, and all of the businesses of a self-sufficient community. The attraction at the restaurant, aside from the low prices, was that all of the food items came from Father Divine's farm and were fresh. We didn't have to join his community to enjoy the economic benefits. It did help if we said, "Thank you, Father," in all of our transactions. I gladly complied with the custom, especially to get second helpings. It worked every time. A breakfast with everything—bacon, fresh eggs, grits, fruit, biscuits, and coffee—was about a quarter. I was not ashamed to be seen there or even to say, "Thank you, Father." I ate there on many occasions.

# CHAPTER 11

# THE PHANTOM RETURNS TO NYU

*T*he autumn of 1940 was the beginning of my junior year at NYU, and it was to be a rather eventful season for me, both on and off campus. Being back in good graces with the Willises meant that I no longer faced a subterranean existence like that cat in *Les Miserables*, but I still was short on funds and always in need of a good gig.

Mercer Ellington rescued me this time. I had helped him out with the band job at Camp Lakeland, and he returned the favor in short order. Mercer came by to see me at 393 in mid-September. He said his dad had given him the go-ahead to form a band of his own, using some of the young cats that Duke was planning to call on later for his own band. Billy Strayhorn was one such individual, and while he did not play piano in Mercer's new group, he certainly gave us some eye-opening arrangements. I had never heard of Strayhorn before that, and his soulful, dreamy style of playing was very impressive. More than that, he was as nice a guy as you would ever want to meet—considerate, sensitive, self-effacing. He was loved and respected by everybody even though he had yet to make his name. He evolved as Duke's silent and sometimes senior partner. Who can forget his arrangement of "Take the A Train"? The A Train (an express from downtown to Harlem) was symbolic of the black jazz musician's return home after a brush with the white world downtown. My favorite piece by Strayhorn is his sensuous and nostalgic "Chelsea

Bridge." That piece reveals a harmonic sense that places Strayhorn right alongside the great impressionists, Frederick Delius and Claude Debussy. I was later to be an apartment mate of Strayhorn's and a member of the We Love Strayhorn club.

George Duvivier was my only competition as the projected bassist, and fortunately for me he was working at the time. It was a large band. I don't remember all the guys in it. We had something like four trumpets (five with Mercer playing on special arrangements), three trombones, five saxophones, and a complete rhythm section. Calvin Jackson and Luther Henderson were our pianists from time to time. Luther Henderson, like Calvin and me, was a member of the Cavaliers social club, as was Mercer. Luther was a Columbia University student and an outstanding jazz arranger. He later became a vocal coach and manager for several female singers, Eileen Farrell and Diahann Carroll among them. If you remember in the movie *Ain't Misbehavin'*, he sat with his back turned to the audience, and only in the last scene did he turn around and say the motto of the film: "One never knows, do one?" He played piano like Fats, and actually he was "Fats" without the extra weight.

Mercer's rehearsals were all held at the Savoy Ballroom and were enjoyable affairs. I tried my hand at writing an arrangement for the band. Almost everybody in this talented group did likewise. With these guys, not to mention Billy Strayhorn, one was lucky to get a hearing. One afternoon Mercer pulled out my arrangement—an original tune, if my memory serves me well. Duke himself sat through the rehearsal, making critical but positive remarks. I had written the trumpet parts all in the neighborhood of high *C*. You see, I wanted this number to be a real screamer. For balance, I had all of the saxophones in their lowest register. The truth of the matter was that I hadn't thought through the results of transcribing a piece from the piano key to the keys of the various instruments. It was a dumb mistake and ruined what would have been a nice piece. As soon as we finished the first rundown, Duke immediately yelled to the band, "Trumpets too high—reeds too low." What a way to have a lesson smashed into you. I subconsciously was trying to impress Duke, so it was doubly painful to hear him pound the obvious. Whenever and wherever he saw me after that, Duke would acknowledge me by saying, "Trumpets too high—reeds too low." That was my name to him, even ten years later when I saw him in Houston.

The band was a group of young lions. It was like a farm system for the major-league Ellington Orchestra. Billy White from Washington, D.C., was intended to be Otto Hardwick's replacement on alto sax in the Ellington Orchestra. This never came about, and my conjecture is that the impending war scrambled the plans. Billy White sounded exactly like Hardwick and was a tremendous section leader. Trumpeter Cat Anderson, who made his reputation on the unbelievable high notes he could hit, later joined the Ellington Orchestra. And, we had Clark Terry on trumpet. I believe he also did some stints with the Duke. Another alto sax player was Sonny Stitt, who was to become famous in his own right. I feel flattered when I realize that the band members were personally scouted by the master himself on the recommendations of his son. I like to think that I would have been in the Ellington Orchestra had it not been for America's entry into World War II. Even so, it is personally satisfying to realize that I had Duke's stamp of approval as a performer—if not as an arranger.

There was just one major fly in the ointment: All of the guys in Mercer's band were unemployed. Nobody had any money except Mercer. We were all scuffling, trying to make it in New York. Some of us were concerned about meals. Mercer did what he could to help with his allowance, but there were too many problems. I told Mercer, "You're not going to have this band long unless you get us some gigs."

As it was, we had personnel turnover problems as soon as anyone got a steady gig. Here we were, rehearsed to a frazzle, with outstanding personnel and no place to play. After a couple of months Mercer wangled a Savoy Ballroom night. It was to be the beginning of the end. This was not the same band with which we began rehearsal. It wasn't a failure, nor was it a smashing success; we just got through the night professionally. Mercer eventually took the band on the road. I couldn't go because of classes at NYU. The road trip was not a success, and soon thereafter Mercer quietly folded the band.

I went into my junior year at NYU in the fall of 1940 with a new wrinkle. I joined the football marching band. The marching band was not an official music department activity. We had an orchestra and a concert band, but a marching band would have been unthinkable to the tradition-minded faculty. Because of this, band members received no academic credit, but we did get a small stipend for transportation and a meal. I think it was something like $2.50 for a rehearsal and $4.00 for the game. Since the bus or subway only cost a nickel, this was good money for me. Nothing like a gig, but it meant survival in the absence of gigs. The rehearsals were in the basketball fieldhouse on the uptown (Bronx) campus, and we only had two rehearsals before a game. One rehearsal would be for music only, and the second would be for practicing the shows. We received the diagrams of the show by mail a week in advance.

When I consider marching bands of today practicing from twenty to forty hours a week, the two- or three-hour rehearsals were remarkable. We didn't try anything elaborate like today's bands. The most we did was march, countermarch, play the school song, "Grim Gray Palisades," and make formations spelling simple messages like HELLO or NYU. We couldn't do much more than that because of our small size (eighty-five members). We attempted to enliven the proceedings with our fast cadences. We were nicknamed the "Track Team" because of our speed marching. The musical fare was primarily Sousa marches with a few Broadway show tunes thrown in. We usually won the battle of the bands and lost the football game. One notable exception was our encounter with Ohio State.

Ohio State came to New York with an unbeaten football powerhouse. They beat us 32-0. The battle of the bands went the same way. To begin with, they had about three times as many musicians as we did. We were simply overpowered by the sheer volume of sound. They had the world's largest bass drum, about ten feet in diameter, rolled on a four-wheeled platform. It took five guys to operate this contraption, one on each corner to move it in formation and one guy walking alongside swinging upwards to beat the drum. To complete our embarrassment, they spelled out words like WELCOME and OHIO STATE while marching faster then we did. Further complicating my peace of mind was that I, the only black member of the band, missed a turn in one of our maneuvers and marched off in the opposite direction from the formation. Not only being black, but playing the tuba (sousaphone) engraved my name in the annals of the Yankee Stadium foul-ups. I was famous when word got back to the downtown campus. It took months to live it down.

Playing in the marching band and attending the football games, I was really Joe College. I even had NYU pennants in my room. I had graduated from sleeping under the piano in the living room to a small cubicle that we called the library. I dated a young lady on campus, Frances Saunders, who was president of the sociology club. As part of our togetherness I attended club meetings. One strange day, for reasons I still can't figure out, I was elected president. I was not even a sociology major; I was a music major. However, it gave me a seat on the School of Education Student Council. This was to have repercussions for me in terms of the notoriety I received relative to the "Bates Case."

Len Bates was our most publicized—and only black—football player. He weighed around two hundred pounds and ran the one hundred-yard dash in 9.8 seconds. He was our main scoring threat from his position at fullback. The trouble started when the University of Missouri requested that NYU not bring Bates along for a game to be played in Missouri. The university's chancellor replied that integration would come along in time but the time was not yet right, so he agreed to the request. That enraged the student body, and the whole campus was up in arms. We got support and publicity from the NAACP, the Urban League, the Young Communist League (YCL), and just about every liberal organization in New York. We sent petitions to the University of Missouri asking that those who would like to see Bates play sign the petition, and we got several thousand signatures in favor. We marched and picketed, carrying signs saying "Bates Must Play."

The YCL was most helpful in all of this activity, purporting to guide and assist me as the only black member of the student council. I got a lot of notoriety and was even interviewed by *The New York Times*. We got nowhere with the administration, only an admonishment to disassociate with the YCL. I was called in to meet with the chancellor, whom I had never seen in my three years at NYU. He told me he understood our feelings about Bates, but that the time was not yet ripe. He asked me why we allowed the YCL to play such a big role. I told him that I was new to any idea of political responsibility and that I would use anyone who could help in the fight against injustice. I went on to say that I had no experience in organizing picket lines or gathering petitions and that I was grateful for the assistance given me by the YCL and any other group that could help in the fight. I felt that NYU had the controlling hand, since Missouri wanted us on their schedule and eventually a game in the New York market. We parted with each side holding its own.

A postscript to this sequence of events was that Bates wound up as a bouncer at the Savoy Ballroom, and I received the Chancellor's Scholarship—based, I guess, on my 3.4 average, membership on the student council, and being black. I took the tuition scholarship and ran.

Late 1940 and early 1941 were still the outer edges of the depression. I could get orange juice, two doughnuts, and coffee at Nedick's for a dime, and this was my standard breakfast if time permitted. I applied for the NYU work aid program and received it. They paid me fifteen dollars a month. I began as a janitor's helper in the students' building. The job gave me close familiarity with the broom and the mop. At home and at 393 I had had plenty of janitorial training.

Fortunately, I was soon moved to the bookstore where my chief duties were package wrapper and sign painter. The joke there was that nobody could see me, a Negro, doing a nonmenial task. I believe that the manager of the store had other ideas, for he asked me to take over the cash register during the term opening textbook rush. Still, I didn't get to wear the NYU bookstore smock that the white, mostly female clerks wore. Some clerk would ask for Thurston's *Introduction to Economics,* and I would point to it. I knew where every book was in that store. I would take the money, make change, and await the next inquiry about the location of a book. The manager, who called me Willie, appreciated this and would leave me out there at the cash register alone. You'd have thought I was the manager if you had seen me giving directions and prices to my white "subordinates." Still, the fifteen dollars a month was not enough for me to buy textbooks and music equipment, to eat, and to date the young ladies. I quit the NYU job to move across the street to the cafeteria.

Mrs. Gorham, a very southern white lady, was the manager. She saw me in the cafeteria and asked if I would like to have a job. The position, busboy, was not an inducement, but the food allowance plus better pay was. Mrs. Gorham asked me if any of the other Negroes hanging out in the cafeteria would be interested. I told her I would ask. In spite of the guys always crying the blues about not having any money, nobody was interested in working. That job entailed the most walking I've done in my entire life, including the army. I would snatch away a plate with food on it in order to finish up and get to a two o'clock class. My friends started guarding their plates about a quarter to two.

Mrs. Gorham came to me and asked, "Willie, do you need money for the spring semester?" I told her I did. She outlined her plan. I would become a dishwasher for a month which, at union wages, was dramatically better than a busboy's pittance. I would have to join the dishwasher's union in oder to do this. Mrs. Gorham paid the union dues. In spite of her pronounced southern accent, she found ways in her managerial position to help young blacks in this northern, overwhelmingly white university. I have to qualify that to say she helped those who could overcome their aversion to working in typical Negro jobs and doing what was required. She was running a very large food service in a no-nonsense way, and you would never know she was a closet liberal from seeing her daily business dealings. Students had to comply with her standards of work, and when she asked to see their grades, then and only then would they get any clue to her humanity.

C. A. ("Skeets") Tolbert, a Columbia University graduate student, rescued me from the dishwashing machine. He wanted me to play bass with his six-piece band of local renown. Skeets had been an alto saxophonist with Budd Johnson and Lucky Millinder. He had a businesslike manner and was as articulate as he was smart. Also, he used no profanity; in other words, he was Mr. Clean. His band reflected him. All were intelligent, the kind you could trust anywhere and with anybody.

Carl Smith was the trumpet player, and while he was no exciting Dizzy Gillespie in style, he was more than adequate and experienced. Lem Johnson, the tenor saxophonist, was a good soloist as well as a singer of blues. (I later played a recording session with Lem as the featured blues singer, recording my first and last solo chorus on tuba. I wish I could find that record just to prove it to the unbelievers.) The band was a rarity: educated black musicians who could sight-read anything. As a result, we were in demand to play shows, especially those with limited rehearsal time. Mac Mackay, who brought Skeets to the house, was our drummer. As the youngest and least experienced, I was teased unmercifully as the country hick of this sophisticated group. Lem Johnson was my principal tormentor, but he would mitigate this by inviting me to his apartment for dinner.

We had a gig in the famous Cotton Club. The uptown show was a real eye-opener for me. The featured fan dancer performed with nothing except fans, tantalizing the audience with only fleeting glimpses of her glorious form. We, the band, had unlimited and unrestricted views since we were behind her on the bandstand. I tried to be cool and professional, but it was too much, and while I didn't ogle, I did warm to this vision of the forbidden. Lem Johnson rode me unmercifully. I had to suffer through his gibes as long as that dancer was part of the show.

These were not the halcyon days of the Cotton Club. Actually, it was closed for several months before this revival, but it was still the Cotton Club with chorus line, tap dancers, and comedians. Normally, there was a big name band like Duke Ellington or Cab Calloway, but for purposes of current economy, the Tolbert band was chosen. We had to get special clothes. The opportunity of a tailor-made suit was a first for me. Until then, all my suits had come from the racks of a men's clothing store or a big department store. We went to Karnak's on Forty-ninth Street, which was well known as the firm that made the uniforms for Tommy Dorsey's and Benny Goodman's bands. I was appalled when Karnak himself came out and appraised me. I say appraised because he did not have pencil, paper, or any measuring device, nor did he at any time use anything to record my non-Apollo-like form. He just looked at me from head to toe. I tried to tell him about the peculiarities of my shape and how I would have to have my suit fit. He dismissed it, saying, "You don't tell Karnak anything. If the suit isn't perfect for you, you can't wear it out of this shop!"

That's the way it was. The suit did fit like a glove and was a bit gaudy, but in good taste. Unfortunately, the Cotton Club closed for us after about four weeks, before we had completed payment for the suits. Eventually, we were sued. It was the most expensive suit that I had owned up to that date.

The Tolbert sextet then moved to the Bronx to the Sky Club. We were completely off the beaten track. When all of the working musicians were going either to Harlem or downtown, we were going in an entirely different direction. The club featured some strange acts, usually refugees from Radio City. We even had acts that had been with Ringling Brothers, Barnum and Bailey. As you can see, it was a different menu from what most black jazz players could handle. This group could read and play just about anything.

One black act, a male and female dance team, loudly and unprofessionally challenged our tempo during a show. The reputation of Mac Mackay, "the human metronome," was so well regarded that the manager fired the dancers. Despite our prestige as a show band, I did not enjoy this gig as much as the Cotton Club because of the strange music we had to play. The music for the Japanese acrobatic fire dancers was finally too much. We had little time left to swing. I was glad when we left.

Happiness at leaving the Sky Club was tempered by the ensuing unemployment. With so many mouths to feed at 393, my funds dwindled to almost nothing. We had to think up some ideas that would get us some money. At the time, I found my classwork mostly boring, but I realized that to maintain the scholarship I had to keep my hands on the wheel, like it or not. Studying, then, became a financial necessity. Today, when I look back on this I realize that even though I got very little from subjects like Educational Sociology, what was rewarding was the discipline needed to get an A or a B. I got a little arrogant with that viewpoint. I believed that I could get a B in any subject the university offered, provided I could read the textbook, attend class regularly, and stay awake.

With that in mind, three of us—Mac Mackay (B.A. English, University of Illinois), a young lady named Gwendolyn Johnson who was our typist, and I—started a term-paper business. I did the research and made the outline. Mac did the actual writing. Gwendolyn typed the paper. We had cards printed that had the statement "A grade of B guaranteed or your money back." Five dollars was the going price for an undergraduate paper. We never had to refund any money even though we had some wide-ranging topics from the school of business and the liberal arts college. We must have done about a dozen term papers. Our reputation was expanding when other interests, more musical in nature, took over.

One of these opportunities arose at an informal chamber music session. I brought up an idea while we were reading through a Mozart quintet. I was the second viola. "Why don't we try to mix the quartet with a clarinet and a rhythm section?"

The reaction was enthusiastic from the members of the regular student string quartet. I said I would recruit a jazz clarinetist, pianist, and a drummer. I would play bass and arrange some music. The quartet members were familiar with the Mozart clarinet quintet and knew that that instrument mixed well with strings. I got Jimmy Hamilton, my old Philly friend who was in a slow period with Duke Ellington, to play clarinet. He was enthusiastic about the idea. He, too, was a lover of classical music. Luckily, Ernie Washington was available for the piano slot and arrangements. Mac Mackay was the drummer. We wanted to rehearse some innovative arrangements and present these to a recording company, or at least try for some club dates.

We practiced at first in the rehearsal chamber on the ninth floor of the Education Building. Later we went to individual apartments or houses, depending on who had a piano. The string quartet was all white, and the rhythm section and clarinet were black. Once when we rehearsed in Washington Heights (183rd Street), I was met at the subway station by a group of young white thugs. They admonished me to "be sure that you go back (to Harlem) the same way you came." There was no violence, fortunately, and the rehearsal at Danny Yale's apartment was productive.

Ernie Washington's arrangement of "Groovin' High" anticipated "be-bop." We later moved downtown to Nola's Studio, a favorite rehearsal place on Broadway, and we used their facilities to make a recording. I took this recording to every studio, booking agent, and club in the midtown area. I received one consistent answer. "We like the group and the music, but we can't use it unless you can make it all white (in which case I couldn't play) or all black."

It was a crusher for all concerned, especially the quartet members for whom this represented their only opportunity to play jazz. It was a sign of the times, but that did not make me feel any better. I had such high hopes for the innovative mixing of the classical with the jazz.

Another sign of the times in that somber spring of 1941 was a double dose of hard reality that I felt pressing in on me: first, that a world war was imminent, with me as a likely participant, and second, that I was almost three-fourths of the way through college and on the threshold of my twenty-fourth birthday. In a little more than a year, if all went according to the script, I would either be a soldier of misfortune in the uniform of my country or an NYU alumnus in search of a real job. Neither prospect was all that alluring.

Turning first to the more urgent of the two, I acted on some information passed to me by a classmate named Wilberforce Simmons, a French horn player in the School of Commerce. Simmons, who understandably preferred to be called by his nickname, "Red," told me he had heard that a Navy band was to be stationed in New York primarily for recruitment purposes. It was to be a black band, and they needed a qualified director, also black. This was exciting news to me. Like practically all young males, I felt that war was inevitable, and I warmed to the prospect of landing a non-combat position. Figuring that there would be a very limited supply of black college-trained musicians, I went with high hopes down to the Navy recruiting office to volunteer. They gave me the works physically, and I was doing fine right down to the end. Then came the eye exam. The officer told me to take my glasses off and walk up to where I could read the second from the bottom line on the chart. I was defeated right then and there. I practically had to put my nose on the chart. They gave me a very polite rejection, and I returned to 393 Edgecombe filled with hurt and anger. The U.S. Navy was not exactly an equal opportunity employer for minorities at that time, and I couldn't help feeling that discrimination had something to do with my rejection. There's no denying, though, that my vision was very limited.

The only paying gig I remember getting in the spring of 1941 came about when I got a call for a recording session from Alfred Lion, who was actively engaged in recording rising black jazz artists. The artist for this occasion was Jimmy Shirley, a young West Indian guitarist with fabulous technique. A virtuoso, he had won many guitar battles with the unusually fine group of guitar players in New York at that time. I don't think that any period since has yielded such a collection of competitive guitarists. Floyd Smith, Buddy Fleet, Carl Lynch, and Charlie Christian were just a few. I had worked with Jimmy Shirley previously in the after-hours club, Monroe's Uproar House. I knew what to expect: dazzling flying tempos, tunes with complicated chord changes, and melodic pyrotechnics. It was as much fun as it was challenging—just guitar and bass.

Two productive and educational (albeit non-paying) experiences of that spring were especially memorable for me, involving as they did some of the giants of American black history. The first came about when Red Simmons approached me one day and asked if I would like to go with him to visit W. C. Handy, the great blues composer and trumpeter who lived over on St. Nicholas Place. Naturally, I leaped at the opportunity.

Though he was nearly seventy and was no longer in the limelight, Mr. Handy, the famed composer of "St. Louis Blues" and his hometown tune, "Memphis Blues," still had active years ahead of him. He liked company, especially young and adoring musicians, and Red and I felt like big shots as we conversed with him. After a little chatter on the current state of Negro music, he brought out a hundred pages or so of pencilled manuscript and asked us if we would proofread it for him. It was the beginning of his memoir, *Father of the Blues*.

Red and I returned, at his invitation, several times after that, whenever we could catch Mr. Handy at home. I was completely absorbed by the substance of the story he was writing, particularly the parts about his early days—from the 1890s to the 1920s—as a pioneer black musician in the South and beyond. I remember particularly his description of a gig at which a gang of white Texans chased and shot at him, and another at which he played for a black square dance. Red and I discussed the format of the book with him, and I think we were a help to him as proofreaders of the manuscript and the galley proofs. Just being with him was a great thrill, because W. C. Handy was already a historic figure.

The other great experience for me that spring came about when the sociology club at NYU, of which I was still the music-major president, decided to have a series of music and literature events in celebration of Negro history. Since I had just met W. C. Handy and already knew such figures as Langston Hughes and Walter White of the NAACP (our near neighbor on Edgecombe), I played a major part in the planning. Mr. Handy came, and he was magnificent, not only in his talk but also with his trumpet. Langston Hughes also made a brief appearance and read a few of his poems, and Mr. White talked about his work investigating lynchings in the South. The real coup, though, was getting J. Rosamond Johnson, who along with his late brother, James Weldon Johnson, had written the Negro national anthem, "Lift Every Voice and Sing."

We held these sessions in the lounge of the students' building, which was basically the parlor of a large brownstone house on Washington Square. The programs, of which there were about half a dozen, were very popular, and each time there was a standing-room-only audience. In addition to the featured speaker-performer, there was also student music on the program, as when some of my friends from the music department ensembles played an original composition of mine. It was an attempt at something like a spiritual, entitled "I'm So Tired of Working (My Soul Is Not My Own)." Both it and a longer piece of mine called "The Negro Suite" were frankly derivative and not well thought out. They were politely received but quickly—and mercifully—forgotten.

Classroom work at the university had become more or less routine by then, and I had little enthusiasm for it. Already, I was beginning to dread the required senior recitals, still a year away. I would have five of these: major instrument (tuba), minor instruments (bass, viola), piano, and voice. Since I had never studied privately in any of these specialties, I could only contemplate these final tests with terror. But that was in the future, I kept telling myself. I had plenty of time to panic.

Fortunately, the Camp Lakeland summer gig was available to me again in 1941. Having no other prospects, I grabbed it without hesitation.

# CHAPTER 12

# GOOD-BYE, NEW YORK

**W**hen we returned to New York in September, war had enveloped all of Europe. Having flunked the Navy physical, I decided to go ahead and register for what should have been my last year at New York University; but circumstances were to change that. I missed my scholarship renewal by one point, with a 3.1 grade point average instead of the required 3.2. But no matter. I had my earnings from the summer at Camp Lakeland. Also, I didn't have to pay for food or housing at my New York home, the Willises' at 393.

Things were picking up economically as the whole country was gearing up for the as-yet-undeclared war. I was assigned to Seward Park High School on the lower East Side in Manhattan to do my practice teaching. This was an all-day gig five days a week, with my only class at the university being a classroom management course. With the high number of male faculty members volunteering or being called up for their military reserve units, I was immediately seized upon to become an unpaid but full-time teacher replacement. I received about one hour of orientation from Mr. Hartley Shellans, the music director, who then put me immediately to work. The principal, teachers, and students all treated me like a regular teacher instead of a student teacher, so glad were they to have a warm body to fill the ranks.

Seward Park High was located in what some films featuring the dead-end kids referred to as Hell's Kitchen. We were in the heart of Little Italy, with a moderate sprinkling of blacks and Puerto Rican students. Strangely enough, there was not a single black regular teacher. In fact, I learned there were fewer than ten black teachers at the high school level in the entire New York public school system. Consequently, the principal really pushed me to become the missing black representative on his faculty. Fortunately, the kids liked me—I guess because my age, appearance, and demeanor were closer to theirs than to the regular teachers. The principal noted that point and told me that he wanted me to come back to Seward Park when I became certified.

One afternoon when I came home, Mrs. Willis greeted me with much consternation. She said, "Get that white chick out of here." I went into the living room and saw a Seward Park student who was a member of the Negro history club. Her name was Estelle Goldman, and she told me how she had gotten my address from the principal. She told him that she needed some materials for an American history class on Negroes. I knew that student-teacher fraternization was taboo, especially for a practice teacher, so I suggested that we leave. We walked over the 155th Street bridge about as far as Yankee Stadium. We were so engrossed in conversation that we doubled back two or three times until late in the evening.

Estelle Goldman became Suzie to me, and the relationship grew until I was sincerely in love for the first time in my life. She was about eighteen and not particularly pretty, but her appearance was striking. She had a ballet dancer's appearance and poise. She was very arty, a devotee of poetry, art, ballet, and classical music. Suzie was also anorexic, self-conscious about her appearance, and paranoid that she might someday weigh more than a hundred pounds. I weighed in the neighborhood of 130 pounds, but loved to eat. I drank beer in order to gain weight.

As the relationship waxed into a full-fledged affair (much to the disapproval of Mrs. Willis), we spent most of the time together walking and talking or attending concerts and art museums. We spent entire afternoons at the Museum of Modern Art, with me suggesting that trying to make sense out of the various grotesques on display was a hard gig.

I had guilt feelings about the affair, not only because of the difference in our age, race, and life experiences (she was an innocent), but because I was the teacher and she the student. I wrote bad, but fiery, love poems, and she gave me little personal gifts like cufflinks and neckties. We discussed marriage and decided that because of the difficulties of interracial marriage, we would wait until I had a steady job that paid enough to support us.

No sex was involved in our daily companionship, although we

came close on a few occasions. My guilt feelings were amplified by fear for my professional future. No doubt Suzie, while not having my guilt, had the fear of her own cultural background and of her family. We had walked together across the street from her home on Webster Avenue in the Bronx, but she vehemently refused to let me meet her family. We seldom had the opportunity for physical expression, as Mrs. Willis disapproved of our use of 393 and such intimacy is awfully difficult in an art museum.

Our intercultural exchange was amusing to me. She was always shocked by my consumption of alcohol and puzzled by my various Negroisms. We differed, too, in our reactions to social snubs. Once in a restaurant in Yorkville, the German enclave of Manhattan, we waited about an hour for service. Suzie was patient, but I was upset. We were about to be at war with the Germans, and I guess their theories about a master race emphasized the restaurant's approach in dealing with an interracial couple. We were not poisoned, but we knew definitely that we were not welcome. Also, I was awfully sensitive about the eyes boring through me whenever we were together on the subway. In the museum or the concert hall, the stares seemed less intense.

I loved Suzie above all else and would have married her then but for our economic limitations. I wonder if our idyllic relationship would have lasted in the face of the practical realities of American life.

One day in the fall of 1941 I received a call from Bill Doggett, a fine jazz pianist from Philly and a graduate of Central High. He had had his own big band, and they were later transformed into Lucky Millinder and the Mills Blue Rhythm Orchestra. Bill wanted me to come to the Savoy Ballroom and fill in for their regular bassist, who was unable to make the week's engagement. I was thrilled—first to be able to play at the Savoy and second to play with Lucky Millinder. The Savoy, advertised as "the home of happy feet," was the dream of just about every black musician trying to prove himself, the supreme test for the black jazz bands. Lucky Millinder was a dynamic nonplaying band leader like Cab Calloway and Tiny Bradshaw, and like them he surrounded himself with outstanding musicians. So it was a privilege to play with the likes of Red Allen and Dizzy Gillespie, trumpets, and Tab Smith on alto sax. I was on a cloud all week. This was a fiercely rhythmic band (the name Blue Rhythm was no joke) and tailor-made for the mood and requirements of dance halls like the Savoy. We riffed and shouted with driving rhythm all night.

Mercer Ellington, Calvin Jackson, and I had occasion to attend

Benny Carter's opening night at the Savoy. We got in free on recognizance. Everybody knew Mercer and Calvin, so I just made it on the basis of having played there recently with Lucky Millinder. It was pleasing to have such status—the doormen and cashiers were ordinarily a mean bunch. Benny Carter was a musician's musician, well respected for his contributions to the development of jazz. He was famous as an arranger, an extremely competent trumpet soloist. It was truly wonderful to watch him pick up a trumpet immediately after a tasty saxophone solo and compete with the best trumpeters around. He had been doing this since his days with the pioneer Fletcher Henderson band in the twenties. What a band that must have been with the likes of Benny Carter, Louis Armstrong, Coleman Hawkins, Buster Bailey, and many others of that ilk. It was an inspiring night, thanks to Benny Carter's sophisticated musicianship.

For the balance of 1941, the news from Europe was, as always, disturbing. The news from the Pacific was almost as bad, but mitigated by the remoteness. Somehow, the events involving Japan and China did not seem as threatening to our future as did the threat to England, France, and Germany. Even the German invasion of Poland and Russia did not have such a catastrophic impact as Dunkirk and the bombing of England. We knew that sooner or later we would be actively involved in France. It was almost as if the rest did not count.

My religious life flowered during this period of uncertainty. I had rebelled against going to church, Sunday school, and BYPU (Baptist Young People's Union) in my high school days. Later, my night life made Sunday morning activity highly improbable. At Suzie's instigation, I occasionally attended a black Lutheran church on 135th Street near City College. The main attraction here was the music of J. S. Bach. I had been used to the traditional hymnals of the black Baptist or Methodist church. I missed the fire and brimstone preaching, but the chorales of Bach, sung by black voices, gave me a spiritual uplift.

With my roommate Calvin, Suzie and I occasionally attended the Christian Science church on Columbus Avenue at Eighty-sixth. I was shaken up, first because there was no collection or collection-sermon, and second because there was a full-fledged orchestra in residence. The talk or lecture lasted about ten minutes. There was a printed program of the concert to be played. It was like going to Carnegie Hall to hear a religious concert, but in a church setting. Handel's Tenth Organ Concerto made a deep impression on me. I got my spiritualism or message, not from the sermon, but from some really great music.

Going into December 1941, Suzie had been almost my daily companion, with the exception of gig nights. Word got around that I dated only white chicks. Consequently, to repair my image I made an effort to expand my very limited circle to include some black girls. In all fairness, there were not many black women at NYU, and gigs (practice teaching and jazz) severely cramped my style. However, on December 7, 1941, I found myself at the apartment of Millie Outerbridge, a beautiful dark young lady of Bermudian lineage. She lived up the street on Edgecombe Avenue and was an NYU student. We had just settled into the usual social banter with the radio playing quietly in the background. About three in the afternoon the announcer said, "We interrupt this program to announce that Pearl Harbor has been attacked." That shattered a blissful afternoon.

Everybody that I knew who heard that announcement could recount today exactly where they were or what they were doing at the time. It was sobering. We didn't realize the scope or significance of that attack but, even then, I had terrible forebodings. The whole thing was a complete surprise, a bolt out of the blue. I dated Millie on a few other occasions, but in this new atmosphere of uncertainty my attempt to widen my circle of female friends expired. Suzie remained paramount.

The first tangible evidence that a war was on was when Harlem's own 369th Infantry Regiment was called up for active duty. I didn't realize how intertwined Harlem was with the war effort until that fateful event. Most of the young ladies that I knew had a brother, uncle, cousin, or boyfriend on that train that pulled out from 125th Street station. Nobody knew, until some letters arrived, where they were going. The 369th dated back to World War I when they had the famous band that popularized jazz in Europe. It had Colonel James Reese Europe as its commander and contained many jazz greats, like Noble Sissle, who later put Harlem on the jazz map. This leave-taking was Harlem's "Noche Triste"—sad night—and it reached into the hearts and lives of just about every Harlemite.

But Harlem got through the trauma beautifully. Everything went on as usual, except that occasionally people were missing. Having finished my practice teaching stint at SPHS, I registered at NYU for my last semester of classes. Shortly after that another bomb fell: the Willises were leaving New York. There would be no more 393 Edgecombe Avenue for me. Albert Edwards, one of our residents, had gotten a job as principal at the New York State Training School for Boys in Warwick, New York, and he offered Mrs. Willis a job as a secondary school teacher and Bill a job as boy supervisor. They would receive an apartment and other amenities besides salary. After having done the after-hours club and trying other ways of making it in Harlem, they grabbed the opportunity for what they thought would be a better life.

Before the Willises left, Mercer Ellington invited me to attend a rare performance of the famous Ellington orchestra at the Savoy Ballroom, an occasion I'll never forget. The main attraction for me was a chance to hear Jimmy Blanton, the phenomenal bassist. He was about nineteen, a precocious rock in one of the finest rhythm sections in jazz, with a most innovative solo style. This guy was a virtuoso who soloed with impressive technique and with exquisite taste. After he and Duke finished their duet, "Jack the Bear," I had serious thoughts of chucking my attempts at bass playing. I realized that I might never reach that level of sheer artistry. Incidentally, Blanton had attended Tennessee State University in Nashville, a school that would play an important part in my later development.

The Savoy audiences were, along with those at the Apollo Theatre in Harlem, the premiere critics of jazz performance. After years of the best black music available, they tolerated only the best. Duke's band passed the test with flying colors. In a dazzling performance, Duke went out of his way to rock the house, and the hardened Savoy crowd succumbed. Not only did the group play their very sophisticated recorded hits, but they out-Savoyed the Sultans with their own game of riffing and swinging.

Early 1942 was real trauma. The Willises did move to Warwick, leaving me and roommate Calvin with no place to stay. We had to split up for the first time in almost four years. Calvin moved to the Bronx, and I moved in with Phil ("Trash") Gordon further up on Edgecombe at 162nd. I stored my string bass and tuba in the basement of the students' building. Severely handicapped in practicing for my senior recitals, I dropped the whole idea temporarily, thus contributing to impending tragedy: my non-graduation from NYU in 1942. About fourteen semester hours of credit were tied up in the senior recitals. I went about regular course work without my former drive and increasingly depressed.

As I look back on it, I had no real excuse. I could have found places to practice, but the will was not there. Suzie was there. She tried to be my conscience, reminding me that the sooner I got to five thousand dollars a year, the sooner we would be able to marry. That was not encouraging; five thousand dollars a year was an executive's salary, inconceivable to me for years to come.

Looking back from almost half a century, I think I can see what was happening to me, though it is difficult to explain logically. I was suffering from the combined effects of war hysteria and the ticking of the body clock. I wanted to be married, and the deal with Suzie was appearing more remote as each day went on. I wanted to be done with college, too. And I also sensed that I probably would be drafted, most likely in some undesirable capacity. All these factors plus a degree of immaturity and the creeping malaise of academic burnout contributed to my depression.

When Mercer, my prestigious buddy, asked if I would like to attend an Ellington record session early in 1942, I jumped at the opportunity. I don't remember the name of the studio or the location, except that it was downtown (below Forty-second Street). It was in the morning, so I took a day off from classes. Duke was there, as were the famous Ellington personnel. I was particularly interested in how the best of America's black bands would record, in contrast to live performance. First, I noticed that there were no arrangements or even parts passed out. From about two staves of music on one piece of music paper, they recorded four pieces. Duke would begin with some improvisations on piano and would then comment, "Do you remember what we played on such and such occasion?" Then he would point to the trumpets and at the same time cue Johnny Hodges on alto sax for a solo. He would repeat this process with different sections and soloists. Everybody seemed to know exactly what to play on the slightest cue from the master. Whole sections would be immediately harmonized, and on completion everything would fit into what one would call a stylistic whole. However, in a way I was disappointed because I had assumed that at this very highest level of musicianship the parts from the charts would be passed out, and I always wondered who was Duke's arranger and what a technocrat he must have been. Or was it that my gods had clay feet? It was unthinkable that at this level there were musicians not proficient in reading. In short, as in the bands that I played with in Philly, much was never written down, which now presents some problems for the musicologists who are trying to assemble the complete Ellington book. The history of jazz is bound up in this collection.

In the spring semester I registered for an elective in sociology. The course was taught by Pearl Buck, the famous author of *The Good*

*Earth* and other books about China. She was also the founder of the "open door" concept, which was more of an idea than formal organization. Its primary purpose was to help disadvantaged women and children. It was fascinating to hear her describe how the concept began in China and her role in the rescue of many women and children from slavery. Miss Buck was an impressive personality who had an incredible love of people, mostly the dispossessed and the poor. I don't remember the name of the course, but it was at the senior graduate level. I had qualified to take it by right of having done my practice teaching. She gave no written exam, but she assigned required reading and we had to do volunteer work in her "open door" concept. As the only music major, I volunteered to work at the Bedford-Stuyvesant community center in Brooklyn. I had to spend Saturday mornings working in some aspect of their music program.

The director of the center, who had known of my playing with various jazz bands, asked if I would form a group of teenagers into an organized band. We posted notices around the neighborhood, and there must have been twenty kids aged thirteen to eighteen who turned out for our initial meeting. It was immediately apparent that we had a number of problems. Playing experience levels ranged from zero to three years. The instrumentation could only be described as bizarre. We either had too many or too few to approximate the various sections. Trumpets? We had too many, so we had to rotate them. Saxophones? Not enough to make a go of a standard stock arrangement. The personnel changed weekly, with only about ten regulars. I can't romanticize this by claiming that we were ever competition for Count Basie, but we did work up an enthusiasm in trying to close the gap. In a way, the results were sensational; at least those kids were not participating in gang activity on Saturday mornings. In that project, the basis for my social thinking was set and would see fruition over four decades later.

One day in that spring, Mercer saw Calvin and me visiting in his neighborhood, and he gave us some good news. Duke himself had suggested that we move into their apartment, at least for the remainder of the school year. It touched me to realize that the great man was aware of our problems. Our basic responsibility was to be musical companions to Mercer, who at this time was also a student at NYU. As near broke as I was, it was a great break for me.

Also, Billy Strayhorn was staying there and it gave me a chance to know him better. Strayhorn was for real, a genuine saint. He had respect for everybody, the knowns and the unknowns (of whom I was a prime example). From what I saw, he had no romantic inclinations toward anybody, male or female. I think he was asexual, not homosexual as rumored, primarily because he couldn't be associated with any particular young lady. His big romance was music. He loved everybody, and everybody loved him. I would like to quote his four freedoms; it was apparent that he lived by them.

1. Freedom from hate, unconditionally.
2. Freedom from self-pity.
3. Freedom from fear of doing something that would help someone more than it does me.
4. Freedom from pride that makes me feel that I am better than my brother.

Ruth Ellington, Duke's younger sister, was the lady of the house. This was a large apartment with at least four bedrooms. There was also a maid, who evidently had been with the family for years and was not a servant in demeanor or activity but more or less a control for the smooth running of the household. Calvin and I ate there only by invitation. Rather than risk the disapproval of the maid we made our own beds and cleaned up our mess. Duke still called me "Trumpets Too High" rather than Oscar.

Duke came by only occasionally. Rumor had it that he had several apartments throughout Manhattan. When he was home, everybody gave him plenty of space. He was a night person, sleeping during the day. Sometimes we heard bursts of piano from ten or eleven at night until the morning hours. He might still be at it when we were on our way to NYU. Billy Strayhorn took up the slack when Duke was not there. Even so, that piano didn't interfere with our sleep.

Mercer had the use of Duke's new Mercury, which the Ford Motor Company presented Duke annually for advertising purposes. I found out that it cost as much to garage the car as to rent some smaller apartments in a lesser walk-up building. All in all, living there was an exciting experience for Calvin and me, and it was to be the last time for us to be together as roommates.

I did not do my senior recitals, and without those required hours of credit, I obviously would not graduate. With my fate thus sealed, I left school early without taking any final exams. Out of respect for my past scholarship, I received no failing grades, just "incompletes" except for that sociology course with Pearl Buck. I received an *A* for my volunteer efforts. About the middle of April I got a call from the Willises up in Warwick saying the need for teachers was desperate because of teachers being drafted. I knew Mr. Edwards, principal of the school, because he had lived with us at 393. I could not be certified as a regular teacher because I hadn't graduated, but with the war on, it made no difference. I accepted a job and became the music teacher at the New York State Training School for Boys.

When I talked it over with Calvin and Suzie, both were against the idea. They wanted me to stay and graduate even if it took all summer. Suzie was particularly upset because we would no longer be seeing each other daily. Psychologically, I felt the need for a change. Most young males were searching for stability, and there were a lot of war brides. Suzie still stuck to her $5,000 condition and since my new job paid only $1,440 a year, we were at odds. I took my tuba and string bass to my mother's house in Philly and returned to New York. Then I told Calvin and Suzie good-bye and with mixed feelings took the bus to Warwick.

Talk about uncertainty! I had no idea what the future would bring.

# CHAPTER 13

# WARWICK

*T*he New York State Training School for Boys near Warwick was in a magnificent setting. The main campus—classrooms,
shops, and dormitories—was on one side of the lake (the lake had a
name, but we just called it "the lake"). The staff buildings were on the
other side, and the entire place was surrounded by green rolling hills.
Warwick, the rustic village, was four miles away and offered the only
social activity.

All staff members had to fill in on almost any gig, with the
exception of administration. After my one-week orientation I was
asked to perform the duties of boy supervisor (a nonteaching position), recreation director, and, finally, cottage parent. This, coupled
with the fact that the music-teaching post was relatively unimportant
and dispensable, gave me thoughts of a short tenure.

I held on as long as I did because of my interest in the boys.
They were from ages twelve to sixteen, and what a bunch of characters—from orphans to rapists, muggers, and even murderers. Each
case was different, interesting, and challenging, especially when I got
involved. I met with a degree of success there because of my youth,
ghetto credentials, and mod appearance, my rather wild band uniforms being the only clothes I had. You would be surprised at the size
and strength of some of the sixteen-year-olds; some of those guys
looked like they could play football for Notre Dame. Practically all
were members of street gangs, and these same gangs were represented on school grounds. We had Harlem's 133rd Street Sultans
practically intact because members would commit crimes just to join

their buddies up at Warwick. School—the academic side—was unimportant, and I have to admit that I was academically ineffective. I was only able to oganize a small drum and bugle corps of about twenty kids. So I had to be up at five in order to have our drum and bugle corps available for the six-o'clock flag-raising ceremony. The early rising stimulated my thoughts about other employment.

It was like pulling teeth to get those twenty delinquents to do anything in an organized manner. Working cooperatively as a group was against the very nature of these rugged individualists. They certainly were not motivated by the flag-raising ceremony. However, the principal required it, and we performed it with mixed results. We finally put together about four different bugle calls. These had to be taught by rote as the guys refused to have anything to do with reading notes or music fundamentals. Fortunately, most of them had good musical instincts and a superb sense of rhythm. This made our modest organization credible, but there were no Louis Armstrongs there. I tried to get some of them to attempt trumpet, trombone, or band instruments in a systematic way, but this broke down as soon as the method book with notation was introduced. I did have one guy who would play trombone the whole school day, but this was his alternative to avoid attending other classes. So I was reduced to baby-sitting instead of teaching music. Give eight juvenile delinquents some snare drums and some drumsticks, and you wouldn't believe the possibilities for utter chaos.

I received a notice to register for the draft at Middletown, New York. I don't remember much about it, but I did sense the beginning of the end. Beautiful as the setting was around Warwick and congenial as it was to listen to music in company with the Willises, my mind hardened. Even though Suzie and I saw each other every weekend on alternating visits, it was not enough. I knew I was not long for Warwick. The county sheriff came by one day and deputized all young male teachers. For this I received a badge (to be worn only on authorized occasions) and a card. We kidded each other about this, speaking of "Sheriff Smith," "Sheriff Blake," and so on. Fortunately, I never had to put on the badge, but I did get a kick out of presenting my card.

Meanwhile, my class at New York University had been graduated—without me.

It was a summer of bad news from the Russian front and mixed news from North Africa. The draft noose was drawing tighter, and I was a thoroughly mixed-up kid. The Willises prevailed upon me to stay at Warwick, as the manpower shortage there was critical. Really, I had no other commitments except to the draft board. I signed on with more assurance than before. But I knew that it was only a matter of time before the draft board called me into the service.

My residential quarter was in the lower staff building, and it was tiny. The eighty square feet were enough for my few belongings, however—some clothes, books, a phonograph, and some records. Warwick itself was Whitesville, USA, and with the exception of some Indians and "Jackson" whites, people of color were very few. (Jackson whites were the descendants of the Hessian soldiers who remained in the United States after the Revolutionary War with their Negro or Indian wives.) All of this added up to an extremely limited social life. Suzie and I made our visits less frequently, so I was a lonely young man with recourse only to my little room and some classical music recordings. My favorite recording in time of stress was the Brahms violin concerto with Jascha Heifetz as soloist.

The boys, individually and collectively, were my main source of interest and entertainment. Considering that their uniforms had no pockets, it amazed me to find cigarettes in the classroom. Little clouds of smoke could be seen in the corners of the room at various intervals. I resolved this by acknowledging that I couldn't stop them and pointing out that it would be better for all of us if the superintendant or the principal did not "see me seeing you smoke." We agreed that we would take smoke breaks away from the classroom proper. They did a good job of protecting my image and, of course, their privilege. We took fight breaks from time to time, leaving the building and getting far enough away to escape observation. The two aggressors would be invited to go at it. Then a strange thing would happen. Without the satisfaction of disrupting a legitimate classroom activity, all of the aggression would be dissipated. The actual fight would last about a minute and a half. I learned a lot that was not taught in any pedagogy class.

Winter and loneliness finally became too much for me at Warwick. I spent Christmas there alone, not having seen Suzie since Thanksgiving, and I was depressed and frustrated about my life in general. I resigned Warwick for the second time at the beginning of 1943 and headed for home—not New York this time, but Philadelphia. At least there was a piano at home. However, this time home was not on my beloved Brown Street, because my mother had moved to 1208 Fairmont Avenue right around the corner. She still owned the house at 1306 Brown, but it was occupied by my oldest sister who had a large family. Mother had remarried Mr. Jack Gee, a Philadelphia auxiliary policeman, who also owned and ran a restaurant on Columbia Avenue. I moved in with my mother.

Almost immediately I spotted the girl directly across the street and proceeded to make her acquaintance. She was extremely pretty—a sepia Barbara Stanwyck—and extremely young (fifteen), but beauty overcame any qualms about age difference. Julia Marie Witherspoon was a fine natural musician. She could sing and soloed in churches almost every Sunday. She could also play any piece she liked on the piano after only a few hearings. I began our dating sessions by teaching her J. S. Bach's "Jesu, Joy of Man's Desiring," which she played beautifully. In spite of our educational and age differences, I proposed marriage to her in about February or March, and she immediately accepted. My advisors, including my mother, suggested that it might be a good idea for me to bring Julia along and make her into what I wanted her to be. I didn't see it at the time, but that notion would prove to be our undoing. We were to be married in two weeks, but before that event three bombshells exploded.

The first had actually landed shortly after I returned to Philadelphia when Dizzy Gillespie came by the house and offered me a steady gig. It was at the Downbeat Club right behind the Earle Theatre. This was a downtown white club that featured big-name jazz. Dizzy certainly had qualified as a big name by this time and was considered one of the three top trumpeters in a very competitive field. It was an honor to be his bassist; in my memory it ranks right up there with my Coleman Hawkins tenure.

Stan Levey was the drummer, a white guy who played well and sort of passed for black. Racially mixed groups were in their beginning stages in 1943, and ours was one of the first. (The very first may have been when Teddy Wilson joined Benny Goodman's group in the late 1930s.) Johnny Acea was our pianist, one of the five or six best jazz pianists I've ever played with. He was an all-around musician who would keep his tenor saxophone underneath the grand piano and ambush unsuspecting visiting saxophonists. Dizzy was our leader and teacher, and he could do it all. He would take sticks in hand and demonstrate various percussion patterns or slide over to the piano and "comp" for Johnny Acea when Johnny played his sax solos.

We had visiting big-name jazz musicians almost nightly, and the group was considered the outstanding jazz happening in Philly. I remember our reunion with Charlie Shavers, the dazzling trumpeter, and our gig with Tommy Dorsey. Charlie had perfected a muted trumpet style from his years with John Kirby's "biggest little band," and it was an unusual pleasure to hear him do his thing on open horn. Then to hear him and Dizzy alternate solos was definitely trumpet at the summit. With all of this musical technique around, it was *de rigueur* for us to display it with dazzling, flying tempos. Most of the time I was the only bass player, and for defensive purposes I developed stamina for about twenty-five or thirty choruses of *molto presto* (very fast) tempos. Somewhere along the line, we added another white player, the guitarist and vocalist Teddy Walters. That cat could sure play, and as a four-piece rhythm section we met Dizzy's concept of harmony. It was a very exciting time, even with the somber clouds of war hanging over all of us.

The second bombshell was a phone call from Suzie, who was at the North Philadelphia railroad station. She was in town and wanted to visit with me for a week. I took my mother's car and met her at the station. I had not seen her in about three months. The first thing she said after indicating that she would be staying with us on Fairmont Avenue was that she wanted us to get married while she was in Philly. She had reconsidered her financial barrier in view of the uncertain times. Telling her that I was engaged and would be married in a few days was one of the hardest things I ever had to do, primarily because I had my own misgivings about the course of events. I still loved Suzie, but my common sense told me that we couldn't make it together. She was white and a New Yorker with social and cultural and financial needs of her own; I was back in Philadelphia in an all-black situation, with a different set of requirements. Had I stayed in New York and worked my way into a position in the Ellington band, things might have been different; but this was clearly the end of the road for Suzie and me.

To her everlasting credit, I think she faced the reality almost as quickly as I did. I took her on out to the neighborhood and introduced her to my family—and to Julia—as an old friend from NYU who had come for a little visit. At first, everyone was uneasy with her, but Suzie won them over with her graciousness; even my grandmother, who had been born in slavery, eventually came around. Julia, too, was very gracious, and if she spied my romantic dilemma, she never let on. As for me, I tiptoed through the week in a state of shock. It was awkward, to say the least, but somehow we all got through it.

On the day after Julia and I were married, the third bombshell exploded in my hands. You might say it was a letter bomb from President Roosevelt. "Greetings," it began, and it directed me to report on

March 26, 1943, two weeks hence, to Governor's Island for an army induction physical exam. Flunking the navy physical two years earlier gave me some hope of remaining a civilian, but I figured this time they were going to get me.

While I was waiting to report, I got a call from Steve Gibson, leader of the dynamic Redcaps, a New York band of great prestige. He had just lost his bassist, Eardlie Hope, to the army and offered me a job at substantially more than my eighteen dollars a week at the Downbeat. I explained to him that I had just bought a marriage license and received a draft notice and had no place to stay in New York. He told me to come on anyway; he would find us a place to stay. He also said there was a chance that I wouldn't pass the physical; then I would be in place for a permanent gig with his band in New York. I grabbed the opportunity and left Dizzy's band. Julia and I took the train to New York with one piece of luggage between us.

Steve Gibson was true to his word; he found a place for us to stay—in his own room at the Theresa Hotel at 125th and Seventh Avenue, the very capitol of Harlem. Steve resided there during the day, leaving us the place for evenings and nights. He explained that it was to be our wedding present and a honeymoon at no cost. We made considerable use of the honeymoon. The Theresa was probably the best known of black hotels in the country, and as such it was a prestigious address. The gig itself was at the Enduro Club in Brooklyn, and one of the features that benefited both Julia and me was the generous food allowance, which was considered as part of my pay. We took dinner at the club every evening, which meant that Julia was present for each night's gig. It was all very exciting to this young teenager, and I'll admit it was new and exciting to me also. Julia even sang some numbers, and the band adopted her as their little sister. As it turned out, this was to be the highlight of our marriage, the sweetest memory of a brief union.

Steve Gibson's Redcaps were different from any group that I had ever played in. They were more into entertainment than into pure music. Every member, except me, had numbers to sing or gag lines. This is not to suggest that music and musicianship were subordinated, but that entertainment was foremost. They could all play well, and Steve himself recorded several jazz albums on guitar. The Redcaps were primarily for clubs rather than dance halls. I should have seen the handwriting on the wall for big bands, but I was having too good a time. Our rehearsals were mostly novelty numbers, as was reflected in our repertoire, but there was enough musicianship around to play a good set of blues or even an Ellington tune.

Aside from Steve, one musician in that band stands out in my memory, and that is Romaine Jackson, the pianist. After watching him play all night standing up and swinging his hips, I was shocked to learn that he had studied viola at the Curtis Institute in Philadelphia. I had never heard of any blacks at Curtis at that time. Romaine tried to talk me into assuming some of the entertainment duties by clowning or singing. I flatly refused, my dignity as a performing musician offended. His main argument was that if he, a Curtis Institute affiliate, could do it, I could do it. I didn't bend.

Anyway, it was enjoyable playing with them and watching them entertain. The guy that I replaced, Eardlie Hope, was about six feet, five inches tall—almost a foot taller than I. I inherited his rather flamboyant uniform as there was not enough time to have one tailored. The pants came up to about six inches above my navel and the coat came almost to my knees. After my first appearance in this outfit, I was known and referred to as "the coat."

But the best times are all too often the briefest, and before I knew it, the day to report for my physical had arrived. I had convinced myself by then that I wouldn't pass, and I reported with hope in my heart, thinking that I had enough physical shortcomings to play it straight and still stay out of uniform. My confidence rose when I took the eye exam; my 20/200 vision and other shortcomings caused one medical officer to lump me with the entire lackluster batch of potential inductees and groan, "How can we fight anybody with physical material like this?"

The protesting officer didn't look in such good shape himself, but his remark didn't offend me. Rather, I thought for sure that I would make it back to Harlem to Julia and the Redcaps. I finally came face to face with the final officer, the one who applied the final stamp that said ACCEPTED or REJECTED. He was a colonel and was constantly shaking his head as he leafed through my file. I was feeling good about his negative reactions when he suddenly looked up and asked me, "Your face looks familiar. Haven't I seen you before?"

"No, sir," I replied. "I don't think so."

Then he asked if I was a musician. I almost choked, but my Christian background made me give him a truthful answer.

Then he said, "The Enduro Club, the Redcaps. You're the bass player with that funny coat."

His next statement really floored me. He thundered, "The

army needs musicians. You're accepted for limited service. Congratu-
lations!"

I was ordered to be at Penn Station on Thirty-fourth Street the
next morning for transportation to Fort Dix, New Jersey. That gave
me less than twenty-four hours to wind up my affairs. I put Julia on a
train to Philadelphia that night and said I would send for her as soon
as possible. All too quickly, our good times had come to an end.

# THE TRANSITION YEARS

# CHAPTER 14

# MILITARY MUSIC

**W**e arrived at Fort Dix, New Jersey, in civilian clothes. I did bring my spring overcoat, but it turned out not to be enough for those March mornings at 4:00 A.M. During the first week, I was put in touch with our two armies, the black and the white. The all-white Fourth Motorized Division of Georgia arrived on the post. In view of racial friction between young white men from Georgia and black recruits primarily from New York, New Jersey, and Pennsylvania, everybody was apprehensive and circumspect. There were, surprisingly enough, only a few incidents. One was at a post theatre where the blacks were asked to sit on one side. The northern black recruits refused to go along with this degree of segregation and ripped out the benches on their side. The situation got pretty ugly, but fortunately the men of the Fourth Division, organized from an existing national guard unit, were well disciplined and walked out quietly. Contact, however, was not to be avoided. One morning I was called out on a detail with about fifty recruits. Assigned to the area where they were building Women's Army Corps (WAC) barracks, we were under the direction of a lone white sergeant, a real sergeant with, evidently, many tours of duty. At first we were given the job of removing rail sections so that a walkway between the proposed barracks could be built. I had no idea that a rail section of about twenty-five feet could be so heavy. That thing must have weighed several tons. It took all fifty of us to pick up one of them. When we had moved them all the sergeant blew his whistle and said, "I want all you niggers to come over here."

This guy was either brave or stupid. There was nobody out there but one white guy and fifty angry, aggressive blacks. Everybody explosively converged on the sergeant, pinning him in the center without even enough room to move his arms. Strangely enough, we were wedged in so tightly that no blows were exchanged. Seeing what might develop and that help was at least a mile away, the sergeant said, "It's time for a break, and I want to buy you all a coke at the PX." We were all relieved and didn't feel we had to avenge the insult. We finished the day without incident, our sergeant displaying his military professionalism.

Work details other than Kitchen Police (KP) usually came off after breakfast. The trick was to disappear right after eating. I would go straight from the mess hall and get on a post bus. There was no charge, and the ride was a long one. It took all morning to go around the post once, with the farthest point being at least thirty miles away. Lots of guys split like that. This escape tactic was perfect, but I knew it couldn't last. I got caught after a few days of sightseeing in Fort Dix, New Jersey.

They caught me one morning before I could get out and onto the bus. I was headed for KP at about four-thirty in the morning. It was still dark out there. When the mess sergeant asked for "volunteers" for the various available gigs, I "volunteered" to clean pots and pans. I didn't realize what I was getting into. All of those pots were about two feet deep and eighteen inches in diameter. They started me off with about six pots, and that took me up to lunch time. As soon as I had finished them, they brought six more. These pots had to be not only squeaky clean, but polished so I could see my face in them. It was a never-ending process for three meals each day. It was also a fourteen-hour work day, and as soon as I got back to the barracks I went straight to bed.

I began to yearn for a pass. I had heard about this marvelous institution from some of the long-term residents. The highest-ranking black that I saw was Corporal Bobby Evans, a former entertainer and tap dancer. He was always well groomed and full of himself. I wrote him a little note in which I said, "In your climb to greater heights in the army, it would be nice if you could not only notice but assist your subordinates in their personal problems."

I immediately got a two-day pass, and considering that Philadelphia was only forty-five miles away, it was sublime. The bus ride from the post was a short one, but in that brief period my horizon widened in reference to black people. There was a group of soldiers on the bus chatting away furiously in a language other than English. They weren't talking ghettoese or southern. It took me awhile, but I finally figured it must have been French. I marveled at this and moved around in front of each speaking soldier to see if he was for real. They all looked like any other black that I knew, say from Harlem, inner-city Philadelphia, or even Georgia. Then I noticed the FFRR patch on their arms. They were free French from Martinique or Guadalupe in the Caribbean. My world of blacks had been small; I only knew or thought of black people from the inner cities or the South. I had heard of Africans but thought of them as exotic, distant people. It was mind-boggling to realize that there was a world of blacks out there, speaking different languages and having different customs and cultures. Even though I couldn't communicate with these soldiers, I rode into Philadelphia feeling a definite kinship.

The two-day pass to Philly was uneventful, and I returned to Fort Dix to an improved condition. Corporal Slim, Slim Gailliard, came by with a teasing proposition that I readily accepted. First, I was to be assigned to maintenance duty at the recreation (rec) hall, in charge of cleaning the stage, sweeping, mopping, and waxing. This was enough to remove me from the barracks legally and consequently from availability for the more distasteful gigs. Also, I got a special tag to hang on the bedpost that identified me as one on an assignment. Corporal Slim was none other than half of the famous instrumental duo Slim and Slam. He could really play the guitar. He knew of me as a bass player in New York, and he planned to place me in the new duo to play the part of Slam Stewart. This was all right except that Slam Stewart was one of the premier developers of jazz bass playing. He pioneered playing bass solos with the bow with his unique style of vocally doubling the instrumental solo an octave higher. The duo was very popular and entertaining with such hits as "Flat Foot Floogie."

Obviously I couldn't be Slam, but I *was* the only black bass player not on shipment and thus available. We played gigs in the officers' clubs for the magnificent sum of two dollars a night. Sometimes we used a drummer, a pianist, or even a saxophonist. Also, we played concerts on occasion for all of the troops including the Fourth Motorized of Georgia. I got a little notoriety on the post for playing "Big Noise from Winnetka." In this drum and bass duo, the drummer uses the bass finger board as a drum. With the bassist sliding his hands up and down the finger board and changing the pitch, the effect was incredible to some people. It sounded more technical than it actually was.

With some collusion from the officers for whom we played those two dollar gigs, we were able to remain in status quo for several weeks. It was the best of a bad deal to remain in Fort Dix, fifty-five miles from New York, and get almost weekly passes. Alas, one morning a white sergeant came over to the rec hall, called my name, and ordered me to report to headquarters as soon as possible.

The army didn't mess around. I found myself with about six other recruits on a train to Fort Huachuca, Arizona, that very day. I was given the tickets and vouchers for food for our little party. The first part of our trip, until we changed trains in Chicago, was uneventful. Still it was exciting since I had never been on a transcontinental train like the Broadway Limited before.

The party was definitely over as we stepped into the 105-degree dry heat of Arizona. We were surrounded by mountains, and I could see objects clearly defined forty miles away in that dry air. Everybody else in our party went to the Thirty-seventh Special Service Company. I was assigned to the 1922 SCU Post Band. I never did understand what S.C.U. stood for. There were two army divisions on the post, both with black enlisted men and mostly white officers. There were a few black lieutenants, but about 99 percent of the officers were white.

Phoenix and Tucson were off limits by collusion of the army and state officials; they didn't want all those black enlisted men running around their bastions of white supremacy and eyeing the white females.

The 1922 SCU band resided in the old post, in permanent-style buildings instead of the regular wooden barracks. The members of the band were not war inductees, but army veterans of many years' service. It was a closed club, and they seemed to resent newcomers. They were all noncoms. I was the only private, and I was reminded of that fact in every way possible. Rehearsals were particularly nerve-wracking because any imprecision was met with scorn and derision. They made no concession for my being new to their style of play. I was permitted to play the baritone horn part and march in this crack unit, but I made no friends among these guys, most of whom were ten to fifteen years older than I and already had their cliques. I can remember only my apprehension over each upcoming parade, concert, or rehearsal. After a few weeks of this tension, I was relieved to learn that I had been transferred to the Thirty-seventh Special Service Company somewhere out there in the boondocks of Fort Huachuca. I would be reunited with my buddies from Fort Dix.

The special service company in the army is primarily a support unit. It was set up to operate the post exchange behind combat zones and to entertain. The Thirty-seventh was headed by Captain Kenneth Johnson, a career soldier and not a musician. We had a complement of 109 men and 6 officers, all black. Of the 109 enlisted men, all but 6 were noncommissioned officers or specialists. My discharge papers list me as a sergeant (T/4) and a storekeeper first class. Most of our officers were products of the ROTC in black colleges and consequently had no real army experience. Captain Johnson had prior army experience through the National Guard. A lot of our men were professional musicians and entertainers, so we were unusually equipped to carry out our entertainment functions. We were also well supplied with equipment, including a sixteen-millimeter film projector and a piano in each of the four platoons. It was a shame to see that studio Steinway painted khaki. We also had a lot of college men, with black colleges prevailing. I had the impression that it was the policy of the army to dump black intelligentsia into outfits like these. Most of us were happy and felt we were better off not being in actual combat units like the Ninety-second Division.

We immediately went into basic training. Again, I didn't distinguish myself. We did the extended order drill in which we used our rifles to break the fall and dropped into a prone firing position. This was all right except that the Arizona sand had been baked into almost solid concrete. After doing this for hours at a time, I could feel the skin coming apart at my knees.

When basic training was over, we celebrated energetically and enthusiastically. One of our first projects was to go to the "hook," the cabins of prostitution right outside the gate. I tried not to go, protesting that I had no money. My new buddies gave me no alternative saying, "Come on, Smith, we got the money (five dollars) and we gonna party." There was no way around this predicament, knowing these guys, so I went. Right outside the entrance gate and across the road from the bus stop was a row of about twenty one-room cabins, a Cadillac beside each one. Inside were some of the most horrible-looking women I had ever seen. There were lines of about a dozen guys in front of each cabin. The guys gave me my five bucks, and I got into a line. I was there about one or two hours while each client was getting about ten or fifteen minutes. To me, this was all too degrading and horrible. My view of sex had more to do with conversation, companionship, and compatibility. I agonized over what I would do after I got inside. A guy walked down the steps, smiling and zipping up his pants, and it was my turn. I went in and the lady eyed me suspiciously while holding out her hand for the five bucks. In defense, while she was getting on the bed pulling aside her dressing gown, I asked her just to let me stay about ten minutes and fake the whole thing. It was beautiful. When we hit the door after ten minutes, she had her arms around me while I zipped up my pants. It was enough to convince my buddies, who asked me, "How was it?"

I told them, "It was good." Everybody was happy, but I could have used that five bucks for, say, a pint of Jack Daniel's.

Although the East Coast seemed so remote, we began to receive letters from civilization. I received a letter almost daily from Suzie and occasionally one from my wife. The letters helped me to settle down and make a go of it.

We set about organizing a band, and we had to decide what to do with so much talent. Eardlie Hope, my predecessor with the Redcaps, was in camp. I decided to relinquish the bass playing post to him in spite of my greater reputation. That way, we could all be happy; he could play and I would write. As it turned out, I was given credit along with Hess Franklin and Pinkney Webster as the organizer of the band. We had guys who had played with Cab Calloway and other bands of that ilk, enough talent for two bands, not to mention a choir, which we also had. We also had guys with organizational skills not necessarily connected with music. We had projectionists, accountants, carpenters, and electrical engineers. With that group I think we could have landed on Mars and established a livable community with an excellent quality of life.

I wrote music daily, composing and arranging on my bed in the barracks, and I was at the top of my game when Lieutenant Wertz came in and had me stand at attention. "What's all this mess on your bed? Get in full field pack and fall out on today's expedition in five minutes."

Nothing to say but, "Yes, sir." So I fell out. We went on a short hike of about five miles and returned to the company area before dinner. At dinner that night Captain Johnson called me over to his table and asked me, "Did you finish the music for our new show? We'll need it in a week."

I saluted and told him, "Sir, I find it difficult to write while walking, Sir." Then I related the afternoon incident.

Captain Johnson stood up and ordered, "Lieutenant Wertz, come over here. Did you order this man out on your little hike? Lieutenant, can you write music?"

The answer was, "No, sir."

"Look, Lieutenant, we can get some more lieutenants, but we only have one guy who writes and arranges music. From now on, you find out what he has to do and help him."

With the help of John R. D. Jones and Howard Roberts (a former Lionel Hampton trumpeter), we developed a credible band and choir. We had some terrific singers and developed some really fine musicales, especially shows built around the war bond theme. I wrote some originals and arrangements for them. We were invited to present our wares not only on the post, but in surrounding towns like Bisbee, Arizona.

During this period I received a letter from my child-bride saying that she would be in Arizona the following week. I was both happy and frightened. Never having been in the military before, I didn't have any idea what to do. I knew of men who had their wives on the post, but they were veterans, not like most of us in the Thirty-seventh who were little more than recruits. Captain Johnson took care of that situation at a routine dinner. He called each of us up, one by one, and handed us our stripes (for PFC, corporal, or sergeant). I was flabbergasted when he called my name as Sergeant Smith. I guess he took into account the organization of the band and the writing and arrangement of the music. I certainly was not promoted for any military qualities.

# CHAPTER 15

# THREE UP AND A T

**N**ew Sergeant Smith (T/4 or Tech Sergeant—three up and a T) had a problem. His wife would soon be arriving in Benson, Arizona, and he didn't have a pass to receive her. Not only that, but we had to find her a place to stay on the post.

Julia arrived, and through some finagling I got her in one of the guest rooms at the service club. They were very strict, saying she could only stay for one week. Julia rapidly became a favorite of the guys in the Thirty-seventh, especially after they heard her sing. Instantly, she had 109 new brothers, which was good in view of the fact that her only brother, whom I never knew, was killed in action in Italy. Corporal Webster had his wife Pauline on the post, and we had lots of fun together. Julia and Pauline were quite a team. We took shopping trips to the the Mexican border towns of Aqua Prieto and Naco, where I first became curious about the Spanish language.

The ax fell when our week was up. We had to find other quarters and a job for Julia. Julia, who had left school after the tenth grade, had no marketable skills other than singing. That left only menial tasks such as chambermaid or waitress. There were no openings on the post except to be a housemaid in the white officers' compound. Here they had homes, family, and tradition on the old post. I took my wife around, and we "interviewed" several wives of captains, majors and colonels. The pay offered was an insult, and I saw America's class system in operation. These white women basically wanted slave labor. Every house that we went into had a plaque with something like Chicamauga 1862 or Colonel Macintosh or United States Military Academy 1884. I was looking at a tradition or a class system. I was reminded that the younger brother did not inherit the plantation and often went into the military. When desirable assignments ran out, he, the younger brother, often found himself in command of black troops.

Julia did find some part-time work at the PX as a sales clerk, but it wasn't enough to give her housing on the post. She had to move from the service club hotel, and we found a room in a nearby town in one of those Mexican courtyard affairs, two floors with a balcony around the second floor and all rooms opening onto the courtyard. Since all of the other occupants were Mexicans, my romance with the Spanish language continued.

But we could not find any work for Julia, so the inevitable came to pass. We had to consider giving up the apartment. My salary of seventy-eight dollars a month could not sustain us. Reluctantly, I bought a ticket to send Julia back to Philly. I was sad, but grateful for even that short interlude.

The next blow came rather unexpectedly. I was ordered to appear at headquarters, where I met a white colonel. He said that along with five other guys in the company, I had been selected to go to college. I don't remember the name of the program, but I was delighted at the opportunity. The selection was made on the basis of IQs. I was amazed to find out that the guy with the highest IQ in the company was a company cook with no college experience. We were ordered to pack our belongings and be ready for a jeep to pick us up at about supper time. I packed and spent the rest of the afternoon in eager anticipation. At supper, Captain Johnson called us over to his table and informed us, "You can unpack. A company commander can request and keep all personnel he deems necessary to the company's operation in wartime."

He had done just that. Hurt, frustrated, and angry, I immediately began formulating plans for getting out of the army. The next morning I went on sick call, complaining about sinus troubles and headaches. This was legitimate; in fact, I've had a sinus condition for practically all of my life. Captain Johnson accused me of malingering but had to comply with army regulations. I went immediately to the post hospital where, to my surprise, I was admitted. I stayed there for over a month, during which time the Thirty-seventh was shipped out, eventually to North Africa and Italy. Since my service records went with them, I was a nonperson, a soldier without an attached group, which meant no pay. I went for a month without a single dime. I had a place to eat and sleep as long as I wore the uniform, but no newspaper, candy, whiskey, or beer for one month. (Fortunately, I didn't smoke cigars then.) I could have gone to the Red Cross for a few dollars but decided to brave it out. It was very hard when I got an unbelievable craving for beer or for a nickel candy bar. I fought off these temptations and survived practically a whole month before my records caught up with me. One thing helped: The operation on my sinuses confined me to the ward for several days. I don't know what they did in the operating room, but my sinuses were worse than ever after the operation. I was ordered to pack and be prepared for shipment to the Beaumont General Hospital, Fort Bliss, in El Paso, Texas.

Julia joined me in El Paso. Because of the general freedom of movement in the hospital, I had time to roam the streets and find an apartment for us. I found a one-bedroom place not far from the International Bridge and the Rio Grande. It was another Mexican courtyard affair, and the neighbors were friendly even with our language difficulties. When Julia put on her Mexican outfits, she was easily taken for one of them.

Beaumont General Hospital was a lot freer than the Fort Huachuca Hospital. I only had to make roll call in the morning. There were no gigs like KP because they had civilians to do that kind of work. I spent a lot of time at our little apartment, which was basically what we call a second floor studio apartment with a balcony. I took a job at a bowling alley as a pin boy. With no automatic setup machines, I had to skip out of the way when a strike was thrown. I survived that because we needed the money. Somehow we made it and even enjoyed living in an atmosphere far different from the urban complexes of New York City and Philadelphia. Living among Indians and Mexicans, away from concentrations of blacks, was a pleasant culture shock.

My money from the Thirty-seventh caught up with me at Fort Bliss. For a while I was rolling in dough—well, maybe not rolling, but I had the luxury of a ten-dollar bill in my wallet. I invested that money on a weird proposition. I bankrolled our leading crapshooter, "the Kokomo Kid" or "Kid Fingers," a character who walked around all day fingering a pair of dice. In the evening he went to the officers' game room and plied his trade. Invariably, he doubled my money. Ten dollars became twenty dollars by morning. What I could never understand was why he had to be bankrolled repeatedly. I never asked him—I just gladly handed over my money. After witnessing "the kid" time and time again roll any number he called, I had the feeling that this was the only sure investment to be made. Anyway, it served me in good stead as musical gigs were nonexistent at Fort Bliss. Kid Fingers was black and had no outstanding qualities except his tactile senses. He could control a pair of dice better than anybody I had ever seen. Because I was one of the few blacks on our ward, he came to me for stake money. He never played in any of the enlisted men's games but looked for the officers' games and found them with unerring precision. Even more remarkably, he was readmitted to these games even after he had cleaned the men out before. We enlisted men rooted for him, feeling that he had achieved a sense of justice, cleaning out those higher paid officers. It was only right.

In the segregated army, blacks and whites living together in a shared barracks was unique. Fort Bliss was the regular army, but Beaumont General Hospital was not. I stayed downstairs in a barracks of overwhelmingly white occupancy. I had been somewhat prepared for this by my summers at Camp Lakeland. I had been used to being around and socially interacting with whites from kindergarten through college. In the wards, however, we had a complete crosssection of the white population of the U.S. We had poor and more affluent whites, educated and uneducated whites, and I assure you the affluent and educated whites were better and easier to deal with.

I had two friends—Mel Perriera of Portuguese descent and Wilbur Hood, a drummer and Stanford University graduate. We roamed the streets of El Paso looking for possible jam sessions. Sometimes we took Julia with us. El Paso was a segregated town, of course, but segregation was a little less rigid here, primarily because there were not that many blacks in the region. A couple of establishments were indifferent to state law, and we even saw interracial dating and dancing.

After a couple of failed sinus operations, I received notice that I would be discharged from the army; they referred to it as "separation from the army." It did not take a crowbar to pry me loose; I was ready to go. When the supply sergeant suggested to me that if I waited a couple of days he could give me a complete clothing outfit (from overcoat to shoes), I asked him, "Can I get to the train in my underwear?" With my discharge in my hand, I was ready to get on the first thing smoking.

Julia and I left El Paso hoping to reach New York in time for me to get to Camp Lakeland and register at NYU. After a brief interlude in Chicago with my relatives, we rode into Philly with the most money that I've ever had at one time. We decided not to party, but to invest it in the future. That was a good decision because our child was on his way.

# CHAPTER 16

# RETURN TO WONDERLAND

*I* left my wife in Philadelphia while I went to New York to register at NYU and to find an apartment for what would soon be three of us. I concentrated my apartment search in an area around Washington Square. After walking through some empty apartments on Fourth Street, I applied at the agent's office only to be told, "The apartment was just rented, and we haven't had a chance to take the sign down."

After about a dozen of these coincidences, I was becoming discouraged when I noticed an old warehouse on Bleecker Street near the Bowery. I saw that while this was no regular apartment building, people were living there. I was desperate, so I inquired at the hardware store on the corner. Luckily for me, the man I asked happened to own the building. He had an empty flat, which he would rent to me for seventeen dollars a month if I asked for no repairs or improvements. The three-room flat was a basket case, starting with the toilet in the hallway outside the apartment proper. We would take baths in a square tub in the kitchen, which was also the entrance to the apartment. The place obviously was not designed for human habitation. The ceilings were at least twelve feet high. We would have had to get up on a ladder to feel what little heat there was in this cold-water flat. The only good thing I could say about it was that it was within walking distance of NYU and later of my teaching job at Seward Park High.

I registered at NYU to redeem myself from all those incompletes of 1942. While I didn't take any courses that summer because I wanted to be free for a gig at Camp Lakeland, I was able to make up all the missed requirements except for major and minor instrument recitals, piano, and voice. That cleared me to register in the fall of 1944 for graduate work. It also enabled me to take the New York City teachers' exam, which would qualify me for substitute teaching even without a degree. With a baby coming, I had to think of a more consistent source of money than music gigs. We bought a piano for seventy-five dollars, and the work of that summer was dedicated to clearing my name and academic reputation. Turning in those papers, assignments, and exams took a big load off my mind. Now I could direct my attention to those four music recitals that stood in the way of the degree.

The mood of the summer of 1944 was one of general optimism. It was the period of the Allied landings in Normandy. We were not getting the bad news of German *blitzkriegs* and encirclements of the previous two years. In New York, business seemed to be going as usual. Jobs were available for just about anybody. Bars and nightclubs seemed to be thriving. Various friends, acquaintances, and relatives were missing, but there seemed to be enough other people to take up the slack. Very few of the black jazz musicians appeared to be in the services, although everybody knew of personnel changes because of the war. All of the major bands kept going, and some new ones came into being. In my absence a revolution in jazz was brewing at Minton's, a club near the Apollo Theatre. I heard about the strange goings-on and some of the key characters involved. While I never had the opportunity to hear or see the action at Minton's because of school or other gigs, the musicians' grapevine brought me word about Charlie Parker, Tad Dameron, Thelonius Monk, and others. The whole business of "bebop" would soon have an impact on my musical life.

That summer of 1944 was spent at my old standby gig—Camp Lakeland. This time I was married and could not get involved with any females. Also, I was busy getting all those missed term papers, book reports, and other assignments together.

When the summer ended, I came back to NYU and the apartment on Bleecker Street. I registered for graduate classes, even though I could not officially graduate until I did my recitals. The GI Bill had not come into being yet, but with the remains of my army mustering-out pay and summer employment, the tuition was paid, and our finances were under control. Busy with classes and possible work as a substitute teacher in the New York school system, I approached my musician colleagues for one-night, or week-off gigs, nothing steady or with an organized group.

I contacted Clark Monroe at an after-hours club on 133rd Street. He now had a club on Fifty-second Street, the jazz capital of the world. He told me to come to work the next week for one week. I didn't know who I would be working with, but boy, did I find out! It was a week-off gig for me with Max Roach on drums and Thelonius Monk on piano. It was Monk's trio, put together by Clark Monroe. I'm sure neither of these two musicians would have hired me, as they did not know me, although I had heard of them, especially about their new, experimental music. I was apprehensive to say the least, but a gig is a gig and has to be treated professionally.

It was a weird week. If I had known the roles these two guys were to play in the history and development of jazz, I would have kept notes. At the time, though, I had some problems. First of all, I was a big band bassist accustomed to a straight, driving, swinging four/four beat. It was unsettling to try to survive in the dislocation of rhythmic patterns and the unsettling "bombs" of the very experimental Max Roach. Even then, he was a virtuoso of technique and could execute anything so that his "bebop" phrasing became credible to all but the most unsophisticated listeners. Max was a great drummer, and with a bass player of similar capabilities he would have achieved wonderfully innovative results. I simply was not that bass player; I played it straight out of my experience. This stuff was too new for me to digest.

Later, in 1945, I took part in a recording session in which Max Roach and Dizzy Gillespie were two of the principals. I was indeed hurt when, as soon as Max saw me come in with my bass, he blurted out, "Oh, no! Not that guy!" I don't think he intended disrespect for my playing ability, but rather for my "old-fashioned" style. I listen today with pleasure to any record that Max Roach is on because I now know what is involved.

Neither Max nor Thelonius was talkative, so it was not a very sociable week. Thelonius had a reputation for being mysterious, and I was not privy to his inner circle of friends and musicians. I thought his hesitating style was primarily due to a lack of technique. I had played with such master pianists as Calvin Jackson and Hank Jones, and I thought that Thelonius was fumbling for the right notes pretty much as I would do on a piano trying to play an unfamiliar tune. I did notice some of his harmonic eccentricities, which later registered as brilliant. He was indeed complex, but with a provocative twist. Having played his music in later years and listened more carefully, I can attest to his greatness as an innovator. My favorite piece of his is the haunting "Round Midnight." We played out the week at the Spotlight professionally if not comfortably. I would not want the experience again, but I respected and now (with some education) enjoy these two musicians. All was not lost because Clark Monroe, the owner and manager of the Spotlight, told me that he would use me whenever he could. I would be the house bass player.

Graduate school at NYU was completely different from the undergraduate program. First, there were significantly more blacks, there primarily in the summer as a result of the southern states' scholarship policy designed to maintain segregation in their state colleges. In most of my undergraduate experience, there were never more than two blacks in a class. In the graduate class there were never more than three or four, but these were much smaller classes. Most of the blacks were experienced professionals. I was privileged to speak with them and learn about life in the South and at black colleges. Many of them were professors in black colleges, but I was surprised to hear them stand up to our white professors. I shouldn't have been because they were teaching the same subjects with the same competency as their white counterparts. I sat next to Ahmed Williams, a music professor at West Virginia State College in Institute, West Virginia, and derived a totally different approach to graduate study. It was to be more aggressive and independent, and to do it I would have to pay my dues in preparation and study. I had the added burden of performing the four recitals left over from 1942 and taking the New York City teacher's exam. The recitals meant practice for piano, bass viol, tuba, and voice. For the teacher's exam in instrumental music, it meant additional preparation for clarinet, trumpet, violin, snare drum, score reading, music history, and music theory.

Senior recitals at NYU were serious business, with printed announcements, posters, and programs. I think the poster about William O. Smith, "tenor," was the most frightening. The idea that anybody would be invited to hear me sing was, at the least, disconcerting. I had the hammers on my piano tufted so that I could practice in the morning without waking my wife. She actually could not hear the piano at all from about fifty feet. I was allowed to do the major (tuba) and minor instrument (bass viol) recitals in one sitting. I guess nobody wanted to hear a whole program with two such unseemly instruments.

The major/minor recital went off uneventfully with no major mishaps. It seemed that every black employee of NYU was present.

One would have thought that the recital was taking place in Harlem. The elevator operators, the janitors, and even the female service contingent were there. I had one of the largest audiences of the senior recital series in this nine-hundred-seat auditorium. Julia and my mother were there, too. I played the Beelzebub variations and other selected beauties from the Kopprasch advanced tuba *étude* book. As it turned out, I would never play this much horn again. As a matter of fact, I pawned my tuba later in a tight financial period and never redeemed it. The bass viol half of the recital consisted of my arrangement of the "Swan" from Saint-Saën's "Carnival of Animals" (the soulful cello solo) and a "Concerto for Bass Viol" by Capuzzi. There were some shaky moments in the "Swan," but other than that, I got away with it.

The voice recital was the most embarrassing. I did get through it, but I was terrified at the thought of standing up before an audience with nothing in my hand. We were taught to clasp our hands in front of us, and I thought that was "sissified." Again the auditorium was filled with my black constituents, so when my accompanist struck up the introduction to the first piece, there was no place to hide. I proceeded with songs like "Caro Mio Ben" (in Italian), Handel's "Where'er She Walks," and a song in German. You would have thought that I was Caruso the way my black supporters applauded. No encore was in the cards—I ran off of that stage like a jack rabbit. I went straight to 4 Bleecker Street and guzzled down a half-pint of good rye whiskey to forget.

My most pleasant memory of these recitals has to do with the piano recital. Probably because I am not and never have been a pianist, I got the most satisfaction out of practicing or performing piano literature. As I had no lessons and only a modicum of guidance from the piano department, I had to be restrained from ignorantly considering virtuoso material for the concert. There was nothing explosive in my recital lineup, and it was just as well because I couldn't handle any piano explosions with my limited technique. The program opened with a toccata by C. P. E. Bach, a piece that suggests more pyrotechnics than it takes to perform it. There were a few tense moments, but no major messups. Anyway, I passed this hurdle and was on my way toward taking the New York City teachers' exam to qualify for a teaching job.

The written part of the teachers' exam was a breeze—mostly music theory, history, and literature, with some methodology thrown in. Coming off a series of senior recitals, I was able to impress the examiners in instrumental performances. I was asked to play the foundational scale and a simple tune on the violin, cello, clarinet, flute, trumpet, and trombone, then a drum roll on the snare drum. Everything was a piece of cake except the drum roll. I simply had not practiced it enough.

The oral portion of the exam was the terror of most applicants. It was administered by Dr. Ruth Mansker and had previously been used to control the number of black applicants. Some of the victims of the system took speech lessons and affected British accents. No hint of a southern accent would pass. I refused to go the British route and suffered the consequences. I did not pass the New York City teachers' exam because of "a condition in speech." All, however, was not lost; I was still certified by the state of New York and could work as a daily substitute teacher.

As soon as I got on the substitute teacher list, I received a call from Seward Park High. The principal recognized my name and put in a request for my services. When I reported the next day, he asked me if it would be all right if I came daily. He was short of teachers because of the war and could not guarantee that I would be in music every day; but while I would not have a homeroom, I would still be considered a regular faculty member. My pay was $9.50 a day or $47.50 a week. While the money was timely, it did put a damper on my gigging. New York gigs were usually from 10:00 P.M. to 4:00 A.M. Also, graduate school courses (evenings and Saturday mornings) put a limitation on my sleeping time, not to mention time with Julia. Fortunately, the baby was not born until January 1, 1945.

The principal had a time-card system and collected all the cards promptly at 7:45 A.M. Anyone who came after that would not find a card to punch. As I was paid on a daily basis, I was afraid to be late and walked to school rather than take a chance on the transportation system. Fortunately, the school was only about a mile from 4 Bleecker Street. But I had only about two hours' sleep after a gig before going out no later than 7:30 A.M. I taught mostly instrumental music, with a few excursions into social studies and physical education. I was the assistant orchestra director and assistant band director and taught most of the beginning instrument classes. I was responsible for the junior string ensemble. It was to be a good year in spite of my lack of sleep. At least I was financially stable, albeit at the minimum.

To further exacerbate my lack of sleep, Clark Monroe, owner of the Spotlight, called me to come to work on a weekly basis. I was delighted and reported forthwith in spite of graduate classes and daily subbing at Seward Park High. I couldn't quit the teaching because that was to be my future, so I just had to brave it out. The appearances at the Spotlight started right after I took the teachers' exam. They began with Charlie Parker and a small group with Max Roach (drums), Al Haig (piano), Teddy Walters (guitar), and later Dexter Gordon (tenor) and Leo Parker (baritone). Miles Davis was the unofficial trumpeter, though he was not hired or paid by Monroe. I was the house bassist and later moved to other groups formulated by Monroe. Curley Russell was to be my replacement with Charlie Parker. With this lineup's reputation as founding fathers of "bop," we became favorites for other musicians sitting in. We also became highly experimental. Many old and familiar tunes were given the "bop" treatment. New tunes, riffs, and clichés were formulated.

Charlie Parker blazed with his dazzling technique while Miles Davis played most frequently with a mute and his trumpet pointed toward the bandstand curtain. I wondered who he was. I found out he was a Juilliard student and friend of Charlie's. The musicians' union would have frowned at the idea of an extra unpaid musician on the stand, but Miles Davis solved this by remaining largely unseen. He stayed very close to the bandstand curtain, usually behind somebody. I was not impressed by his playing, and no doubt he was not impressed by mine. I had no personal relations with anybody as I could not hang out or party but had to beeline back to the apartment to get a few winks before my classes started.

Fifty-second Street was probably at its liveliest in the fall of 1944. Stuff Smith, the great jazz violinist, was across the street and I could hear him up and down the street with his electric amplification. On occasion, Art Tatum, the great virtuoso of jazz piano, held forth, and he was like a magnet drawing all would-be jazz pianists to his court. Errol Garner was almost in perpetual residence with his unique hesitating left-hand rhythmic style sounding like a guitar background. Errol was such a character that I really thought he was crazy.

The usual hangouts for intermissions were either an apartment close to the Spotlight for tea (marijuana) or the White Rose bar. I thought it was an insult, but police identification was required of all musicians playing on the "street." The police were in evidence on the street moving all passersby along. They were particularly adamant about mixed couples. Such couples were rather common in this freer part of the city's entertainment system. Theoretically, black patronage was not encouraged. The prices were high enough to dis-

courage most blacks, especially the ones I knew. The blacks we saw
were either celebrities—actors, boxers, entertainers, and so forth—
or relatively obscure sidemen like myself (but known to be employees). Duke Ellington, Joe Louis, or Lena Horne were always
welcome, but people like me could get in if we took a back table.
Strangely enough, this was not the situation in Harlem. All were welcome in Small's Paradise and like establishments if we had the money.

Monday afternoon was payday at the Spotlight, and everybody
was there. The Spotlight, the only black-operated club downtown,
had financial problems and was basically a shoestring operation. The
musicians were paid forty-five to fifty-five dollars a week, depending
on the prestige of their name. My name was never on the marquee, so
I got the smaller figure. Interestingly enough Charlie Parker did not,
to my knowledge, receive a leader's fee (usually double a sideman's
pay). Actually with his bar tab he usually took home less than I did. I
know this because on several occasions I was in line right behind him
when Mr. Monroe paid off.

I usually arrived at the club a few minutes before 10:00 P.M.
That gave me a chance to strike up a friendship with the bartender,
who usually got me to sample some of his newer concoctions. One
day, however, feeling flush with my position at the club and sneaking
in a few more minutes of sleep, I arrived at work about fifteen minutes
late. Although I was the only musician there at the time, I was con-
fronted by the assistant manager, who asked me, "How come you
late?"

I pointed out to him that I was the only musician there and that
Charlie Parker was late. He immediately applied the crusher: "You
ain't Charlie Parker." Much chastened, I was never late after that.

The Spotlight was probably the favoritie "sit-in" spot for the
younger and soon-to-be-famous musicians. It seemed as if the musicians were walking up and down the street looking for action. If Ben
Webster, then with Duke's band, showed up, just about every tenor
sax player with any reputation would be inside the club within fifteen
minutes.

One night there was a tribute for a Scandinavian jazz journalist, and union rules were relaxed to permit more than five men on
the stand at the same time. It seemed that the journalist was much
loved by the black jazz musicians and was in New York because of the
war. Duke Ellington himself was a sponsor of the event and took over
the piano. It was fascinating; away from his own band, Duke proved
that he could play with anybody. I had never heard such artistry from

a backup pianist. He actually fed the soloist with ideas, rhythms, and riffs. Also, I had never heard that much piano from Duke. He actually orchestrated the jam session while presiding at the piano. Fortunately for our journalist friend, the whole session was recorded so he could take this gift back to his war-torn country.

At the intermission I made one of my regular trips to the White Rose bar and took my place amidst the conclave of bass players. The bartenders not only knew us all but knew our alcoholic preferences. Without a word being spoken, they handed me a jigger of Carstair's 1788 whiskey with no chaser, no ice or anything. I thought that I was showing sophistication here in not ordering the cheaper Carstair's White Seal. I also thought that actions like this were commensurate with my position as one of the lucky few musicians employed on the street. A young man walked up to me and introduced himself: "I'm Ray Brown from Pittsburgh, Oscar." (I was flattered that he knew my name.) "How do you get a gig here?"

I answered that the usual procedure was to sit in for sets in the various spots so the musicians could hear you play. I told him he could sit in for me anytime. I was taking a chance here because I had never heard him play. However, if he could sit in for a whole set, I would have ninety minutes free for studying or even going home to Bleecker Street for a snack. In a way, I took advantage of him, getting him to play while I got paid.

When Dizzy Gillespie asked me about going on the road with his band, I suggested that he go down to the Spotlight and hear this new kid Ray Brown, who was sitting in for me. Dizzy liked what he heard, and he and Ray made a fruitful liaison for the history of jazz. I didn't realize how fruitful until three years later when I heard the record "One Bass Hit." I feel proud of my role in helping one of the premier bass players of all time get started.

The year 1944 ended explosively, with Julia and me making a mad dash to Riverside Hospital on the upper end of Manhattan Island, all the way from Bleecker Street. William O. Smith, III, was the first baby born in the New York area in 1945. Arriving just a few minutes after midnight New Year's Day, he was awarded a free layette from *The New York Times,* and a paragraph noting the event appeared in the paper.

# CHAPTER 17

# THE SPOTLIGHT

*T*he year 1945 began with a promise of life and hope for the future. The graduate classes proceeded normally, and I got out of the club gig just in time to succeed. Only one class made a lasting impression on me. Creative Rhythms for the Dance was a course for both music and dance majors. A committee of teaching specialists was in charge of the various aspects of the course. Martha Graham taught elements of modern dance, and Norma Lloyd (later director at Juilliard) taught composing for the dance.

The first few weeks of this class were devoted to the fundamentals of ballet (the primary positions) and elements of modern dance. The latter orientation presented a problem. The unusual movements required for modern dance often use muscles in an unusual way. Try crawling like a baby (something you used to do) and see if you don't break out in perspiration. Even bending an elbow in a direction not usually taken will provide the suggested effect. We got through this rather embarrassing (for me) phase in passable shape.

When Martha Graham, the godmother of modern dance, selected me to lead in one of her infamous "follow the leader" games, I reluctantly complied. I was terrified. Everybody waited for me to do something and then imitated my movement. I started out doing some rather awkward leaps and on inspiration from a Tarzan movie, tried to make out as an African spear dancer. I would leap periodically in time with an imagined tribal war chant. The leap consisted primarily of extending both elbows and knees and pointing the imagined spear in sudden alternate directions. With a few irregular runs in between

155

leaps, the whole thing was rather strenuous, but Ms. Graham was ecstatic.

She exclaimed, "How primitive! How African!" She had me repeat the whole thing—I guess not realizing that I was coming off a 4:00 A.M. gig. The good part is that I received an *A* for the course, and I'm sure my African heritage influenced that grade.

My day gig at Seward Park High proceeded uneventfully, but with some satisfaction. I felt good on my shopping forays in the immediate neighborhood when some white kid introduced me to his parents with, "This is Mr. Smith, my music teacher."

I felt like an honored person in the community. One evening we had a program in honor of Eleanor Roosevelt, and she was there. Much beloved in such lower-class communities as the Lower East Side and Harlem, she came across as the protector and spokesperson for the poor, blacks, and women. The program was the high spot of the school year, and we brought everything in our cultural arsenal into display. The kids all loved Mrs. Roosevelt—I could feel it. They felt honored that she would even notice us. Since I was not the director of any of the organizations that performed, I was not required to be there. I had a possible gig on Fifty-second Street, but I turned it down, as it was for me unthinkable not to be present on this critical occasion. I made my presence effective by helping the orchestra director and the kids in all of the little things they had to do in order to give a good performance. And they gave a good performance. In fact, they outdid themselves. The principal was so proud that he even included me in his effusive thanks. I didn't realize it at the time, but Mrs. Roosevelt noticed my presence (possibly because I was the only black teacher in the school). A few weeks later when I was shopping for groceries at the Cooperative on Sixth Avenue, Mrs. Roosevelt came in. I couldn't imagine the wife of the president of the United States coming into a routine, commonplace store like this without an honor guard, police escort, and sirens, not to mention the flag. But here she was, looking like everybody's grandmother very quietly shopping. She stopped when she saw me rolling a baby carriage and said, "Young man, I certainly enjoyed that program at Seward Park." I was even more flabbergasted when she reached down into the baby carriage to pat Billy on the head while saying, "Oh, what a cute baby." Billy, my son, didn't realize what was happening, but I was thrilled.

I had begun 1945 by taking on the responsibilities of fatherhood. I also took on additional financial obligations such as paying Riverside Hospital, not to mention the doctors. With this in mind and after successfully completing the first semester of graduate study, I began to seek some gigs. Again, Mr. Monroe came through. He was in the process of formulating a new trio featuring Tiny Grimes, the great jazz guitarist. Grimes had just completed a stint with a dream trio led by Art Tatum, the fabulous pianist. Slam Stewart was the bassist, and although they didn't record very much, musicians regarded them as an all-star group.

Monroe hired me as bassist and Kenny ("Kilo") Watt as pianist. Grimes evidently wanted to showcase himself, especially after his last gig. I was not known as an all-star but as a reliable and capable bassist. Kilo Watt's reputation as a pianist was primarily that of accompanist for the top jazz singers, such as Billy Daniels and Ella Fitzgerald. While not an Art Tatum, Kilo could be counted on to provide a tasty background for a soloist. He could also play a pretty fair solo. Our specialty as a trio was flying tempos. Tiny Grimes had dazzling technique but could also play a soulful, slow blues. We lasted for about six weeks, even without any rave notices. We played very little bop but relied on up-tempo versions of standard tunes. Actually Watt and I were basically background for the brilliant Mr. Grimes. Our egos were not damaged because I knew I was not Slam Stewart, and Kilo clearly understood that he was not Art Tatum.

The return to the Spotlight carried us into the spring of 1945. This time around we had an added advantage. The club had hired a relief piano player who played a half-hour set. If somebody like Ray Brown sat in for me, I had a two-and-one-half-hour break. So, I could sleep or study back in the storeroom. It meant that I could hang on longer in spite of my day gig and graduate classes. Our relief pianist was none other than Sarah Vaughan, who was not then universally acclaimed as a great jazz vocalist.

After another leave of absence from the club, I returned for what would be my final stint at that location. I was grateful for my little break from the night gig, which let me catch up on my graduate work and remain more alert on my day gig at Seward Park High. Julia had the main burden of child care. We even got in some socializing, mostly with my NYU friends (Julia knew very few people in New York). One of the strangest events was a "hootenanny," a party the young Village-type bohemians attended in as much Western garb as they could improvise—big handkerchiefs around the neck, ten-gallon hats, and, to really be in style, cowboy boots. Everybody sat on the floor in a sort of round-the-bonfire arrangement. Of course, there was no fire, but there were a couple of guitar players. Between sips of cheap jug wine, we sang songs of social consciousness. Pete Seeger was our model. Usually there was no hanky-panky at these affairs, and I thought the whole thing ridiculous but enjoyable. The very idea of the urban cowboy was a joke, but the hootenanny was popular among the young, serious college set. All of the kids except Julia and me were white and mostly middle class. The basic repertoire was Western cowboy, prison, Mississippi blues, and protest songs. Of course, I did no singing, but I did drink the jug wine and thus got into the spirit of the event.

My return to the Spotlight after the brief break was pure enjoyment. Mr. Monroe had put together a new trio with Buster Bailey on clarinet, Hank Jones on piano, and me on bass. Charlie Parker and his group were still the main attraction. Parker's group now included Dexter Gordon, a newcomer to the New York scene. I can still see him, a tall penguin flopping over the saxophone. He soon was the talk of musicians in the know about the new music.

As for our trio, Buster Bailey was the leader. To me, he was the impeccable and the immaculate rolled into one. A former Fletcher Henderson great, he exuded class and played the same way. He had been places and had performed in the most exclusive of circumstances, and he was very much the boss of our little outfit. Hank Jones and I were novices by comparison. Next to Art Tatum and Calvin Jackson, Jones was the best jazz pianist I had heard up to that point. He played with adequate if not dazzling technique, but his rhythmic ideas and pretty harmonies were outstanding. His chords were not simple but contained tension. He could hide dissonance so that you might not notice it—but it was there. We, the trio, did not play any bop but attempted our own version of new music.

Buster Bailey, urbane and dapper, set the tone for the club. He exuded a quiet dignity and class that Hank Jones and I tried our best to emulate. Even Charlie Parker's boppers toned down their boisterousness and profanity. Our relief act was another example of class. It was the song stylings of Billy Daniels. I had heard of Billy Daniels but had never heard him perform. I was intrigued by his consummate artistry. He was a male Lena Horne in his management of audiences with his sophisticated repertoire. He controlled the mood of the crowd and manipulated them with timely selection. For this he had the perfect accompanist. It was none other than my old sidekick, Kilo Watt. Watt was better suited for this pianist role than as a foil for Tiny Grimes of our recent trio. I have to give Monroe credit for his putting together the groups at the Spotlight. It certainly paid off as the crowds grew larger.

The audiences were the *cognoscenti* of black jazz in its most contemporary form. Most of the principal performers were not yet the big names that they would become. Our salaries were lower than in other places on the street; but, after all, this was a shoestring operation. I for one welcomed the opportunity; just playing with my group and hearing others made my day.

Just before the Bailey trio left the Spotlight, there were some mildly unusual developments. First, the musicians had been integrated. Charlie Parker's group included Al Haig on piano and Teddy Walters on guitar. Clark Monroe took this a step further when he hired Harry ("the Hipster") Gibson as a relief pianist. Harry the Hipster was a young white kid out of school but with a lot of talent and piano technique. His specialty was playing two well-known ballads simultaneously. An example would be "Tea for Two" and "Lady Be Good." Beyond that gimmick, he could really play some swinging jazz. However, he was crazy as a loon or just naive. He was evidently new to the game as he would experiment with concoctions like a "benny" (aspirin and Coke). I had no evidence of his dealing with drugs like marijuana but only of crazy combinations like a benny. He discussed the relative merits of these concoctions nightly. I finally suggested that he give it up, adding that that was not the route to being accepted among musicians as "hip." I heard him recently on Marian McPartland's "Piano Jazz" playing better than ever, four and a half decades later. Evidently the hip program didn't affect him, or he learned to control it.

It was well into the spring of 1945 when we closed at the Spotlight. I felt as if it was the end of the world, but it turned out not to be that bad. Buster Bailey kept the trio in rehearsal, and since the rehearsals were in the afternoon at the Spotlight I had to forgo some days at the high school. The bad news was that the whole package seriously impaired our family income. We weren't too bad off because I had saved some money from the two gigs (Spotlight and Seward Park High), and we were able to meet our financial obligations. Also, I was able to beef up my work in graduate school and spend more time with Julia and the baby. The biggest bonus was that I was able to get a full night's sleep.

Before long, the Buster Bailey Trio was rewarded with a few weeks' engagement at the prestigious Waldorf-Astoria Hotel, a pinnacle gig for any jazz musician. We were hired as the background group for Hildegarde, the acclaimed international singer. This was a class gig that paid the most money I had ever made, the astronomical sum of a hundred dollars a week. For this, we played a short half-hour set of our own stuff, followed by a four- or five-song set with Hildegarde. Then there was a brief fifteen- or twenty-minute intermission after which we repeated the whole process. Hildegarde was a real *chanteuse,* who could sing in many languages. She was also an actress who could put a song across regardless of your understanding of the language. She had the most dazzling array of costumes I had ever seen. Without great beauty or voice, she was able to communicate a song, a story, or a mood. It was educational for us, especially since we were part of the act.

With a hundred dollars a week coming in, I dared to ask the principal at Seward Park High for some days off. I had to do it because graduate work and assignments were catching up with me. He reluctantly agreed but stipulated that if he was in a bind I had to come to work. In the four-week period, he only called me about six times. I needed his recommendation, so I came to work on those occasions, sometimes with three hours of sleep.

# CHAPTER 18

# BEHOLD THE SCHOLAR

When the gig at the Waldorf terminated in midspring, I was relatively well-off financially. We could pay the rent, eat, and buy a few necessities. Without the weekend gigs I was free to baby-sit while Julia spent some of the weekends in Philly. I couldn't go because of a Saturday morning class and the necessity of studying and preparing the required papers for my first year of graduate study. I did take some one-night gigs (days off for the regular groups), usually on a Monday in what we called pickup groups, just filling in. I was lucky here in that while I was not a star performer, I was considered capable and dependable enough to be a regular substitute in a number of clubs on Fifty-second Street. I finished the semester in good shape academically and received my bachelor's degree in music. True, it was three years late, but I was proud nonetheless. My mother came up from Philly and attended the convocation with my wife and Calvin Jackson. I was disappointed that the Willises (formerly of 393 Edgecombe) could not be present, but we celebrated heartily at 4 Bleecker Street in a somewhat different ambience than an uptown location would have afforded.

Summer came, and the mood of the city was much more relaxed. The Germans had surrendered, and America faced only the opposition of the Japanese. I think we in New York felt a little more secure because in a lot of minds all we had to do was to switch our European war resource to the Pacific theater.

In this atmosphere, I took the summer job at Camp Lakeland. Again we had our interracial group with veteran trumpeter Cliff Bryan as our glue. I was so relaxed as leader that I asked other members of the band to collect the money on payday to demonstrate that there were no secrets between us. It also freed my time for tow-boating, table tennis, and sheer relaxation. I even appointed Boots Battle, our drummer, as my personal athletic director. He was also my roommate, and he saw to it that I got into as good a physical shape as I would be in my entire life. Julia spent the summer in the apartment, and at the Italians of the Bleecker Street environs; for her the summer passed uneventfully.

There was one event that I really don't like to talk about. Lakeland employees had driven to New York on our day off when somebody suggested that we stop in a Bronx neighborhood bar for a parting drink. We went into the bar in a party of about a dozen characters of whom only Cliff Bryan and I were black. Cliff didn't drink. The atmosphere seemed okay, so I ordered my usual bourbon with water on the side. It didn't hit me until I got on the D-train to go to Bleecker Street that they had slipped me a mickey! I was so sick that Cliff offered to ride home with me. He was scheduled to get off at 145th Street station, so I told him I would be all right. I changed to the A-train with the idea of getting off at Fourth Street. I looked up from my stupor to see Fourth Street as we were pulling out of the station and rode on until the end of the line in Brooklyn, whereupon I got off and curled up on one of the benches. The station attendant told me that I couldn't stay there, so I got the next train back up the line. I wound up at the end of the line at 207th Street in Manhattan. Again I took the train back, but this time I got off at Fourth Street. The air hit my face, enabling me to walk home slowly; but my stomach was still queasy. Looking back on this episode, I can only conclude that it was an example of New York racism. In the South they would have been more direct with signs or direct physical expulsion. Somehow I would have preferred that to the extended torture I suffered.

After we entered the nuclear age, the war was over, and people began returning home. Everybody was on the lookout for friends and relatives from New York's own 369th regiment. There were parties and celebrations. There was also sadness when a particular individual did not come back, especially after we had heard that his outfit was in New York.

With the war over, my calls from Seward Park High became fewer and fewer. The regular teachers had returned to the scene. But this was not a disaster for me, partly because the GI Bill had come into being and partly because I had more time to study, sleep, and be with my family. I registered for my last year at NYU (1945–46) in hopes of having a master's degree by June 1946. The home life was all right, except that Julia was becoming lonesome for her Philly friends and restless. She took as many weekends as possible in the City of Brotherly Love. Little did I suspect that this was the beginning of the end for the two of us. Most of Julia's friends in Philly were single mothers and had what I call the "ghetto syndrome" of existing on child support and minimizing responsibility as a way of life. I suggested to Julia that she not listen to advice from these "friends" as I regarded them as failures. Looking back, I'm sure that my attitude pushed us farther apart. Anyway, we went through the last year on a respectful but strained basis. Julia was still a teenager in 1945. That fact, along with her being a high-school dropout, must have made it uncomfortable for her with the graduate-school friends who were my main social companions.

The courses that I took for my final run at NYU were, with few exceptions, complete bores. Courses in educational administration merely served to point up my lack of experience in the educational process. Considering that the classes were made up of school principals, superintendents, and veteran teachers, I had my work cut out just to maintain crediblity. In lieu of writing a thesis on education, I elected to take four additional hours of credit. One gave me the opportunity of studying composition with Phillip James, the well-known American composer. It was a good antidote to all of those stifling education courses. The year went well, and I was able to chalk up my highest grades at NYU. I give my army experience, enhanced maturity, and a realization of responsibility for my new family credit for this. It was to be a common experience for many returning GIs.

Early in the fall of 1945, my old friend Nat Rudnick came by the apartment with a job offer. He had a position with Decca Records, and he wanted me to be a part-time staff arranger, turning out arrangements on demand. Usually the time frame was forty-eight hours and could be as low as twenty-four hours before a scheduled session. Fortunately, the arrangement was not for the sessionists but for the purpose of filing. When Rudnick came to me for an arrangement of blues for Dizzy Gillespie, I argued that Dizzy did not need an arrangement to make a distinctive blues recording. As a matter of fact, an arrangement would hold him back. I found out then what it was all about. As a sort of general manager of the session, Nat Rudnick had a budget for arrangements. He got me to do the actual manuscript, and we split the fee, usually seventy-five dollars. Since I was pushed for time, I did just a lead sheet with the chord symbols underneath the notes. It was a racket that profited the sessions' managers, and since most of them could not write music, put a few dollars in some hack's hands. I think that Decca Records found out about it because by Christmas both Nat and I were gone from Decca's employ.

Somewhere in the beginning of this last school year at NYU, I received a call to come to the Village Vanguard. I don't remember who contacted me, but I soon found myself in the presence of Mr. Max Gordon. He would play a role in my life similar to the one played by Clark Monroe. Gordon wanted me to be the house bass player regardless of other changes in personnel. This suited me fine since the Vanguard was on Seventh Avenue, in walking distance from my Bleecker Street apartment. At 4:00 A.M. I didn't have to wait for a subway or a bus. Gordon was a friend of the owner of Cafe Society, at that time one of the most prestigious jazz clubs in the city. My first assignment was to accompany Clarence Profit, whom I would classify as a society jazz pianist. He could play all of the popular show tunes in a swinging jazz style. While Clarence was not an Art Tatum and he did not indulge in the new bop style, he certainly could please audiences with his unlimited repertoire of Broadway hits. The one fly in the ointment was that Clarence was continually in ill health. I probably was hired because he was a frail little guy with health problems everywhere. As a solo pianist, Clarence really didn't need a rhythm section. I was there to front for Clarence and cushion him from the crowd, especially in his sicker moments. Our unlikely duo played for several weeks without realizing that Clarence was on his deathbed. He died before the year was out. Again, I was not out of work for long. Mr. Gordon brought me back into the club with a new trio.

The Village Vanguard was not a big room, nor was it small enough to be called intimate. Part of the new jazz scene in Greenwich Village, the club featured the new and unusual. For instance, we had Sir Lancelot, the West Indian Calypso singer. He featured black music with a Caribbean flair. I was intrigued by the facility with which he could make up lyrics on the spot, usually to put down an unruly customer. The customer would be devastated publicly, in reply to an uncalled-for remark. A whole song would be spontaneously composed with our unfortunate friend as the subject. It was fascinating but sometimes cruel, especially if the victim had some unfortunate physical features. I was not aware of it at the time, but Sir Lancelot was considered one of the giants of calypso (a forerunner of reggae). Also, we had Muriel Gaines who was a black and jazzy Hildegarde. She could do songs in various languages as well as suggestive versions of folk classics such as "The Girl with the Delicate Air." Even the bartender was my friend, and he tested all of his new drinks on me. I was a willing victim, like a hog in hog heaven. I have never had a more congenial gig before or since.

My new group was the Leonard Ware Trio, and our extended tour of duty lasted almost to the end of the semester in 1946. Fortunately, with the war over, Seward Park High called upon me to sub very infrequently. I was able to concentrate on graduation and the Vanguard. We weren't rich, but with the GI Bill and the Vanguard money, we weren't complaining. Leonard Ware was, of all things, a banjo virtuoso, which was very unusual since the banjo had virtually disappeared from the jazz scene in the '40s. The guitar, with its softer and less percussive sound, had replaced it. I had heard of Banjo Bernie, who had a good reputation with jazz musicians, but Leonard Ware's name was new to me. I was very apprehensive when I reported for our first rehearsal. My fears were put to rest after a few minutes of playing. This guy was a master of the instrument, one who could obtain all gradations of tone and had the technical equipment to play anything. In short, it was to be an unusual but fun engagement. I compare Leonard Ware on the banjo with our present-day Chet Atkins on guitar. Without an amplifier, Ware made the instrument less abrasive and even more persuasive. He could play anything from blues to bop and even Broadway show standards. Leonard himself was a rough-hewn big man, more like a Chicago Bear tight end and obviously not college educated. Still, he was a gentleman with great sensitivity for all around him.

Clarence Williams on piano was the third member of our trio. I had never heard of Clarence before the gig, but that really meant that I was the unknown. Clarence was a real New Yorker, who had been around for years. He could play anything, any style, and was at home in an intermediate size room like the Vanguard. While not up to Art Tatum standards (who was?), Clarence could play a decent solo and accompany like crazy. He was what I would call a "banker" of the gig. He showed me his little notebook, which contained a record of every gig he played and—even more importantly—the money he was paid. Mind you, this happened in the days before the IRS got us all in their clutches. I wish I had done that, not for the money but to keep a record of all the people I had played with. Both Clarence and I were small, five feet, eight inches, and about 135 pounds; and here we were playing with this big banjo picker. Ware had me play in a style not used by bass players at the time. In ballads he liked me to play notes on the first and third beats and pat the fingerboard with my palm on the second and fourth beats. In effect it lent an element of percussion and gave the illusion of the presence of a very quiet drummer. I didn't particularly like the idea, but it did add to our ensemble effect. That, along with the banjo, enabled us to sound like no other trio in New York. I was excited to be able to do even that in the Vanguard.

Dizzy Gillespie came by the apartment late one afternoon, bringing with him another musician, who turned out to be Milt Jackson, the vibraphonist, later of Modern Jazz Quartet fame. This was his initial foray into the New York jungle. After a brief social period, Dizzy asked if our new brother Milt Jackson could stay with us for a few days. It was okay with Julia, so Milt moved in later that evening, vibraphone and all. He was from Detroit and completely unknown to the New York musicians. He soon took care of that under the guidance of the old veteran, Dizzy himself. I didn't get a chance to talk with him much because of the Vanguard and NYU. However, I did hear some snippets of his playing. Believe me, I was impressed, and I had some lessons on the vibes from my old friend Mac Mackay. This cat could play! When he got on his feet in New York and had gone through Local 802's six-month probation period, our paths never crossed until years later—in 1956 when Milt and the Modern Jazz Quartet came to Iowa City to play a concert at the university. By this time Milt had become famous and the MJQ had upgraded jazz to the classical. I regret to say I haven't seen him since, but I have purchased many of his records. Who can forget "Bags Groove," my favorite piece to play?

One of the benefits of working at the Vanguard was its proximity to Cafe Society. On my off nights I could go into Cafe Society as a Gordon employee, which was a financial blessing as it was higher-priced than the Vanguard. I heard Pete Johnson and Albert Ammons, boogie-woogie piano masters. It was a fascinating evening. They needed no amplification or accompaniment; they were overpowering, individually and collectively. It was a whole orchestra of effects and colors. They probed the blues in all of its varieties, but theirs was mostly happy music, house party music stretched on a blues frame. I didn't realize that the left hand could be so potent in piano. The experience raised my consciousness about old music.

I finished out the school year at NYU and received my master of arts degree. Again, I took the summer job at Camp Lakeland. The season there was uneventful except for the return of pianist Wesley Walker. We still had our white saxophonist Gunnie Borraclovich, and he was more experienced. In fact, we sounded more like cool professionals. My older brother, C. S., Charles, was hired as a pantryman. Even though we were there daily, we still did not hang out together. He had his special crowd in the older workers. He did introduce me to Andrei Gromyko's (the Soviet ambassador's) chauffeur at a nearby bar. The guy did not speak a word of English, but they were having a fabulous time drinking vodka amidst shouts of *tovaritsch* (comrade). When I saw them, they each had five jiggers of vodka in front of them. Nobody would let the other guy out-buy him. I was introduced, and the Russian promptly ordered five drinks for me. I didn't know enough Russian to tell him no thanks. Besides that, both he and my brother were rugged types. I bought five rounds and C. S. promptly ordered five more rounds. That afternoon and for the rest of the evening I took to bed with my room revolving in one direction and the bed undulating in the opposite direction. Sadly, I missed playing the evening engagement for the first and only time at Lakeland. My band, faithful troopers that they were, carried on without me.

A phone call interrupted the Camp Lakeland proceedings. It was a request for me to be an emergency replacement for a "Jazz at the Philharmonic" concert in Washington the next night. Since I was only the bass player, my own group could get along without me for one night. The next morning I took my bass and my toothbrush on the early train from Poughkeepsie to Grand Central Station. A cab got me from there to Penn Station where I took one of the Limiteds. It was not the Congressional, but it got me there in good time and style.

As I remember, Errol Garner and Billie Holiday were the headliners for the jazz group, and Pee Wee Russell, clarinetist, was the main figure for the Dixieland group. The black musicians met at the home of a Dr. Minor where we ate and refreshed ourselves before the gig. The main talk was about the sound set and the telephone in the bathroom. Dr. Minor was a jazz fan and evidently a very successful physician, as his house and furnishings made everything else I had known in terms of black residences look like Uncle Tom's cabin. Before the concert at Griffith Stadium, I received the news that I was to play the Dixieland end of the concert. In other words, I was the replacement for the white Dixieland bassist in an all-white group. I was disappointed, but the money I earned for the gig eased the pain.

Milt Hinton was the bassist for the jazz sets, and they brought

Griffith Stadium down with their brilliance. This major league ball-park was packed with jazz fans. I didn't realize it at the time, but this concert was among the first of a series that would become famous. "Jazz at the Philharmonic," under the promotion of Norman Granz, would go on for years. The music was different from anything I had become accustomed to. However, Dixieland is really exciting and re-warding when played by musicians of this caliber. As the only black musician in the group, I was thoroughly enchanted and engrossed with the ideas and inventiveness of these white musicians. I couldn't keep my eyes off Pee Wee Russell as he contorted his body and squinched and grimaced while playing his clarinet. They were living the music. While not strictly Dixieland, Red Norvo was an exciting performer on his vibes. Jimmy McPartland demonstrated how effec-tive a trumpet could be.

When we closed at Camp Lakeland for the summer, I headed to Phila-delphia instead of Manhattan. As Julia didn't have many friends in New York, we opted for Philadelphia. Julia and I bought a little two-bedroom row house with hardwood floors and French doors in North Philly, courtesy of the GI Bill. My mother helped me locate a place near both of our mothers' homes. We closed out our apartment on Bleecker Street and, with the aid of C. S. and a rented truck, moved the stuff to 1735 Stillman Street in Philly. The house was listed at $3,500, which I thought was too much. I lost some friends in New York who wanted me to use my GI money for buying a home in Queens. But with New York's racist hiring policies, I was not op-timistic about getting a regular job with the school system. It wasn't too good in Philadelphia, either, but at least I would be home and the cost of living would be less. Julia was happy to leave New York; I left reluctantly, not realizing that it would be one of my better decisions.

During the summer of 1946, I received a telegram from NYU's placement bureau suggesting that I apply for a job at Morgan College in Baltimore as a band director. I promptly set up the interview. When I got to Baltimore's Penn Station, I felt the overt racism in the air. I waited for over an hour for a cab until some kindly brother walked up and said, "You can't get a cab here—black cabs are not allowed. Go out to the street level entrance and try there."

My interview with Dean Grant and Dr. Holmes, the president, went well, and I was hired at the lowest salary they could give me ($1,800, or $200 a month for nine months). I asked them if they wanted to see my transcript, and they said no. Graduation and the M.A. degree were all they required for the moment.

The joke was that Morgan College had never had a marching band. I was to develop the program, report to work on September 1, and have a group ready to play for the dedication of the Carnegie library on October 19. I was foolish enough to say that I would try, knowing that I had to start from scratch.

# CHAPTER 19

# BALTIMORE IN

**W**hile uneventful and pleasant, the train ride to Baltimore found me apprehensive. I was filled with fear of going south. Actually, Baltimore was not that bad. At least they tried to hide most of the expressions of racism, or so it seemed. They did not have a segregated transportation system, but I hardly noticed that when the trolley I was riding was 100 percent black-occupied. There were very few points of contact to reveal the segregation policies in action. Examples could be seen in downtown department stores and restaurants. (I actually saw a black guy go into a white restaurant, but he had on a turban and spoke with an accent.)

My grandmother was fiercely against the idea of my going south. I tried to explain to her that Baltimore was only ninety miles from Philadelphia and that Philly was not all that good. But her experiences in Georgia had soured her on anything closely or remotely relating to south of the Mason-Dixon line. (In fact, that famous line of demarcation was only about fifteen miles from our home on Brown Street.)

I got a room on Druid Hill Avenue (the Park Avenue of the black community), where the rules were no smoking, no drinking, and, of course, no women. I tried to break the no-drinking rule on my first evening in the room. Exploring the neighborhood, I found a liquor store on North Avenue that had a small bottle in my budget range. It was a bottle of potato whiskey, guaranteed to be three months old, for forty-five cents. When I got back to the room, I took one sip of what promised to be my escape from loneliness. I could not force myself to take another. Since I didn't get any pay until the end of the month, I became a teetotaler, dry as a bone until payday. That potato stuff was so bad that if it had been the only alcoholic drink available, I would have become a model of abstinence for the rest of my life.

Morgan State College, an all-black institution, was located in northeast Baltimore. Most of the faculty and students lived in the southeast and southwest sectors. As a result, they made heavy use of the city's transportation facilities. There were a few dormitories, but Morgan was primarily a city college for black Baltimoreans. It was the pinnacle of local public education for blacks. Morgan State was then thought of as a Notre Dame of black colleges. They had gone through something like nine years undefeated in football. Consequently, there was tremendous local pride in this institution. Most importantly, they also maintained a high academic standard.

Dean Grant informed me that the band could only practice four and a half hours a week. We needed special permission from the dean's office to practice another minute, even to prepare for the grudge game with Howard University. Dean Grant's reasoning was that we had to provide time for the kids to study, even if they didn't do it. I had never been in an all-black educational situation before, and I was impressed with the general academic seriousness.

In a pleasant development, the state of Maryland passed a cost-of-living raise of three hundred dollars for all state employees. Consequently, I never received the $200 a month that I had signed a contract for. Even better, the state legislature passed a bill making twenty-seven hundred dollars a year the minimum wage for all higher-education faculty, a 50 percent raise for me by the time I had received my second check.

Only the growing estrangement from Julia tempered my happiness and outlook for the future. With the signs of the impending breakup of my marriage increasing, it was hard to be optimistic about what lay ahead.

Morgan College was a delightful school. It was small enough for everybody to know everybody. You could actually witness Dr. D. O. W. Holmes call every student by name as he strolled down the main walk of the campus. Dean Grant could do the same thing. Faculty meetings were exciting; it seemed that every session got down to a rousing intellectual debate such as I imagine the British parliament could produce. J. O. B. Moseley, my department head, explained these lively proceedings to me. "We have such a collection of black intellectuals who have little opportunity in the U.S. except for teaching," he said. "They take their frustrations out in brilliant displays of argumentative skills, intellectual depth, and pure cussedness in the faculty meetings." The meetings were competitive, almost combative. In my first experience with a college faculty, I didn't say a word. I just listened while these Ph.D.s and would-be Ph.D.s put on a lively show.

With an October 19 performance deadline, I had to get the band into high gear almost immediately. We were supposed to be ready to play for the dedication of the new Carnegie library on that date, just five weeks away—and we were starting from scratch. There were no band veterans around, but there were some service veterans who had some band experience. In the first week we were able to scrounge up about twenty-three members with varying degrees of instrumental experience. I talked a trio of guys whom I observed dancing in the rec hall into trying to handle the cymbals and bass drum. This worked out pretty well in terms of rhythm but broke down whenever we had to read music. I showed a big fellow how and where to hit a bass drum and told him, "Don't get fancy—just keep the rhythm steady." This worked very well for us in our limited repertoire.

When we played the dedication ceremony on the entry steps of the library, we were able to get away with three numbers: "America the Beautiful," "The Morgan College Fight Song," and a simple Sousa march. My cymbalists and bass drummer offered a strong rendition of the pieces we played. My mixed unit of former GIs and college-age undergraduates numbered about twenty. We doubled that the week after the concert—not that the concert was all that good, but I believe we overcame the problem of credibility in a school that never had an instrumental ensemble.

A lot of the credit for our modest beginning had to go to the Coffee twins, who were coffee-colored—without cream. They were two female freshman live wires. Every time I became depressed or discouraged about our prospects for success, they came through with some positive action—like recruiting a trumpet player for our organization. The Coffee twins were well known on campus for their dedication and hard work; they were even popular with the upperclassmen. Dame Fortune smiled on me when she had these charming twins cross my path.

I also had good luck with the war veterans returning to school. These guys brought a level of discipline that made it easier for me to handle what was to become a large group. In view of our off-campus socializing, they agreed to call me Mr. Smith on campus. Some of them lived near us, and we shared refreshments, liquid and solid. On occasion we had a dinner of Campbell's pork and beans—right out of the can. These occasions depended on who had the money. Since I didn't get paid until the end of my first month, the vets got me through a difficult and financially embarrassing beginning.

Not having a car in 1946, I was confined to Baltimore on weekends. This was particularly lonesome for me as I had no friends in town except for the war vets and people on the music faculty. I did not try to visit the latter as they were all older and more established people. Besides, I did not have the clothes and felt generally overmatched in their presence. J. O. B. Moseley was my mentor in many ways. He advised me about organizing the band. He had been a band director in the army and had just retired from the armed forces as a warrant officer. He also informed me about life and politics on all-black campuses. I think I would have failed in my first college job without his guidance. As the newest and least experienced instructor, I inherited all of the details that no one else wanted. This was primarily a voice and piano music faculty, so I taught all of the brass and woodwind students and classes. They even had me teaching functional piano to most of the nonpiano majors. For instance, associate professor Blanton (a well-known recitalist) taught only eight piano students as her full teaching load. By contrast, I taught all of the instruments—individual and class, piano for nonpiano majors, and a couple of academic classes in addition to administering and directing the band. I had five times the teaching load of Professor Blanton but received about half of her pay. I didn't think about it then, nor did I resent it later in view of all of the teaching experience I was getting. I still thank Mr. Moseley for giving me the initial opportunity to develop into a real university professor.

With football games every Saturday, I was unable to get to Philly on weekends. My marriage really began to crumble. My mother advised me to send a weekly allotment by postal money order. That turned out to be good advice, as I was hauled into the Philadelphia domestic court system for child support. The day of my appearance, the judge was annoyed and bad-tempered. She lectured the court between cases about men not taking care of their responsibilities. When my turn came, she asked me, "What's your problem?" I started to lay out the whole situation for her when she cut me off with a very sharp, "Shut up!"

I took all of my postal money order receipts and dashed them across her desk without saying a word. The judge then called Julia, asking her, "What's the problem here? This man is taking care of your baby." When the judge found out that I was working in Baltimore while Julia was residing in Philly, she ordered me to continue the support. Then she ordered Julia to move to Baltimore, saying, "I can't ask this man to support two residences."

Considering that the judge was sending guys to jail all morning, I felt that it was fortunate that she smiled as she dismissed the case. Even so, I felt powerless and lonely. Powerless in that I couldn't be with Julia to offset the advice of her "ghetto syndrome" advisors. I was even more disturbed when the Philly neighbors told me that an interloper lived right across the street from our house. The loneliness intensified because I couldn't do anything about it until I had organized a suitable residence in Baltimore. And until the football season was over, the marching band had to be my immediate priority.

This period was not all bad. I had a lot of support from many sources on campus for developing a representative band. The legendary Coach Hurt of the football team came to my office in Washington Hall. He brought with him six football players who had had some instrumental experience. These were freshmen or marginal players that he couldn't include in his travel squad. The idea was that they could make the trips anyway as band members. That one gesture by Coach Hurt made the band a popular activity on campus. We went overnight from about twenty-five pieces to forty full-time effectives.

Reverend Howard Cornish, the director of the religious center (a sort of student union), suggested to me that I formulate a jazz band to play for student activities. He offered guaranteed weekend gigs and money for music and equipment from his activities budget. This really fired us up. It was also needed because Morgan was a little distant from the city proper. Many activities were sponsored on campus, and professional bands were too expensive for some of the smaller clubs. It was a good move that would pay off in the popularity of the instrumental movement at the college. It also increased my personal credibility as a new faculty member. We expanded to about sixty-five members in the marching band in the second year of operation.

Toward the end of the school year (spring 1947), I found an apartment near Fulton and Edmonson avenues. I bought furniture and moved my piano from Philly. Fortunately, there was a real refrigerator (not an ice box), and after I bought food and supplies, the apartment, really a first-floor flat, was ready for Julia. In high anticipation, I made the call to Julia, and she reluctantly agreed to come to Baltimore as ordered by the judge. She and Baby arrived, but it was more like she came in going out. She immediately got on the phone to people in Philly, and I don't know whom she called or what was said, but I could sense that my bubble was about to burst. She left for Philly the next day, and I knew this was the end. We were divorced a few weeks later.

The divorce was not bitter, and I didn't contest it. I did regret that she would not be around for the benefits of that schooling. She got the custody of our baby, but she sent him to me fifteen years later. She and I are still friends, and we both make the attempt to keep in touch.

The school year finished. I closed out the apartment, moved into a room, and headed for my summer standby, Camp Lakeland. Camp Lakeland was basically the same as the previous year, except that this time I was single. More than that, I was on the rebound. Surprisingly, I did not want to be involved with women. I didn't go to Baltimore or Philly and was more or less a loner. I didn't even date the young ladies at Lakeland because I was more aware of our age differences. I felt ancient and rejected. I did associate more with my band members, and I was able to talk our drummer, Boots Battle, into coming to Morgan College as a freshman.

As I was at Lakeland for three months, I let my paychecks pile up in the business manager's office. With those three checks I made a down payment on a 1947 Plymouth business coupe from a black car dealer. He gave me special attention, and I was soon the proud owner of a black, almost sporty, two-seater. It had an enormous trunk into which I could put a bass violin and close the lid. When I would arrive at a gig, the guys would worriedly ask me, "Where's your bass?" That car was an omen of good things to come.

I was introduced to Catherine Leeds quite accidentally. I was with a nice young lady, who is now a member of the Baltimore city council, and she wanted to go for a drive in my new car. We stopped by one of her Morgan College friends' house. The friend turned out to be Jacque Leeds, whose family's apartment on Druid Hill Avenue was a popular stop for a select group of young Baltimoreans. We were having a pleasant afternoon when Jacque's sister Catherine came in from work. I knew on sight that this was it for me, and I made arrangements to see Jacque's sister again. We dated for the balance of the school year, caught up in a whirlwind romance that culminated in marriage. Catherine undertook to feed me after she had visited my apartment and found no food but a full case of liquor. In my depression, I got in the habit of drinking a quart of bourbon or rye whiskey every day. I started on a bottle after I got home in the afternoon and finished it (sometimes without food) by 11:00 P.M.

The relationship with Catherine Leeds reduced my depression and my drinking. The coming school year would be filled with excitement.

# CHAPTER 20

# BALTIMORE OUT

**W**ith a new car and a new love interest, I began the second year of the band and jazz orchestra with enthusiasm. I didn't realize that it would also be my last year at Morgan. Actually I thought that I would be there for life. Boots Battle, my drummer at Camp Lakeland, became a freshman at Morgan and moved in with me at my new apartment on Francis Street. He was a tremendous help to me in keeping the instrumental program moving forward and in keeping me level-headed about my newfound love. I did most of the cooking, and everything progressed smoothly until I put some sardines in with the spaghetti. Our various concerts and football performances showed progress, if not perfection. At least the administrators were appreciative, not in money but in their comments.

My euphoria received a heavy dent when news came to me that my grandmother had passed. My maternal grandmother, Mrs. Rosie Wright, practically raised me, since my mother frequently worked outside the home. With heavy heart, I drove to Philly to attend the funeral. Julia was there with our baby, and we were cordial if a little formal. The members of the marching band sent flowers, and I received much sympathy from the Morgan College faculty.

When I got back to Baltimore, Mr. Moseley had a project for me. I was to get a viola and go with him over to the Peabody Conservatory of Music. We were to participate in a reading of Moseley's new string quintet, and I was to play the viola part with members of the Peabody faculty. I felt very insecure about this as I had not touched a viola since my NYU orchestra days. The director of Peabody Conservatory was, believe it or not, Felix Mendelssohn, grandson of the famous composer. Not only did he serve us some delicious Austrian pastries, he bolstered my confidence. It was a very enjoyable evening and my first interracial experience in this completely segregated town. I also enjoyed the musical conversation between Mr. Moseley and Mr. Mendelssohn and developed increasing respect for this level of music composition and performance.

Catherine Leeds didn't become "Kitty" until we were married, and then she took the nickname because of the convenience of the sound of "Kitty and Smitty." We spent every available weekend going somewhere in my new car. We went to Philly so I could introduce her to my mother. We went to New York City, to Warwick (to meet my old friends the Willises), to Washington, D.C., and to places around Baltimore.

I took one trip without Miss Leeds to find my brother Charles who had been missing (out of contact) for several months. My mother gave me his last known address along with orders to find him and bring him home. The last known address turned out to be what musicians called a "hat." That means no results.

Somebody had seen him on the Bowery, which is really Third Avenue, a section of which was inhabited by derelicts, jobless and homeless men. I put in some real detective work, going into each of the flop houses on Bleecker Street and the Bowery. I had Charles's picture and asked each manager and anybody on the street if they had seen that man. This went on all day until I ran into one guy who had seen him and told me that he was in the Veterans' Hospital in the Bronx. It was late, so I went up there the next morning. Inquiring at the reception desk, I received the information that there was a Charles S. Smith in the consumption ward. I located the ward with apprehension—it could be another guy. When I got there, it was Charles sure enough. He looked healthy enough to me, so I outlined mother's orders. He said quietly, "I like it here."

He had a splendid view of the East River, and in a way I couldn't blame him. So I left New York empty-handed and related the message to my mother. Charles did finally come home to Philly after about a year; I would be in Texas when he came. He moved into my mother's house and lived for about twenty-five years in a somewhat run-down state. His health was such that he could only hold a job briefly. I saw him only when Kitty and I visited Philly. He passed in the 1970s, and I was able to keep a promise. I had told him decades earlier, "I will bury you." It was eerie that right in the middle of the funeral ceremony the funeral director brought the bill straight to me.

I didn't know it at the time, but word went out on the black college circuit about the instrumental program at Morgan. It would turn out to be the basis for my next job offer in Texas.

With the success of the band program, I began to think about my position on the campus. I was the lowest-paid faculty member in the music department, and so I went to the president's office to solicit a raise. Dr. D. O. W. Holmes had what I would call an open office. Anybody could see him without an appointment with the only holdup being if somebody already was in the office. Dr. Holmes was a spellbinding minister and a charmer. He called me in his office as soon as he saw me with, "Come in, Mr. Smith. You are doing great things for Morgan."

We talked for about an hour during which he told me, "We are going to build a great school around such brilliant young faculty as you."

He even rolled out the college budget to show that there was not enough money to give me a one-dollar raise. He charmed and praised me so much that I walked on clouds all the way back to Washington Hall. It didn't hit me until I opened my office door that I didn't get a single dime.

There were some outstanding black musicians in Baltimore during this period. Ellis Larkins, the pianist, was one of them. I gigged with him just once at a private party in Whiteville. I heard him forty years later on Marian McPartland's radio show, "Piano Jazz," and he sounded like one of the ten best jazz pianists that I've ever heard. Another musician in Baltimore was Bill Swindell, a tenor sax soloist. When I heard that he was the composer of "Young Man with a Horn," I couldn't believe that someone that I knew wrote a jazz classic like that. When I heard Swindell play, however, it became instantly believable.

The third musician who had an effect on me was Doris Robinson, an Ella Fitzgerald-type singer with a Sarah Vaughan voice. She was a freshman at Morgan and was popular in Baltimore. She sang occasionally with the school jazz orchestra and gigged professionally all over town.

On one of our weekend forays into the surrounding countryside, Kitty and I drove to Westminster, Maryland. There was a black country club there operated by a Baltimore numbers baron. It was unusual for blacks in that it was a first-class operation. On the way up, I began talking about our future with probing questions and statements. "Wouldn't it be nice if we could do this every weekend? . . . We could buy a nice two-bedroom house . . . . If we had two or three children, I'd get a larger car . . . . You can quit your barmaid job and go back to college."

I was rolling along effusively when Kitty interrupted with, "How are we going to do all of this unless we're married?"

Right then I popped the question, and she answered affirmatively. Actually, I don't remember her words, but the general tone was a yes. We went on to have a nice time at the country club, and I was on clouds all afternoon. Driving back to Baltimore, we made plans to get married the following weekend. We selected the minister, Reverend Levi Miller, who was a professor of philosophy at Morgan and a friend of ours. Although school was not in session, we notified all of our close friends, and I began that week of waiting on the nicest high that I've ever had.

In our discussions prior to the wedding, Kitty and I agreed that at the first opportunity we would leave Baltimore. Actually, the decision was for us to build our future in neutral territory, away from our immediate families in Philly or Baltimore. The opportunity soon presented itself when I received a telegram from a W. R. Banks, acting president of Texas State College for Negroes. He offered me the band director's job at $4,500 a year. Since I was only making $2,700 at Morgan and had been turned down for a raise, I decided to show the telegram to Dean Grant. He called me late that same night and told me that Dr. Holmes had authorized him to raise my salary to $3,600. I gloated with satisfaction as I had some measure of revenge on Dr. Holmes for charming me. I told Dean Grant that I would be married in a couple of days and my bride-to-be had already decided that we would take this new offer. With great joy and anticipation, we waited for the wedding and the trip to Houston.

The day came for our wedding—August 2, 1948—and while it was a momentous occasion, I don't remember much about it. We did pack our immediate necessities in the car. We planned to leave for Houston by way of Indianapolis, St. Louis, and Little Rock immediately after the wedding. It was a small, private affair with only members of Kitty's immediate family and our close circle of friends, including Boots.

Our car was packed with books, records, and clothes. (We left our furniture in Baltimore.) There was little room in the car to wiggle around. We proceeded through Texarkana to the outskirts of Houston where we were greeted by a sign on an overpass. The sign right on the entry highway said, "Next time, try the train."

# CHAPTER 21

# HOUSTON

**W**hen we crossed over into Texas from Texarkana, I could sense that we were in for a different experience from the East Coast. First, a two-lane Texas road was as wide as a three-lane Arkansas road. Not only that, but the roads were in better condition. Everything seemed bigger, better, and less crowded. It was a bit disconcerting to see solemn bridges over rivers with no water. Though it was hot and muggy (we could see steam vapors on the street at night), there seemed to be a relieving breeze from the gulf in the evening. We soon found that we could sleep at night in spite of a lack of air conditioning. In fact, air conditioning was unknown except in some motion picture theaters and restaurants.

There were open sewers and gutters along the curb in black neighborhoods, even in upper-class black neighborhoods. A fine mansion might be set smack in the middle of some slum shacks. I got my awakening when I went up on Dowling Avenue. I saw several men drive up in front of a store and hitch their horses to a post. This was the frontier! Also it was quasi-rural in that often houses with any pretensions of ground had a stock of farm animals—chickens, pigs, goats, and so forth. If it had not been so big, I would have hardly believed that Houston was a city. It was more like a city downtown where there were streets without open gutters, but with shops, skyscrapers, paved streets—and where I didn't see anybody hitching up a horse. Anyway, this was to be our home.

Texas Southern University was then known as Texas State College for Negroes. Organized from Houston College, it was in its first

185

year as a state college. When we got there, everything was new—the faculty and the buildings, with the exception of the Fairchild Building, the home of the old Houston College. Some of the students had attended Houston College, but most were freshmen and transfers.

There had been a small band before my arrival, but I was expected to put a major band on the field. There was plenty of money available, but Texans expect immediate success for their money. My salary at $4,500 ($2,700 as an instructor plus $1,800 from football revenues) put me on par with most associate professors. There were to be no excuses, only results.

Will Henry Bennett, a high school band director, had been the part-time director of the Houston College ensemble and had expected to get the job as the new college director. However, fate intervened as I, an outsider, got the job primarily because Mr. Bennett did not have a master's degree. He was my enemy at first and did not come around as a supporter until well into my second year. He began by sending all of the scholarship students he had rounded up (in anticipation of his own directorship) to other black colleges, mostly Tennessee A & I College in Nashville. That presented many problems, but luckily a significant number of freshmen with band experience had not been approached by Mr. Bennett. He returned to his high school job and heckled our initial efforts with his many loyal supporters. The story ends well, for in our second year we became friends.

After two weeks of being a homemaker, Kitty was "stir crazy" from preparing dinners and doing crossword puzzles. She would snap my head off when I came in after a late rehearsal. We both recognized the problem and enrolled her in school even though it was late. With her in classes and later a campus job, our life became more bearable. We even enjoyed it.

The music department was entirely new, but we all cooperated to help produce a representative band. I was authorized to spend $10,000 on instruments. Imagine the clout I had with the downtown music stores when they saw my authorization letter. Miss Constance Houston Thompson, a great-granddaughter of General Sam Houston, was our advisor, advocate, and door-opener. Widely respected across the state, she got us connections in strategic situations that I or members of our administration could not obtain. I was amazed that white Texans could overlook the fact that Miss Thompson was black. After all, she was General Sam's living relative. She accompanied the band on road trips, and whenever the kids were hungry, she had the bus stop at a well-known, white-only roadhouse restaurant. She went inside, and in a few minutes she and the manager approached our buses waving all of us inside for a meal. She also knew most of the business and power-structure people. This was a great asset to us, especially to me, a newcomer on the Texas scene, in getting the band operative. When you go to the San Jacinto monument just a few miles from Houston, notice that the portrait immediately to the right of General Sam Houston is that of a black woman. I believe her name was Rachel, and she was the general's housekeeper. Nobody mentioned it, but she was Miss Thompson's ancestor.

Our first band trip was to Okmulgee, Oklahoma, where the football team was to play Langston University. I blame my inexperience for not making any housing arrangements. Miss Thompson took care of our feeding, but thinking that Okmulgee was not that far, we planned to return after the game. I did not take into account that the Greyhound bus drivers were limited to eight hours of driving and were guaranteed eight hours of sleep or rest before proceeding. Well, it took us eight hours to get to Okmulgee. We walked around town while the drivers went to a hotel for rest. Fortunately for us, the superintendent of Okmulgee schools was in the audience when our football team proceeded to lose to Langston University by something like 25–0. The superintendent and "Zip" Gayle, the Langston coach, heard of our plight and opened a junior high school building for our use overnight. The kids used overcoats and soft instrument covers as bedding. I took some flak for my ignorance from the administrative types, but the kids forgave me and—their enthusiasm for having an operative band put it behind us.

We proceeded to develop a creditable band, thanks to the prolific Houston public school system and their competent bands in the black schools. We needed a place to rehearse, and we were assigned one of the larger rooms in a temporary classroom building. This was all right at the beginning because we were in rehearsal before academic classes began. However, when classes did begin in the middle of September, you can imagine the confusion.

Freshman English was in the very next room, and when we opened up with the likes of Sousa's "El Capitan" march, there was much wailing and gnashing of teeth. I suggested to the poor young woman teaching the class that we had to rehearse for football games. I also suggested that she complain to the college administration people to find us another place to rehearse. I followed this up with all of the other instructors in the building. We continued to rehearse louder than ever in order to give them additional incentive.

We gave them some relief through another tactic. We formed in front of the classroom building and marched down the main walkway to the administration building. We used drum cadences until we reached Fairchild, where we opened up with horns blaring the loudest pieces in our repertoire. We paused in front of President Lanier's office and serenaded him for about twenty minutes, again with our most forceful style. With eighty-five young and enthusiastic people, we accomplished our purpose. Dr. Lanier called me to his office the next morning. He had received complaints from the instructors. Sympathizing with our need to improve while complaining about the disruption of his office, he immediately got on the phone. We got our band building that same afternoon. They cleared out one of the temporary storage buildings and moved our chairs, stands, and other equipment into the building before our regular rehearsal time at 2:30 P.M. We not only got the building but a couple of acres of level ground in front of the building to practice our football routines.

The band had another problem that called for devious strategy. We had no uniforms. We started the season wearing dark pants or skirts and white shirts or blouses for a uniform look, but toward the end of the season, our traditional rival Prairie View College was coming in. We knew that they had an ROTC band and that they would be wearing smart military uniforms. I had a meeting with our band members and suggested to them that we could not compete appearance-wise with our usual makeshift look. We decided to look as bad as possible in order to get some campus support for new uniforms. We decided that anything would do, from jeans to overalls, and with no regard to a color code. Prairie View showed up and won the appearance battle; I think the music battle was a draw. Anyway, it worked beautifully. The general comment from the crowd was how bad we looked. Again Dr. Lanier called me to his office. When I got there, several people were sitting in his office. They were the newly formed uniform committee. Dr. Lanier was our friend, and though we had money to buy instruments and other equipment, other methods had to be found to finance uniforms for eighty-five to ninety people. It was too late for the 1948 season, but we would be in good shape for 1949.

Toward the end of the year and after the football season, I took a few gigs, more for pleasure than for the money. We played mostly in downtown Houston clubs on weekends. I worked for alto saxophonist Gus Evans, who had made quite a reputation with Lionel Hampton. Gus was an excellent featured jazz soloist and had a good reputation in the Houston area. We had Tucker, the main drummer in our school's marching and concert bands, on drums. Our pianist was a genuine "wino," whom I'll call "Al." Al was a competent journeyman pianist except for one number, "Tea For Two," where he reached brilliant heights. He would charge himself up and then unload a dazzling half-hour rendition of that piece. Al was such a wino that he had to be delivered to the gig, and we took shifts supervising his drinking, with me usually getting the final or delivery stint. Al would show up at our apartment at about four or five o'clock with a bottle of wine inside his belt next to his stomach. He liked room temperature or warmer wine. Kitty and I would tempt him off the wine with food. That plan worked, and I would get him to the gig in shape (sober) to play. And play he did, as if he had saved all of his pent-up emotion for the gig. Al was an unforgettable character with a fondness for pretty women. I saved his life once when he approached our pretty next-door neighbor not realizing that her husband, who was home, was a professional fighter.

After a year of being together, the Gus Evans Quartet finally got a steady weekend gig at a club on South Main Street near where the Astrodome is now. The club was run by a Chicago mafia person and was peculiar in that there was no liquor license. They only sold set-ups and food, but it was still an illegal operation. There were a half-dozen taxicabs across the street, all with many bottles of just about any alcoholic beverage you could name. The idea was that the customer would place an order for food and a set-up (ice, ginger ale, and so forth) and indicate the bottle of his choice. The waiter would dash across the street and deliver the bottle from the taxi to the customer. Of course, this was illegal and at inflated prices. The customer was supposed to keep the liquor out of sight.

However, the Houston police were aware of the illegal operation and raided the club almost daily. These were serious raids in that everybody was taken downtown in paddy wagons except the band and the kitchen personnel, who were all black. On the first raid, a policeman asked the captain, "Are we gonna take the niggers down?"

The captain answered, "No, let the niggers go."

I was standing next to the police officer when they said that, but was not at all offended by their terminology. It meant that I would not have to go to jail and have my name (a TSU instructor) in the papers the next day. It also meant that with only the black band and kitchen personnel left in charge of the fort, we could feast to our hearts' content on the goodies in the club's food stock. Further, it meant that we would have a two-hour intermission before the manager returned and business as usual was restored. Sometimes it pays to be black.

Al, our wino pianist, was no longer in the band in the second year of operation. He had been replaced by Alex Sample, a much more formidable pianist. But the whole Gus Evans saga came to a sudden end sometime in 1949 when Gus, a young man in his twenties, died. This brilliant virtuoso of the alto saxophone succumbed to an overdose of cocaine. I knew that Gus drank plenty of liquor, but I never saw him use drugs. School band members who attended the funeral ceremonies rumored that Gus's whole body had turned green.

Mrs. Evans asked me if she could address our whole marching band. I agreed and set aside a rehearsal for her. The story she told was terrifying and effective. In our band we had several young aspiring jazz performers who wanted to make it big in New York. They all sat bolted to their seats while Mrs. Evans spoke. I fully appreciated her taking the time and making the effort to do some good for Gus's peers. I feel certain that her quiet talk had a positive effect on our young players, especially in the face of the death of one of their favorite role models.

Kitty and I had an apartment within walking distance of the college. Most of the students and faculty walked down the railroad track until they reached the Fairchild administration building, which fronted on the tracks. To Kitty and me it was a degrading approach to the campus. Kitty decided that we should take the long way, through a white neighborhood, to the campus. Her rationale was that we should get the white folks used to seeing black folks in a legitimate capacity. It ultimately paid off; the area today is totally racially mixed. On her way to school, Kitty stopped and talked with a white homeowner on Cleburne Street. She suggested to the young housewife that if she ever wanted to sell her home, we would be interested in buying it. We had persuaded a few dozen other students to use this route to the campus, and within a few weeks the For Sale signs went up. Kitty and I had already made our agreement with this nice young couple. We would purchase the house without an agent, splitting the difference in the agent's fee.

Finding the financing for the property was really weird as it was located in a "white" neighborhood. I got a variety of put-offs, such as "We can only make you a 50 percent loan. . . . We don't make loans to the third or fifth wards" (the main black wards). The house at

3107 Cleburne was close enough to the black wards to be classified as such.

The wildest put-off occurred when an agent told me, "We can make the loan if we can get a white man to sign for you!"

I was flabbergasted and asked, "Even if I have a master's degree and state of Texas job, do I need a white man probably less literate and less financially solvent to do business?"

The guy was unflappable: "That's the case." I left his office hurt and frustrated, but not for long. I called the FHA office in Houston, and they found an agent for me. The loan agent arranged a loan from a Minneapolis insurance company, and the outcome was amazing.

Again Mrs. Constance Houston Thompson came to our rescue in the matter of clearing the down payment hurdle. She arranged a conference for me to talk with Houston millionaire Craig Cullinan, who was on our board of trustees. He immediately dashed off a check for $1,500 payable in easy installments (with no interest), and we were over our last hurdle. I got the money, word got out to the black community, and soon the Houston real estate financiers had visions of all of those potential profits going out of town. Within a few months, we had some black neighbors.

The house was basically a hunting lodge with only one bedroom. It was knotty pine, rustic throughout, and had an eight-foot real fireplace. As it was right across the tracks from the college, it soon became a popular stopping point for faculty members on their way home—so popular that we named the house "Crossroads."

We had sold our car earlier in order to buy furniture and other necessities, and there were some problems whenever we had to ride the bus. Once, when we went shopping for groceries at Weingartens on Main Street, I experienced trauma. We got on the Dowling Street bus loaded down with grocery bags. Kitty was tired and flopped down on the first seat in back of the bus driver. This was legal only as long as there were no white passengers. However, we had gone only a few blocks when some whites got on. They made no issue and took seats all around us. Fortunately, the situation didn't get sticky until we were close to our stop. The bus driver looked at us but didn't say anything until we were about ready to get off. You could feel the tension, but Kitty was adamant so I braved it out with her. About a block from our stop, the bus driver told us that we would have to move. Knowing that Kitty would not move to the back of the bus, I told Kitty, "Let's get off here."

We got off, and it meant only an extra block's walk loaded down with groceries. During the walk, I reflected that given Kitty's aggressive nature, it would be expedient for us to buy a car even if we couldn't quite afford it. Within a few weeks, I bought a 1950 Chevrolet powerglide. It was the first car commercially available with automatic transmission. The only embarrassment was that driving home from the dealer, I ran out of gas.

We really put "Crossroads" on the map when we gave a party for Coleman Hawkins, Ella Fitzgerald, and Ray Brown. They were in town for a jazz concert, and I contacted the booking agent and arranged for them to have some refreshments before the concert. We invited only a few close friends, but word got around that these jazz giants would be at our house. When the time came, we were crowded out. Many not-so-close friends crashed, but they did bring extra refreshments. Booze was plentiful, and by the time for the concert, I was almost out of it. I did manage to talk with Coleman about old times but couldn't get close to Ella Fitzgerald, who was always surrounded by the "crashers." Ray Brown acknowledged to everybody that I got him his first break in New York with Dizzy Gillespie.

We suggested that our stars return to the house for breakfast after the concert. Unfortunately, everybody in attendance heard it. We had a full house again after the downtown concert. I was really inebriated by this time, and Kitty was weary—so weary that she had to call on a TSU faculty friend to prepare the breakfast. Mary Perry, a math instructor, saved the day for us. Kitty was not missed, Coleman Hawkins did not show, and I was still "feeling no pain." After this near fiasco, we were well woven into the social fabric of young, black Houston professionals. It meant barbecue cookouts, parties, and even attendance at the Houston symphony. As one friend, Dr. J. Timothy Ashford, put it, "I will not let segregation interfere with my cultural development."

At the beginning of my second year with the band, the university hired an assistant for me. I recommended C. A. ("Skeets") Tolbert. He was a graduate student at Columbia University when I played bass with his band in New York. Not only did we need an assistant, but we had enough players to set up a junior band. Skeets was in charge of our "B" band and made them so competitive that they challenged our "A" band on occasion. Skeets also took charge of our jazz orchestra. It was a tribute to the number of real jazz performers coming out of the Houston area high schools that we placed second in the *Pittsburgh Courier* college jazz band poll. The poll was based on the number of the newspaper forms that you mailed in. Tennessee State in Nashville won the poll and went on to play the prize-winning concert at Carnegie Hall in New York. I was very grateful to my old band buddy Skeets Tolbert, and it is with nostalgia that I recall that he stayed at Texas Southern much longer than I did.

Dean Doty of the University of Texas School of Music was assigned by our board of visitors to oversee and evaluate the establishment of our music department. I didn't know it at the time, but in less than a year I would be under his jurisdiction as a graduate student at the University of Texas.

When a prospective black student applied to the University of Texas to become a percussion major, he was referred to Texas Southern. I told Dean Doty that we couldn't offer a percussion major because we didn't have the necessary equipment. He instructed me to write up a list and budget for it. I felt bad about this because it would prevent a black person from attending the university at Austin. I made the list as extensive and expensive as reasonably possible. It didn't work because I received a check for ten thousand dollars with instruction to buy everything on the list. It was ironic that after blocking one black's attempt at desegregating UT, I would become the first black to attend that lily-white institution. Dean Doty did offer me a scholarship to the University of Indiana, but I told him that since Texas was our home that we preferred to attend UT. I think that he himself really didn't object to my coming to his school but that he had to deal with his political and financial peers.

The day of reckoning for our overexuberance at a November football game in New Orleans came at the end of the spring semester the following year. At the annual inventory it was revealed that the band was seventy-five dollars short because of missing citation chords. When I received my monthly check, it was seventy-five dollars short, too. I was furious, so furious that I did not even heed our business manager French Stone when he laid out procedures for being reimbursed. The source of my anger was our department head, Dr. Dorsey, who did not have to turn in the information in the first place and had authorized the deduction from my paycheck. I walked off the campus with my reduced check. Our house was up for sale that afternoon. I didn't know where we would go, but it wouldn't be Houston.

Kitty was in Baltimore to see her old doctor, who had told her she could never have children. She was about three months pregnant. I called her to tell her about the incident and about the sale of the house. After the call, I got into our car and drove to Austin where I went immediately to Dr. Doty's office. I was in class the next morning. A court case, the Sweatt case, had integrated the university. However, Mr. Sweatt was having marital problems and did not show for the 1950 school session. That made me technically the first black attending the University of Texas. I had some qualms about this as our salaries would be pared down to the GI Bill money. Also the fact of attending a southern white university did not help my blood pressure, but it turned out all right.

I never did officially resign from my job at Texas Southern as band director. I just walked off the campus, never to return. Austin, here we come.

# CHAPTER 22

# AUSTIN

*I* drove straight to Austin on the wide two-lane highway. It was a fast trip of about three hours. I had mixed feelings about going into the unknown and about race relations in what was then a midsized city. The only addresses I had were those of Bertrand Adams, a Sam Houston College band director, and that of Dr. Doty (head of the university music department). My first visit was with Dr. Doty, who helped me register at UT. The registrar was friendly and told me that I would be registered, but that there would be no publicity in regard to UT's first black student. Frankly, they were tired of all the media attention about integration of higher education in the South. That suited me fine as I certainly did not want the attention that other blacks had received at other universities—like the University of Arkansas where they had a curtain around black students in the classroom. It worked out fine also because none of the disruptive elements in the area knew I was there.

I then went to the only other address that I had in Austin, the home of Bert Adams, where he offered me a part-time job at Sam Houston College, a small (about five hundred students) black college about ten city blocks from the university. The salary was $1,800 for nine months. The job also carried with it a house and free telephone (except for long distance). This helped our financial picture, and it was helped even more when Kitty arrived on campus and accepted a job as secretary to the dean-registrar at the same salary. With the imminent arrival of our baby daughter, we felt blessed and considered Austin our permanent home.

Austin was a pretty town with lots of trees and the look of a small town even though there were about 100,000 people there. The black community was small, and just about everybody knew everybody else. A Mexican community bordered the Sam Houston campus, but the two communities did not mix. We could hear their nightly fiestas, but we did not get to meet a single Mexican socially during our two years there.

The university was unlike any that I had seen. It was big, sweeping in scale, and full of Spanish architecture. Some of the buildings were air-conditioned, and that was fortunate, in that I considered Austin a hotter city than Houston. There were some Mexican students, but the prevailing mix was a few Mexicans and overwhelming numbers of whites. I thought that race relations were relatively good in that there was no overt hostility between blacks and whites. My being on the campus was a new experience for them, but in the main I was not even noticed. This suggested to me that desegregation could have happened on this campus years earlier and without incident. I was amazed at the cheapness of the tuition. I had enrolled for a full course load of fifteen hours for fifteen dollars and received a six-dollar refund when I reduced my load to nine hours because of my part-time job. This was a true *state* university, albeit a rich one.

Since I already had a master's degree in music and that was the highest degree in music offered by UT, I enrolled in the doctoral program in education. However, I was able to pick and choose among many of the music courses that interested me and took musicology and composition courses. One reason for taking these courses was that they were in the relatively new and air-conditioned music building. That was a plus, especially when Austin got up to 105 degrees.

The professors and students were very cordial. I did get a bit concerned when I heard that on occasion a class met at a bar across Guadalupe Avenue with the professor to informally discuss an exam or an assignment. But I felt better about it when I realized that they could not invite me because of the segregation laws. I rationalized that I got everything I was supposed to get in the classroom and that I was here to get an education, not to socialize. It still was a bit disconcerting to take a final exam in the professor's apartment, complete with a bottle of Old Crow bourbon on the coffee table and available to students. They do things differently in Texas, or so I thought. Anyway these were mature graduate students, and the relationship between teacher and student was much more informal than at NYU. I think that my having a master's degree from NYU impressed them more than my blackness.

Our first daughter, Jacqueline, was born before the end of the fall semester of 1950. Fortunately, we had a campus house for twelve dollars a month and a campus full of babysitters. I took a gig with Professor Nat Williams of Tillotson College, right down the street from Sam Houston College. Nat was the head of the music department at Tillotson and a fine musician. The gig was at a white club on the outskirts of Austin. I remember Dizzy Dean was one of our main customers when he was in town promoting Falstaff beer. He was great and talked to everybody (including me) as if he were his long lost buddy. We had more of an entertainment unit than a jazz band. We had Nat on piano, "Rebeat" on drums, a female singer, a saxophonist, and me on bass—and, would you believe, viola. We had a nightly broadcast in which I played our theme song "Gypsy Earrings" on viola.

After the gigs with Nat Williams, I hooked up with Carl Owens and his quartet. Carl was a local high school teacher. While not the pianist that Nat was, Carl was a much better jazz player. In fact, he reminded me of Earl Hines. Carl primarily played weekend gigs in San Antonio. This arrangement suited me fine as I could teach three classes at Houston Tillotson and take three classes (nine hours) at the university. My main memory about the group has more to do with food than music. We would leave a gig in San Antonio at 11:00 P.M. and try to drive eighty miles to Austin to arrive at a fish sandwich shop before the midnight closing. The proprietor was a Mexican who made his fish sandwich the talk of the town. The name of the joint was Kingfish, and he could not have been more correct. Obviously, we had to drive at speeds in excess of ninety miles per hour in order to make it by midnight. Actually, we never made it, but my memory includes the anticipated taste of the sandwich while we made our flying effort. We would usually turn the corner at Eleventh Street just in time to see the lights go out. If you have never seen grown men cry, you should have been with us.

The Austin black community was very close-knit, and everybody knew everybody. If you did not have an extramarital affair, one would be provided for you in the gossip scene. Somebody called me once and related to me, "Did you know your wife was seeing so and so?"

I told him, "My wife is a very busy woman, what with a full-time job, a new baby, and me to take care of. If she can find the time or energy to have an affair after all of that, more power to her." The guy hung up. Our president at the college was an ordained minister who absolutely forbade alcohol or smoking on the campus. After all, Sam Houston was a Methodist-sponsored college. However, one weekend Dr. Harrington hosted the minister's alliance meeting. He approached me very furtively to buy some whiskey for the esteemed clergymen. I was surprised at the knowledgeable way he named the various brands. He asked for two quarts of Old Granddad, two quarts of Johnny Walker black label scotch, a Texas fifty (half-gallon) of Gilbey's gin, and so on. He was precise in a way that told me that he had covered this ground before. I made the purchase and later regretted it. Our houses were back to back, and Kitty and I were acutely aware of these religious "meetings." We didn't get to sleep until about five in the morning on either night.

Duke Ellington came to town and provided us some more fame with Austin's black affluent and professional class. Jimmy Hamilton, Ellington's famous clarinetist, came over to the house almost daily while he was in town. Each time he brought at least one of Ellington's sidemen (Harry Carney most often). Before the booze and food we read through some classical music of the chamber variety. For Jimmy I would secure a campus pianist, and we would read through Jimmy's favorite Mozart trios involving the clarinet. Word got around about our recreational activity, and soon the living room was crowded with local musicians and *aficionados*. I generally played the violin or the viola part. I might add that Jimmy provided the music from his extensive collection of classical music. Looking back, it was a revelation for me to realize the depth and variety of Duke Ellington's sidemen. These guys were real musicians, no matter what they played.

The next gig I got was with a black homosexual pianist whom I'll call "Roger." A fine cocktail pianist, Roger was very shy. I was hired primarily to shield him from the general public and to field requests. It was a good gig that finished early enough for me to get a little sleep before my duties at UT or Sam Houston. There was, however, one fly in the ointment. Roger's jazz quartet was placed in a position of involuntary servitude. It seemed that J. W., the owner and manager of the club, had just been released from a mental institution. It was known that he had shot and killed several people. J. W. went around like a prototypical Texas rancher with a ten-gallon hat, cowboy boots, and a gun strapped to his side. He professed a fondness for our band, saying, "This is mah band." He would not allow us to quit, even for a better job. We were really scared. J. W. periodically ordered the band over to his apartment after the gig. "I'll cook y'all some steaks." I would want to get home and to bed as soon as possible, but I was afraid to tell J. W., "No, thanks." Everybody thought of that gun and J. W.'s rumored record. We went and enjoyed the steaks.

We finally got a better job offer in San Antonio, but the question was would we be able to show up? I went into the club one afternoon, and seeing J. W., I told him that I needed to take my bass home for some needed repairs. The drummer was luckier in that J. W. had just stepped out when he came to get his drums. We loaded up around the corner, terrified, glancing up and down the street for any sign of J. W. What would he do when he returned and found the instruments gone? We drove at breakneck speed down the highway to San Antonio with everybody looking back to see if we were being followed. We knew we couldn't tell J. W. that we had another gig and stay in the same town. That was the reason for the San Antonio location. Anyway, the escape ended a period of involuntary, if somewhat pleasant, servitude.

Before the year was out, I was able to get a measure of satisfaction from my scurrilous exit from Texas Southern. President Lanier of TSU sent none other than Dr. Dorsey, my former department head, to Austin to pay me the seventy-five dollars deducted from my check. I took the check before I denied his request for me to return to TSU. I wouldn't even talk about it. Instead, I focused conversationally on the topic of baseball. In 1950 major league baseball was the religion of the black community because of the exploits of the Brooklyn Dodgers and their new black ballplayers like Jackie Robinson and Roy Campanella. I ignored all of Dr. Dorsey's attempts to get me to return to TSU, so he finally gave up and left. I was really satisfied since he was the guy who caused the break in the first place. It turned out for the best.

At the beginning of the 1951 school year, Carl Owens, a jazz pianist with whom I had worked, gave me a tip for a possible gig. He told me to see Jimmy Wiginton, owner of a new club, the New Orleans Bar, and offer him the possibility of my forming a trio to play there. At that time Austin had three to four times as many bass players as jazz pianists. I couldn't find a piano player free for the gig, so I decided to try the piano spot. I was completely inexperienced as a working jazz pianist, and in addition I had limited technique. Kitty couldn't believe it when I auditioned at the piano and passed the test. In truth, no one else was available. Fortunately, I had a good bass player and a drummer who sang well. I practiced daily to add tunes to my limited repertoire. My list of tunes—and keys—that I could play was divided into fast, medium, or slow numbers. I played what one might call arranger's piano—straight melody and chords. The slow numbers exceeded the fast numbers by a ratio of about five to one. My bass player was my left hand, and the drummer's singing provided some relief for my unadorned playing of the melody. At least the tune was there even if there was no solo improvisation. I confess that 80 percent of my repertoire was in the key of C. Anyway we lasted for almost a year, with "Stars Fell on Alabama" being our main tune to revive flagging interest. Another reason for our lasting a year was that there really was a shortage of jazz pianists in Austin and an oversupply of clubs.

The New Orleans Bar was a club primarily patronized by middle-aged people. As a trio we could concentrate on the slower, romantic ballads and well-known tunes from the popular Broadway shows. We tried to imitate the general style of the King Cole trio, which was hot. It would have taken more pressure off of me if we had a solo guitarist as King Cole's group did. We had to make the best of it with my limited piano playing and the drummer's singing. We played a lot of blues because that was the strength of my piano experience. We also played a lot of King Cole's hits like "Straighten Up and Fly Right" with our drummer almost sounding like Cole himself. Our main weakness was that I could not hold up my end as a pianist in comparison with Cole. With the older crowd, we got by because everybody knew what we were attempting to do. One customer, who evidently liked our trio, said that "we sounded like the King Cole trio without King Cole." After the first few weeks, the frightening nightly experience got better and less frightening. I even added a few keys from the key of C, branching out to F, B-flat, E-flat, and G. I attempted to play the Broadway tunes in their original keys. It was a great learning experience. I never did get to the level of what I'd call a piano player, but I must have done something right. After all, we lasted at the New Orleans Bar for almost a year.

The school situation at UT was going well, but I became restive. I was developing academic burnout from all of those education courses, with graduate courses in statistics being the chief villain. I had foolishly elected fifteen hours of graduate statistics in place of the language requirement for an Ed.D. Statistics forced me to realize that I was a musician and would be happy only in musical pursuits. Kitty and I decided to leave UT and apply for a position elsewhere. In keeping with the times, I applied only at black colleges like Stowe Teachers

College in St. Louis. We got several answers and proposals, but we pursued only two. The first was a position to head the Ph.D. program in music at North Carolina Central (then College) in cooperation with the University of North Carolina. I was flattered at even being considered for the post but realized that I had no business giving someone else a Ph.D. when I had not earned one myself. Also, even though the proposed salary was good, I resented the possibility of being used to maintain racial segregation in higher education. After a brief exchange of letters, we informed the University of North Carolina that we would not take the position.

The other position that interested us was at Tennessee A & I, now Tennessee State University. It came in the form of a telegram from Dr. Herbert F. Mells offering a position as director of graduate studies in music education, teacher of music methods, and violist in a newly formed string quartet. The last part caught my attention. I played the viola in the University of Texas' opera orchestra and was intrigued with the idea of a black string quartet. In spite of our very pleasant experience in Austin, we decided to pull up stakes and head for Nashville. We both resigned as of June 1952 and spent the summer on the East Coast, mostly in Baltimore. In Baltimore I received the call to come to Nashville for an interview. I arrived in Nashville on the hottest day of the year (107 degrees) and had my interview with Dr. W. S. Davis, president, and Vice-President Flowers. The only sticky point came when Dr. Davis asked me why I left Texas Southern without resigning. I told him about the seventy-five dollars deducted from my salary. He then said, "I don't blame you."

With that I was hired as an associate professor with a salary equal to my peak year at Texas Southern ($4,500). I flew back to Baltimore and told Kitty. We were pleased that in a few weeks we would be on our way to Nashville with our new baby and that we would be half the distance away from our homes in Philly and Baltimore.

# THE
# NASHVILLE
# YEARS

# CHAPTER 23

# COUNTRY TOWN

**A**s Kitty and I drove into Nashville from Baltimore, we became acquainted with the Shenandoah Valley and the Lee Highway, or U.S. 11. We were impressed with the scenic beauty of the route, but very tired after the seven-hundred-mile journey. On Dr. Davis's recommendation, we checked in at Don Q. Pullen's house in South Nashville. Don Q. was the preeminent black jazz band director. He was a TSU graduate and a junior-high-school instrumental music director. He was also a good jazz pianist who had studied at Juilliard with Teddy Wilson. We got along famously.

I learned something of the Nashville music scene from him and his wife, Wilma, who was the manager of his well-known band. We didn't stay long as we were looking for larger quarters in order to bring our baby daughter, Jackie, to Nashville. To me, Nashville was just one overgrown country town. It had that rural look, and in 1952 there was very little traffic. I could drive across town five miles to the TSU campus in less than fifteen minutes with no more than four traffic lights. For one coming from the New York-Philadelphia area, it was pure delight. We finally found a house in North Nashville within walking distance of the campus. This turned out to be ideal later when both of us had jobs and we had only one car.

Dr. Herbert F. Mells, who had hired me at Tennessee State, was the very authoritarian head of the music department. He immediately admonished me to stay away from the band room as he had hired me to play viola in the newly-formed quartet. However, as we talked about my previous experiences or my job possibilities, he told me, "You will die here." I have been haunted by that remark ever since.

Dr. Mells ran a tight ship. There was never a departmental meeting except to hear his latest decree. There was never a democratic discussion of policy. He assigned and the teacher did. Mells was not a person to take no for an answer. At over six feet tall and about 235 pounds, he was definite and firm, but with a benevolence and concern for others. He knew what he wanted for the music department and Tennessee State, and he moved toward that goal unswervingly, brooking no interference. We had many discussions privately in his office, and I learned a lot from our teacher-pupil relationship. He planted the first notion in my head about going for a doctorate specifically in music at his *alma mater*, the University of Iowa. Alas, it was not to last. Dr. Mells died before the school year was out.

The quartet, which was the only string quartet associated with a black college, was Dr. Mells' personal pride and joy. Brenton Banks, a fine violinist and jazz pianist from the Cleveland Institute, was our first violinist, and Maureen Stovall played second violin. I played the viola, and Dave Kimbrell, a graduate student who had played bass with Duke Ellington, was our cellist. We were given rehearsal time as part of our teaching load. We had lots of fun even though our rehearsals were very serious and intense. Our repertoire was mostly Haydn and Mozart quartets, or the Schumann piano quintet with a guest or faculty pianist. I will never forget the challenge of our feature selection, the Ravel Quartet in F major. I learned more from trying to play the viola part than from any previous experience. In chamber playing of this stripe, you are constantly exposed, and you are the only one who can carry your weight. I heartily recommend the experience for the development of musicianship and teamwork.

As business manager of the quartet, I booked a tour, which took us through Arkansas to Texas. We were a novelty, a black string quartet playing classical music. Later we were to play as much black music as we could get our hands on to break down the barrier between black audiences and classical music. A musical elite in the black community have always known and understood operas, symphonies, and chamber music. However, to the general masses, classical music was a foreign subject. This is the point that Dr. Mells was trying to address on the TSU campus. Toward that end we played monthly concerts on the campus, as well as appearances at Fisk University and some of the leading black churches.

We got some publicity, and our concerts were well received. Brenton Banks wrote a really jazzy quartet, which was unfortunately lost. I thought it was a significant work, and it was a real crowd-pleaser. In the context of 1952, we filled a void. With integration, nobody notices a black face in a quartet or a symphony orchestra any more. The other side of the integration coin is that the gap between the general masses and classical music is widening. Dr. Mells was right in believing that frequent exposure of black audiences to classical music by black performers would breed familiarity. Unfortunately, Dr. Mells died in 1953, and thereafter our quartet did not get the support he gave us.

At our first departmental meeting in 1952 I was introduced as a new faculty member. On that occasion somebody said out loud, "Oh God, here's that thug from Philadelphia." I looked around and recognized John Sharpe, the university organist, whom I had known in both Philadelphia and New York. He was a neighborhood piano teacher in Philly and must have seen some of my Forty Thieves gang activity. It couldn't have been much because I was such a reluctant participant, but it was enough for him to remember. All of the rest of the music faculty were new to me. Marie Brooks Strange was the oldest faculty member in point of service. She did not have our academic credentials, but she was one of the finest natural musicians I have ever met. She was a wonderful music history teacher, especially when the topic was opera. She would play the overture on piano and proceed to sing all the parts while accompanying herself. She actually lived the opera while she told the story.

I have already mentioned Brenton Banks and Maureen Stovall as members of the university string quartet. I met Frank Greer, the band director, on rare occasions. Since I was a former band director, Dr. Mells gave me instructions to stay away from the band room. I was curious, however, and did sneak in a couple of peeks, especially because of the program's reputation as one of the finest. Greer impressed me because he was everything I was not. He was formal and strict, and his rehearsals were the epitome of order and purpose. I found out later about his concern for every student under his jurisdiction. Wilhelmina Taylor, our music appreciation teacher, was, I found out later, a friend of my older sister, Willie Mae. Her father was the pastor at Zion Baptist Church in Philadelphia when my sister was in high school. Taylor was a revered teacher of music appreciation, which I suspect is a difficult subject to teach in this day of rock and rap. Eddie Goins and I became very close, and I was able to influence him to go to my school, the University of Iowa, for his doctorate in music. "Chick" Chavis directed the famous and competent Tennessee State Collegians. They had just done a Carnegie Hall concert in New York, and some of the student musicians in that band would become famous in their own right. Jimmy Cleveland (trombone), Andy Goodrich (saxophone), and Sonny Turner (trumpet) were later to be nationally known jazz figures. Jasper Patton, our youngest instructor, was a very fine pianist. He was often mistaken for a student rather than a competent and conscientious faculty member. It was a very able group, and working with them was pure serendipity.

My job aside from the string quartet was primarily with the graduate program in music education. As it was a new program we had only one student. Dr. Mells had planned the curriculum to cover as many bases as possible and at the same time meet certification requirements. Poor Edward Louis Smith, our one student, had to take many courses, all marked down in credit to one or two hours. Worse, he had to take them all from me. Our one-to-one relationship through five graduate courses a semester was very curious. It did give us a lot of scheduling leeway. However, with Dr. Mells everything had to be accounted for. Every assignment, every exam, every lecture, and, of course, the official roll and grade sheets with just one name on them. We survived that first year with our sanity intact and laid the groundwork for a growing graduate program. Louis Smith was a remarkable trumpet player, similar to Wynton Marsalis. He was very intelligent and knowledgeable, so it was a pleasure for me to transfer to him what I knew about music education at that time. And I learned to organize and discipline myself as a presenter of graduate materials. I had to do research and devise outlines and lesson plans. Louis held me up to a high standard, for which I am grateful. In spite of our gigs and familiarity, he and I maintained the formal dignity and respect of a graduate class.

Kitty and I found a house not far from Meharry Medical College, Fisk University, and Tennessee State. It was a relatively new house on Twenty-fourth Avenue in the middle of a triangle of the schools. We moved in on a rental-purchase agreement. This was a three-bedroom house, and our two-year-old daughter had a room of her own. Before the year was out, we would need a room for our new baby.

After Dr. Mells died, the music department hired Dr. Edward C. Lewis to take over an existing program not of his making. In my opinion, he was diplomatically successful in keeping the morale and *esprit de corps* we had developed. He was almost the opposite of Dr. Mells in that we had democratic departmental meetings, and faculty input was generally taken into account. Dr. Lewis was an able performer on piano as well as a brilliant administrator. He was also a pragmatic leader, the opposite of Mells' idealism; both were experienced in the ways of black colleges. I would be with Lewis for practically all of my TSU career. He did give me support for nearly all of my sometimes futuristic ideas. The roadblocks usually came from further up in the university administration, generally based on budget. For my part, I would say "lack of imagination."

Being around so many good jazz musicians turned my mind to gigging, if only for recreational purposes. President Davis made a speech warning faculty members not to take part in extracurricular activities, especially off campus. He specifically mentioned jazz gigs, and he went on to say that he knew most of the black club owners. That held me up for a little while, but the pull of all those good jazz performers around me was too much. Besides, with a new baby on the way, we needed the extra money.

TSU had a fine jazz tradition and provided many fine bassists over the years, beginning with Jimmy Blanton, Duke Ellington's revolutionary bassist. Others included Cleveland Eaton who played with Count Basie and was one of my bass students, and Charles Dungey, one of the ten best jazz bassists that I ever heard. Ed Moon, Rick Maness, who had played with Chuck Mangione, and Mike Doster, who is with B. B. King, are others. Besides the people already mentioned from the Tennessee State Collegians, we had faculty members with excellent reputations as jazz performers. Frank Greer, our band director, had played trumpet with Walter Barnes, Nat Towles, and others. Dave Kimbrell, our cellist in the string quartet, was a brilliant bassist and had performed with Duke Ellington. Brenton Banks, the violinist with our quartet, was an excellent jazz pianist, and his jazz violin reminded me of Eddie South, the black angel of the violin. This list is not complete, but should give an idea of the jazz climate at TSU when I got there.

Nashville was a hotbed of black jazz. The rub was that nobody knew about it except for the black community, some white jazz performers, and *cognoscenti*. This was a town deeply mired in country music, the product that gave it national recognition. However, the jazz practitioners knew or knew of each other, black or white, and some of the country music cats crossed over to the black clubs and looked for jam sessions. That didn't work the other way, of course. There were no blacks in white clubs. There were rare exceptions, but in 1952 I was not privileged to experience one. The change would come in a very few years. One favorite meeting place was the Revilot, a black club on Jefferson Street, black Nashville's main drag. Here we could hear people like Ted Robinson, a brilliant tenor saxophonist, and Calvin Jones on trombone. Also playing at the Revilot were Brenton Banks on piano, Dave Kimbrell, our cellist on bass, and Morris Palmer, the singing drummer. Some of the sessions were legendary and comparable to some of the best I've heard on Fifty-second Street in New York. There were other clubs, for example the New Era, which was primarily into rhythm and blues—a young Jimi Hendrix was in the house band there—but with occasional jazz. The Del Morocco occasionally had "name" jazz performers but was basically a cover for the gambling in the back room. I was reminded of what the scene in Kansas City (around Nineteenth and Vine) must have been like in the early Thirties.

Another aspect of the jazz tradition in Nashville was the influence of the black colleges, which produced many of the players. Fisk University, after all, was the real birthplace of the famous Jimmy Lunceford orchestra. Meharry Medical College had many great jazz performers, including students and faculty. Dr. E. Perry Crump, a respected pediatrician and faculty member at Meharry, had been a Count Basie sideman (on clarinet and saxophone) in the early thirties. Jimmy ("Fingers") Minger, a dental student who played like the present day Ramsey Lewis on piano, was to be heard at the Del Morocco. I luckily had occasion to work with him, and it was a joyous experience. Tennessee State also produced Robert ("Bob") Holmes, who was an art major when I first met him. I persuaded him to change his major to music primarily because he came into my classroom and thumped out some really innovative jazz every chance he got. Bob was a versatile musician and later replaced Dave Kimbrell on cello in our faculty string quartet. He went on to become a composer and arranger for motion pictures and video productions. I'm proud that I "discovered" Bob.

Don Q. Pullen (now deceased) was the band director at Washington Junior High School. He discovered and developed many fine jazz performers. Charles Dungey on bass and Little Harry Allen on drums were two of them. I first heard them when they were in junior high school, and they sounded amazingly like veterans. Pearl High School and later Cameron High School turned out many able performers, some of whom later played with "name" bands. The amazing

Thurman Grant, an *avant-garde* tenor saxophonist, was playing most of his "Coltrane" ideas while still in high school. Some others from Pearl High included Harold Nesbitt (drums), John Hunt (trumpet), and Milt Turner (drums), who were later to be integral parts of the Ray Charles band in the seventies and eighties. If I couldn't be in New York, Chicago, or Los Angeles, black Nashville was the next best thing.

With the advent of Dr. Lewis as head of our department of music, my teaching load changed. I had fewer graduate classes to teach, along with some undergraduate classes. I enjoyed teaching primarily for the pleasure of interacting with people, and this new mix of classes provided more people like Carl Russell. Carl had a reputation as a brilliant student—on the days he came to class. However, he also had established a university record for cutting classes. When he registered for my class, I called him to my office for a conference. I told him, "Carl, your reputation has preceded you, so I have a deal for you that you can't refuse. Your final grade will be an *A* or an *F*. If you are late or take one cut, don't bother to come back to class as your final grade will be an *F*. Otherwise, it will be an *A*."

Carl not only came to every class on time, but did brilliant work. He was head and shoulders above the rest of the class. Once, when there was a severe storm warning on campus, he was the only person in the class to show up. I looked out of the classroom window and saw Carl huddled up, but fighting his way to class against an eighty-mile-an-hour wind. I told him, "Carl, I would have excused you if you didn't make it to class."

He answered, "That's all right. I had to prove to myself I can do this."

Carl got his *A*. Years later he returned to the campus in his Cadillac and, with his new job as director of community services for a large city in Michigan, with a salary double mine. He came to thank me for our special deal.

Another advantage of undergraduate teaching was the increased opportunity to interact with the younger students. Dr. Lewis gave me permission to seek a student chapter franchise of the Music Educators National Conference (MENC). In 1953 we obtained probably the first chapter granted to a predominantly black college. I thought it was a great opportunity for our students to gain information about what was going on in our field in other colleges around the nation. Toward that goal we got permission and some funds to attend the southern conference in New Orleans. This was to be a first, not only for our students, but for the up-until-then lily-white southern conference. We made arrangements for our students' room and board at Xavier University. I would be at a black hotel.

We were apprehensive about the drive through Mississippi, but as it turned out the experience was pleasant. We had about nine students in two cars, one of which was mine. We were fortunate in having with us a couple of students from Mississippi, who were able to guide us through the maze of segregation and other possible unpleasantness in that state. We even stopped at their homes, which were on our route.

When we first approached the MENC meeting at a major hotel, we had a problem. At the lobby elevator the black operator stopped us and said we could not use it. We could use the freight elevator or a stairway, which we refused to do. The session was on the mezzanine, which was only one flight up, but we congregated right in front of the lobby elevators. Finally, Dr. Wiley Housewright, president of the southern regional conference, came on the scene and inquired as to the problem. When he found out, he escorted us all on the elevator for the one-flight ride. We never had any trouble from our black operator after that. We decided not to sit together as a group but to sprinkle our blackness throughout the audience. We got full acceptance after our students formed the basis of the student chapter choir. It was a new experience both for the association and for us. I drove around to the black colleges in and around New Orleans, notably Dillard and Southern universities, to spread the word that we were welcome, but they were apathetic and didn't show up at any subsequent meetings. I guess it was too much to expect after years of separateness and segregation.

Probably my biggest reward from the conference came at the black hotel where I stayed. A. Philip Randolph was in residence there. The noted civil rights fighter, whom I had long admired, was very approachable. We took most of our meals together.

I was thrilled by my good luck. Every morning and evening for about five days, I received an education in problems of the American Negro from this famous civil rights advocate. He said, for example, "We [Negroes] never will get any respect in this country until the various African nations are free and sovereign. Every other minority here can claim a sovereign origin but us."

He probed me for my ideas and reactions as our discussions became more intense with each meal. My consciousness was very much raised. I saw the truth in his statements and predictions all the way up to the steadily unfolding civil rights drama of the sixties. I still am grateful for the opportunity to meet one to one with this outstanding contributor to successful race relations. It was a learning experience for which I thank God.

At home, Kitty was carrying our soon-to-be-born son. At the time we didn't have a telephone. I thought it would be good economy not to have this unnecessary expense. My mother, who was visiting us, roasted me on that point. "What if you had to call a doctor or hospital?" she asked.

Sure enough, that's exactly what happened, and I found myself trying to locate a public telephone at three in the morning. I finally found one about four blocks away, and that sealed my decision to have a phone put in the house. We have had a phone ever since. I learned my lesson.

The gig picture in my early years in Nashville was sporadic but choice. I had a weekend two-nighter with Jimmy Witherspoon, the blues singer. "Spoon" used only recording-quality musicians as he had the reputation of his many albums to uphold. His gigs were in higher-level places than the chitterling circuit, and they paid more. This suited me fine except for rehearsals, which were frequent and without compensation. On the other hand, the rehearsals were easy since they encompassed mostly blues.

I had another fruitful set of gigs with Johnny Shaw, who was an announcer on the black radio station (WSOK). Shaw was a Fisk graduate and an excellent jazz guitarist. His gigs often took us into the white community, frequently in fraternities, sororities, or clubs connected with Vanderbilt University. It was an awakening experience, particularly at a time when there was a curtain between the black and white communities in Nashville. "Blind Jimmy" Osborne was our pianist and was quite a competent jazz performer. He was a crowd favorite. Blind Jimmy and Blind Sonny were two remarkable pianists considering their blindness. I got the feeling that they were in competition with each other. Jimmy played more in the refined style of Teddy Wilson while Sonny was more honky tonk. I never had the pleasure of playing with Blind Sonny, but heard him on several occasions.

At TSU we added a music theory teacher in the person of Esther Cook. She was an Eastman School of Music graduate and former trombonist with the Sweethearts of Rhythm. The Sweethearts were an all-female jazz band who were classed with the leading jazz orchestras of the time. Esther was tough, rough, and ready, and also effective and competent. The more serious male students admired and respected her.

We had such an understanding in our "clique," which consisted of Brenton Banks, Maureen Stovall, Eddie Goins, and now Esther Cook, that all I had to do was to walk into any classroom and silently put fifty cents on the teacher's desk. This was a signal for the rest of the clique to ante up. I would call it "fifty cents on a fifth," although that phrase was never mentioned aloud. Somebody in the group would give me the amount needed for a fifth of Scotch or bourbon within the hour, and I would make the trip and the purchase. We then met in someone's nearby apartment, usually Brenton Banks' place in College Hill adjacent to the campus. Within an hour, everybody in the clique was there and the party would begin. Since we were all kindred spirits and dedicated musicians, a good time was had by all and the music department *esprit de corps* benefited as well.

On one of my trips to purchase supplies for our informal meetings, I happened to be on the corner of Seventeenth and Charlotte. A crowd of people stood on all four corners, and there was also a squad of policemen led by a white captain who was having a good time yelling, "A nigger president, ha, ha, ha."

It was loud enough for me to hear every word although I was diagonally across the street from the captain. It occurred to me that I had read in the morning newspaper that President Paul Magloire of Haiti was in town to visit Fisk University and Meharry Medical College. The official motorcade was to be held in a few minutes. I waited out of curiosity to see the president. The captain never let up on his denigration and merry-making until the sirens announced the coming of the motorcade. When the motorcade crossed that corner, the police squad, along with its captain, came to attention in a very precise military manner. Not a sound was heard except that of the motorcade and its sirens. I should say not a sound from the police squad—the crowd of people behind them were cheering wildly. I recall the incident as a microcosm of blacks and their relations with the police in Nashville. I thought it was extremely ironic for our friend the captain to be at attention in front of the very person whom he had held in such disdain. The joke was on him, but I'll bet he never recognized it.

One day early in 1955 my dear wife, Kitty, came to me with a nonnegotiable ultimatum: "We are going back to school this summer." The only item left for discussion was where. We drew up charts for about ten universities. They would have to have good departments in journalism for Kitty and music for me. They would have to meet our budget limitations as I only had one year of the GI Bill money left. We listed and compared such schools as NYU, Northwestern, Indiana, Iowa, and Yale. The deciding factors for Iowa were the well-known departments of music and journalism, as well as the relatively low cost. It was primarily cost that eliminated Yale or my return to NYU.

When I discussed the plan with several senior professors, they unanimously suggested that I go for it. The Ph.D. degree was like a union card, and it was becoming impossible to achieve full professorship without the card. I had previously, cynically, denigrated the degree after I had observed some of the "fools" who had them. I thought it would be easy to get and seriously questioned whether I really needed to go to that trouble. Dr. Kermit King, a former Olympic broad-jumper, and Dr. Ed Lewis, my department head, both pushed and supported me in that direction.

We gave up our lease-purchase arrangement on our home, withdrew my state retirement money, cashed in our mutual funds, and headed for the unknown wilds of Iowa. This ended, for the time being, our introduction to Nashville, but we both knew we would be back.

# CHAPTER 24

# CORN BELT HIATUS

**I** drove to Iowa ahead of the family to receive the furniture and prepare the residence. It was a long drive—650 miles—without a stopover. Around the 400-mile mark, and after eight hours of night-driving, I became overwhelmingly sleepy. Near Peoria, Illinois, I pulled into a truckstop and asked for something to keep me awake. The waitress suggested coffee and something called No Doz. I will never forget that stuff. I was wide awake for several days. Since I didn't even take aspirin, my system was not used to stimulants.

The furniture had not arrived when I found our quarters, but there were a few things like a stove, a refrigerator, and beds with no mattresses. I lay down on the coil springs to try to rest—and possibly sleep—but it was no good. I was wide awake with my heart racing. This went on for two days and two nights until our furniture and supplies from Nashville arrived. Kitty came the day after that with our five-year-old daughter. She left our baby son, Jay, with her mother and father in Baltimore because we were going into the unknown. At best, it would be temporary. With the family there, I was able to go about my business at the university and, above all, get a good night's sleep.

On about the third day in Iowa City I began to worry about our limited funds. I bought *The Daily Iowan* and browsed through the Help Wanted ads. I found a possible job that I thought would not interfere with classes—short-order cook in a very popular fast-food diner on Dubuque Street. I was nervy enough to call them. They told me there was no immediate opening, but they would keep my phone number and for me to be prepared to come to work on a moment's notice. Now I had another worry. What if they actually called me to work as a cook? I had never really cooked in my life. My culinary skills were limited to things like boiling an egg. Could I remember the various orders under the pressure of a crowded, early-morning breakfast time?

I hoped the guy would never call and proceeded to introduce myself by phone to selected members of the Iowa City musicians' union. At about 5:00 A.M. on Friday of the following week, the phone rang, and sure enough it was the owner of the diner. He wanted me to get there by 5:30. Fortunately, I had received a gig offer from the president of the local, a blind pianist. He didn't realize it then, but he saved my life. I turned down the cooking gig with a few guilt feelings because, after all, I had called and applied. Even today I have nightmarish fantasies of what I would have done trying to be a short-order cook.

Iowa was a typical Big Ten campus in that it was huge, but it didn't appear that way since it was in a small town. The music department was established and was one of the earliest to grant a Ph.D in music. There was a large staff with specialists in just about every phase of music and so many doctorates that most of the lower-rank teachers, the instructors, possessed one. Most of the professors used their first names on their name cards rather than "Dr." I could not bring myself to address Dr. Thomas Turner as "Tom." He even asked me about it, and I told him that as long as I was a student, I wanted to pay the respect of a title whether it be doctor, professor, or mister. About the only person who did not have a doctorate in music was the head of the department, Mr. Himie Voxman. His degree was a master's in chemical engineering. In our first conference he basically told me to "go for it, do your work, and everything will be all right." As it turned out, he was exactly right.

Dr. Neal Glenn was to be my advisor, and he permitted me to branch out in other areas, since I already had most of what Iowa offered in my specialization (music education). I had a chance to concentrate in musicology and my favorite pastime, music composition. Dr. Phillip Besancon became my composition advisor, and Mr. Albert Luper was my musicology advisor. You will note that it was Mr. A. T. Luper rather than "Dr." The standard gossip was that he knew so much about musicology that there was nobody around who could give him a doctorate. He didn't need it for prestige as he already was nationally respected. Another advantage of the music setup at Iowa was the university orchestra, which was rated as one of the best college orchestras in the country. I didn't realize the impact that it would have on my future, but I am thankful for the opportunity and experience of playing major orchestral literature on bass violin and, later, viola. I enjoyed the whole atmosphere so much and was so busy between school and other work that it took my mind off of our impending financial demise.

Iowa was a musicians' paradise. The department practiced what I would call total immersion in music. Music itself was the final arbiter in any question about procedure. Even the orchestra rehearsals were well attended. It was more like a concert presentation before students, all equipped with scores. The professors all spent time in the library. I had rarely seen this at NYU or Texas. Even in composition class everybody except me turned out copious amounts of new music. With other subjects to take, I did not have the time to write a whole movement of a symphony or a string quartet every week. After all, most of the guys in the class rated themselves as full-time composers. Most wrote in the style of Bartok or Stravinsky, who were the hot composers of the 1950s. There was no letup of intensity in the musicology class. Our first assignment was a book report due in two weeks. Unfortunately, none of the books were in the English language. I drew *Musik der notationskunde* by Johannes Wolfe as my assignment. Fortunately, I knew Reinhard Grossman, the bartender at Kessler's Beer Emporium. Reinhard was born in Berlin. With his aid and a German dictionary, I was able to complete the assignment successfully and on time. I swear that the only thing in that entire book (some four hundred pages) in English was the date of publication.

Winter came to Iowa, unexpectedly for us, sometime in early October. I had gone to the music building in the morning without a jacket, sweater, or overcoat. I got the message when I came out of the building in the late afternoon. The temperature had dropped about fifty degrees. I knew that Kitty and Jackie were equally unprepared for this early freeze as we all had left the hut in the morning dressed for a bright, sunshiny day in the seventies. I proceeded directly to Sears Roebuck with a credit card to buy sweaters, scarves, gloves, and earmuffs. I delivered the emergency goods to Jackie at Lincoln School and to Kitty, who was at work. It was to be an omen of things to come. Even though we were from the East Coast, we had never experienced cold weather like this. In January everybody cheered when the temperature got up to six degrees. Many mornings I had to shovel two feet of snow to get to our car parked five feet in front of the hut. We had a one hundred-watt bulb burning all night under the hood to keep the engine block from freezing. We found out about the goodness of neighbors as we all pitched in to help anyone in need.

The gig picture in Iowa City was really bleak. There were a few fraternity or sorority parties, but the main action was during the football season. I had the good fortune to join up with the leading jazz band in the area, a five-piece group, occasionally with a singer. Larry Barrett was the band leader and trumpeter, and his wife, Bobbie Barrett, was the occasional singer. It was a well-organized group with a fine tenor sax player, who had previously played with Gene Krupa. We had interchangeable pianists, and both were good jazz soloists. Dale Convey was white, a serious student of jazz in that he could improvise with some of the best I had ever heard. Our black pianist was a senior at the university and was equally good. Clarence Williams was a Chicagoan with a style reminiscent of Errol Garner. I think he was a premed student with jazz as a hobby. In other words, the two top jazz pianists in an area from Cedar Rapids to Davenport were in one band.

We had three drummers during my tenure with the Larry Barrett band. Byron Burford was the main drummer, but occasionally he wasn't available since he was a professor of art. Actually, I was surprised at his competence since this corn-belt country town provided no competition except for some university students who had no bigleague experience. Byron must have listened to a lot of records as he was knowledgeable about all of the "name" drummers of the period. Bud Brammer, a shoe salesman in Cedar Rapids, was our backup drummer. Bud was somewhat eccentric, and one Christmas he even told me he wanted to "rent" some children for the usual Christmas day festivities. He wanted the kids to come down in their nightgowns and open the gifts, which he would supply. When Bud told me about this, he was a bachelor and would work himself up into a weeping fit. He was, however, a good drummer who knew Larry Barrett's book from memory. Our third drummer near the end of my tenure with Larry Barrett was Jack Loghary, a doctoral candidate in psychology. Jack had previous professional drumming experience in Oregon. Again, the drums were in competent hands. I would like to have seen what this group could have done in New York or Chicago. It was buried in sporadic gigs in a country town with a major university. For me, it was enjoyable, if not financially rewarding.

Barrett's band had an occasional gig in a jazz club in Rock Island, Illinois. I looked forward to these events as the leading jazz performers of the tri-state area would be in attendance. Everybody would want to sit in. We had some amazing jam sessions. These were usually guys who had returned home to regular jobs like shoe sales-men from playing jazz elsewhere. They poured out emotions and pent-up ideas in the rare opportunity to release them. It made for a cathartic experience, if not a total artistic success. Probably the strangest gig we had to play was for the Elks in Cedar Rapids. The strange part is that this was for the Negro Elks. I didn't believe that there were more than 50 blacks in Cedar Rapids, a city of over 100,000 people. Iowa City only had six black families at the time. The dance was in a small hall and was packed with happy black and brown faces. "Where did they come from?" I asked Larry Barrett.

"They come from about a hundred-mile radius of Cedar Rapids. All of the farms, packing plants, and factories from here to the Mississippi River and to the Missouri state line have a few black employees. The place is jammed because this is one of the rare social events they have access to."

The whole scene reminded me of Canada where blacks live but are usually invisible. Also strange about the gig was that a white jazz band was playing for a black audience. One reason for this is that there was no organized black jazz band in the corn belt.

Toward the end of our first school year in 1956, we were becom-ing financially pinched. Kitty and I had paid out two tuitions and rent for our student quarters in one lump sum. The football season was over, and the dreaded Lenten season made for a scarcity of gigs. Kitty started as a chambermaid in the city's largest hotel. However, this didn't last because the work was long and confining. She also complained of back problems. Eventually, she got a better job as a waitress-cashier at a restaurant on Highway 6. That connection would last her until we left Iowa City. She was so popular and effective that in the second year she became the evening manager of the restaurant. That meant that I had to become the evening manager of our house-hold. It also meant that I had to do the meal preparation and most of the household chores as well as parenting our two children. Our daughter, Jackie, was in kindergarten, and our son, Jay, was a three-year-old toddler. We handled the toddler situation without a baby sit-ter because one or the other of us was home between classes.

One cold winter day, I was detained at the music building and was unable to pick up Jackie at her school on time. It was snowing, and the snappy cold wind made visibility terrible. I almost panicked when I parked our car and proceeded to look for her on foot. Jackie knew the way home, but the low visibility caused some problems. After about half an hour, I finally heard some crying. I walked to the source of the crying and saw a lonely huddled figure trying to find home and warmth. It was Jackie, and she cried until we got near the stove at home. Thirty-five years later, Jackie still recalls the incident as if it was the most traumatic in her life.

I mentioned to Dr. Tom Turner that I thought we would have to leave Iowa City at the end of the school year because of our finances. That night Mr. Pearl West offered me a part-time job as a janitor for his music store. It was great because most of the hours were on the weekends. I went for one or two hours in the mornings before class and spent practically the whole day on Sunday when the store was closed, and with nobody there to check on me, I could watch the professional football games between mopping and waxing. It was also a quiet place to study. The hardest job was polishing the Steinway grand pianos.

I was satisfied; we had food money for the balance of our time in Iowa City. I was also grateful for the type of community this was. When word got around that someone was in trouble, the faculty and members of the business community came up with help. I might quibble that it was a janitorial gig and beneath my dignity as a doctoral candidate. But I didn't quibble because I appreciated the opportunity for Kitty and me to complete our studies with some financial peace of mind.

We realized that we had to accumulate some funds for tuition, especially since my G.I. money had run out. My weekend gigs would not be sufficient to raise the tuition, pay housing costs, and cover an occasional car-repair bill. I took a civil service exam for railway clerk (postal service). To my regret I passed the exam, and with a 10-percent veteran's preference was accepted and appointed with duties beginning immediately in Omaha, Nebraska. The gig paid well enough, but it required travel away from home on a train sorting mail. I had to turn it down. Then I went to Penick and Ford in Cedar Rapids. They were manufacturers of corn syrup and related products. I applied for the maintenance worker, or janitor, job. Everything was going all right until the interviewer asked me about my work and job experience. I had to tell him that I was a musician and doctoral candidate at the University of Iowa. He was unimpressed even after I told him that I could swing a mop or a broom. In short, I didn't get the job.

Chastened by this experience, I went to the Proctor and Gamble soap-making plant about eight miles from Iowa City. There I not only took a written exam but underwent some two hours of psychological testing. I tried to interject from time to time that I was only applying for janitor. The payoff for a whole morning and afternoon's testing was that I was told I was overqualified. I don't think the matter was racial in view of the job I wanted. Rather, I think they were tired of doctoral candidates applying. All was not lost, and shortly after that experience I received a University of Iowa graduate fellowship. At least my tuition would be paid, and it carried a fifty-dollar monthly stipend. This reduced our mountain and made it possible for us to stay in Iowa for another year.

With the financial roadblock off my mind, I decided to try the language hurdles. I remembered my Texas experience of taking fifteen hours of advanced statistics in place of the two required languages. I could not go that route again, so I elected French and German. I did have two years of French in high school, but no German since my adolescence. The exam was to be at the end of the summer of 1956, so I decided to go for it. I soon found out that my high-school French was no match for what was required: the ability to read a professional or technical book in my major field. I was glad that it was a reading requirement because my limited French with a Tennessee accent did not allow me to be understood. In the spring semester, I began reading an hour of French each morning and an hour of German each night. Of course, all of this was with a language dictionary. I followed this up with a language-reading course in the summer of 1956. It paid off because I took both exams in the final two weeks of summer and passed. Iowa had a history of doctoral candidates staying around an extra year or so trying to pass either one of these exams. I think I was fortunate in the selection of the book to be translated. In both cases, I selected a history of Russian music. The Russian names of the composers were recognizable in any language, as were most of the musical terms. Anyway, it was an achievement to meet both of these language requirements within two weeks of each other. Now the way was cleared for me to take the most fearsome of all hurdles, the dreaded comprehensive exam.

To get ready for the comprehensive, I had to curtail the gig scene. While we were barely able to make it financially, there was no period in Iowa that we were rolling in dough. However, Kitty and I had considerable help from our support group of young married graduate students. We enjoyed our children along with a community social life and never felt that the kids were in the way. We traded off baby-sitting assignments to meet the various needs of our support group. It seemed that this was a tradition at Iowa. I got so that I could even study with a living room full of young kids. The female black undergraduates took a liking to my daughter, and we got a lot of help there. I regretfully had to drop music composition as it was too time consuming. That's the reason that my sonatina, "Long Song for Viola and Piano," was not completed until three decades later. Along with a lighter class load, I had considerable guidance from a black Ph.D. candidate who had passed the comprehensive several years earlier. He even scheduled a session at our apartment for all of the black potential comprehensive takers. He told us that some white fraternities kept a ten-year file of the exam. This was to be the lull before the storm. It was probably the busiest period in my life before or since. I was heartened by the knowledge that others had passed this hurdle, that it was do-able.

The time for the dreaded comprehensive came fast. However, there were some diversions like having my own trio at Kessler's. Even though my policy was to scale down the time-consuming gigs, this was football season and we desperately needed the money. I had a percentage arrangement at Kessler's for all home games. The place was deader than a doornail at other times. Anyway, it was very profitable. We had five or six home games, notably those with Notre Dame and Ohio State. Clarence Williams or Howard Brockington were my piano players. I played bass, and we had Carroll Calloway as a guitarist. Calloway was a good-looking white guy I met at Miller's Music Store. He was an instrument repairman, but he could play good jazz guitar. We split the profit on all beer sold, which could be considerable, especially when Ohio State was in town.

Mr. Kessler asked me to do something about the black football players and their white girlfriends. This was a ticklish moment as Mr. Kessler and I had developed a good friendship and trust. Even though Calvin Jones, the all-American guard, and John Nocera, the fullback, considered themselves fans of our jazz trio, I didn't think it was my place to broach the subject with them. I knew that it didn't help community relations for Jones and our star halfback to drive up and down Iowa City's main streets in a convertible (with the top down) loaded with the cream of Iowa's white femininity. I explained to Mr. Kessler that I had no leverage with the football team, and I think that Mr. Kessler saw my point. Since the team eventually went to the Rose Bowl, most of the community backed off of any animosity. It's funny what a victory over Michigan can do for race relations.

My colleague in martyrdom, Howard Brockington, called me often to make sure I was studying. He would open the conversation with, "Put the bottle down." He was not far off the truth, as both of us had discovered an inexpensive bottle of bourbon called Old Quaker. We were what you might call drinking buddies. He knew that if I got off track, Old Quaker was the probable cause. Howard and I were supportive friends. We would listen for and report all rumors relevant to doctoral candidates. This was important because we both sensed that admission to the Ph.D. club depended upon a lot of factors, objective and subjective. For instance, I shouldn't be a known atheist, Communist, or rapist. I couldn't make it if I was dating a white woman. I even played the game of taking my children to the church most of the music faculty attended. I made certain that Kitty was with me at all social occasions, whether graduate or faculty. It helped to be a family man. All of these guys, faculty and graduate, were educated and smart. Mess up, and I could be stopped. It could happen with the questions posed in the comprehensive, road blocks in thesis writing, or finally in the oral defense of the thesis. I know living examples of people who were stopped for violations of the club rules. Some of these unfortunates were smarter than I could ever have hoped to be.

The day came, and I thought I was as ready as I could be. It was a two-day, six-hour affair with questions and projects submitted to the five people of my supervising committee. My final hope was that none of these people had it in for me. I went to the examining room and noticed that it was right next to the music office. Theoretically, I was on the honor system, but I couldn't predict who might be keeping an eye on me. I put my books in a pile right outside the door. In the room was a small phonograph, a typewriter for those who could use it, pencils, exam answer books, and music paper. I went to the music office at 8:30 A.M. to get my first set of questions or projects. I got the second set at 12:30 P.M. I had roughly three hours on each. I don't remember the order, but one of the projects was to write a three-voiced fugue. Another was to analyze a complete symphony (mine was the Beethoven Seventh). That's what the phonograph was for. However, if I got too entertained listening, I would penalize myself on score reading and analytical time. There were music history and theory questions that called for complete recollection of just about everything that happened in music from Greek civilization to yesterday.

A week later I was informed that I had passed, and we celebrated. At Iowa, if you pass, you don't get your papers back. Only if you fail do you get the pleasure of seeing your marked-up handiwork. I had achieved a higher rung of status among the graduate students, and I was flattered when some of the white guys visited us and asked my advice as to procedure.

Christmas 1956 loomed on the immediate horizon and found us critically short of funds. The football team was on the Pacific Coast, and I had had no gigs since our last home game. Kitty was approaching her last trimester of pregnancy with our third child and had cut her work schedule at Loghry's restaurant. We decided that we couldn't go through with any celebration of the holiday. After we bought food, there was not enough money left to buy a Christmas tree, much less gifts for the kids. We hoped that we could explain it to Jackie and maybe Jay was too young to realize what was happening. Kitty did come up with ten dollars, which she put in an envelope. Somehow the envelope was lost, and we racked our brains trying to locate it. Finally, I remembered putting out the trash in the area dumpster. I vaguely remembered seeing an envelope and went immediately to the dumpster. Although it was about three-quarters filled with everybody's trash and garbage, I proceeded to climb up to the top and lower myself into the pile of trash. I was not proud; ten dollars was all there was between us and oblivion. I rummaged around, and finally spotted a soiled envelope near the bottom. I prayed as I opened it, and thank God, the money was still there.

I returned a little smelly and dirty, but happy. Shortly after I had cleaned up, a car drove up and somebody knocked on the door. It was Mr. Luper, my musicology professor, and his wife. He handed me an envelope and said, "Merry Christmas." The envelope contained ten dollars. I immediately thanked Mr. Luper and told him that I would try to repay him in a few weeks. He said, "The money is a small gift. Pay me back by doing the same thing to somebody else later in life."

I was overcome with happiness and gratitude. Kitty decided to wait until that night, which was Christmas Eve, to buy the tree. It paid off as she found one for $1.50 from a guy closing up shop. We stayed up practically all night, decorating the tree and improvising gifts. Twenty dollars couldn't buy impressive gifts for two kids, but we did the best we could, and when the kids woke up early and saw the tree, we all felt a sense of accomplishment and pride. The day went well. My friend Howard Brockington came over with his wife and a small bottle of Old Quaker. It was my happiest Christmas of all time, and I'm sure Kitty felt the same.

Passing the comprehensive and becoming a Ph.D. candidate greatly improved our social status. Kitty and I were now invited to an occasional faculty party. This meant that we were considered to be part of the establishment, a fledgling part maybe, but still a part. One party we were invited to was in honor of J. A. Westrup, the famous British musicologist. Kitty was unable to go as she was called for an emergency appearance at the restaurant. However, I was not without female companionship: Alice Cisco, a graduate piano major and a classmate in our musicology class, asked me for a ride to the party. I picked her up at her apartment and drove to the party. I had to park about two blocks from the house, so Alice, who was free, white, twenty-one, and pretty, grabbed my arm as we walked the distance. When we got there, I found that I was the only person of color in the building. This wasn't so bad in itself, but I was accompanied by the most attractive white female in the place. Alice didn't know many people there and stayed with me everywhere I went. I spent some time as bartender, trying to make myself useful as a junior partner in a senior situation. Alice was right there by my side. I was afraid that people would not realize the true nature of this situation since I am sure that most of them did not know me or Alice. Anyway, Alice disappeared close to midnight. A red-faced professor then told me that "Miss Cisco is ready to leave and wants you to meet her at the doorway."

I got my coat, and as we left the same professor told me, "The party is still going on, and you can come back."

I took my cue from that remark and drove across the river to Alice's apartment and back in six minutes. Of course, being as nice as she was, Alice invited me up for coffee after thanking me for the ride. I told her, "I'll take a raincheck—they're expecting me back at the party."

It was indeed a command performance—I was ushered into the room where the faculty was with our main guest, the British musicologist, J. A. Westrup. I did my best to hold at this level of conversation. Dr. Westrup was interested in my background but also in Alice's background. I begged off as I knew very little about her. The party eventually broke up, and I went home disturbed. If they were thinking what I thought they were thinking, I could see all of my hopes for a Ph.D. flying out the window. First thing the next morning I went to Mr. Luper's office and explained to him that Miss Cisco was a classmate without a car who had asked me for a ride. I also added that she was the girlfriend of the guitar player in my trio at Kessler's beer and pizza place, that I was simply doing her a favor, and that my wife couldn't come because of an emergency. His reply was, "I'm glad you told me."

By spring 1957 I had submitted a thesis proposal, and it was accepted. This gave me the "perk" of an office in the library for research. It was a small cubbyhole about the size of a large walk-in closet, but it did have a desk and bookshelves. I would sit for hours and not get down one line of an outline. I refer to this as "thesis doldrums," and every Ph.D. I know admits to having undergone this experience. A glance at the calendar reminded me that the whole thing had to be finished by mid-July if I was to make the summer 1957 graduation. This was seriously important if Kitty and I were to go back to a regular income. In short, I had about five months to research, write, and defend my thesis. Kitty's eighth month of pregnancy was another weight hanging on us. I got to work with that realization and spent from six to eight hours a day at that office. Most importantly, I wrote something every day, even if I had to throw it out later. At least I had something to show for the day's effort. The thesis was a comparative study of the supervisors and state agencies for music in ten midwestern states. I wanted to show their relationship to the music education programs of the schools in their states. I was granted time and a state car to visit the ten midwestern state agencies for purposes of research. Before the scheduled trip, I had an unusual experience, even for me.

A nonstudent friend called me one night offering me a weekend janitorial job that was to pay fifty to sixty dollars. The job required cleaning Younker's department store. This could only be done after the store was closed Saturday night, and it had to be thoroughly cleaned by nine o'clock Monday morning. I was soon to find out why the pay was so generous. This was a continuous gig, day and night. Tom advised me to bring a bag of sandwiches, and he supplied the coffee. We started on the first floor by moving the stock to one side, and I found out how much a rack of men's suits weighs. We then swept and scrubbed the floor (I operated the scrubbing machine). When the floor dried, we waxed it (I operated the waxing machine). While waiting for the floor to dry, we attended to details like restrooms and offices. When half of the floor was waxed, we moved all of the stock to that side and did the other side. When that was done we put all of the stock back in its original place. After working all of Saturday night, we just finished the first of two floors by Sunday afternoon. I had never worked that hard in my life—I mean pure, physical labor.

Toward Sunday evening I was about out on my feet when the

phone rang, and Tom answered. It was Kitty calling me to say that her water had broken, and she felt she should be going to the hospital. I told Tom that I'd have to leave. Since there were only five men in our crew, Tom was very reluctant to let me go. I explained that I had the only car in the family and this was Kitty's eighth month so it probably wasn't a false alarm. He finally paid me about thirty dollars for what I had done so far and curtly said good night. I drove out, feeling somewhat guilty for leaving just four men to do the second floor. I was dog-tired and happy to leave, and to this day I thank my younger son, Joel Charles, for getting me out of the hardest work of my life.

The arrival of our child did not, at first, change our lifestyle. Joel was premature and underweight. He had to stay in the hospital for almost a month, and that permitted us to go about business as usual. I scheduled my fact-finding tour of ten midwestern states almost immediately. I decided to use my own car, a 1953 Packard, instead of the state car. I still got mileage expenses. The states to be covered were Iowa, Nebraska, North and South Dakota, Minnesota, Wisconsin, Michigan, Indiana, Illinois, and Ohio. It was to be a whirlwind tour, but I hit it lucky, interviewing three of the state supervisors at a meeting of the North Central Music Educators in Omaha, Nebraska. I took off for Omaha concerned about our baby staying at the hospital (and the additional expense), but at least Kitty could manage in my absence. With that in mind, I proceeded to touch all bases in as short a time as possible. I think I made the capitals of the listed states in less than two weeks and was back when Kitty finally brought the baby home.

My first stop was in Omaha, Nebraska, where I was to stay at the new Sheraton Hotel. The $7.50 a night for a room was a little steep for me, so after conferring with the black doorman, I took a room around the corner at the Rome Hotel for $3. The doorman wanted me to return at the end of his shift. I came back as suggested, and he took me to the employees' locker room about three basements down. We proceeded to have a party with the black employees, all of whom seemed to have a pint of liquor in their lockers. After about two hours of drinking and comparing Iowa to Nebraska for black people, we went out on the town to the most popular black clubs. Wherever there was a band that had a bass fiddle, I sat in. This made me very popular with these doormen, bellhops, and maintenance men of the Sheraton. One would have thought that I had the presidential suite the way they treated me on my return the next day.

Amidst the revelry, I did do some business. Three state supervisors of music were interviewed, and I had pages of notes on their comments. I started off with a standard list of questions and then went wherever the conversation led. I was able to do Nebraska, Iowa, and Ohio in one day.

Shortly after I crossed the border at Yankton, South Dakota, I encountered the biggest snowstorm of my life. It was so bad that I could only see a few feet in front of me. I got down to about ten miles an hour but decided to push on to the next town. At one point, I could only make progress by driving right behind a highway snow plow. A state trooper came by and told me, "Don't leave the car—otherwise we might never find you."

That shook me up, but he added, "The next town is Menno. It's only about four miles, and there's a hotel there."

It took about an hour behind the snowplow, and I almost didn't recognize the town when I got there. The snow was piled so high on one side of the street that I couldn't see the houses behind the pile. Fortunately, the hotel was on the side that I could see. I say hotel with reservations, because the next morning I found out that it was also a jail. There was no one in the building when I arrived at night, so I went back on the street and found one lonely individual. He advised me to go upstairs and take a room and pay in the morning. The room was small and unheated, but there were plenty of blankets on the bed. There was also the standard Gideon Bible on the dresser. When I left the next morning, there was still nobody around, but I saw a sign listing the room rates. I left the two dollars on the desk and still wonder if anybody ever knew I had been there.

The further north I drove toward Bismarck, North Dakota, the more civilized it looked. There were people, cars, and towns. Bismarck is a larger city than Pierre, and the hotel was more like a hotel in the East. I got to thinking about going up to a desk clerk and asking for a room like a real person. I couldn't do that in New York, Philly, or Baltimore, and certainly not in Houston. I was in a part of the country where there were very few blacks. Maybe that was the answer. These people just did not think in terms of segregation.

Further down the road in Saint Cloud I was driving down the main street when I saw a black man on the sidewalk. It hit me that I hadn't seen a black person since Omaha, a distance of more than a thousand miles. I felt homesick and immediately pulled over and parked. It startled the man when I walked up to him and introduced myself. We chatted for only a few minutes, but I left Saint Cloud with the satisfaction of knowing there were some black folks even in this cold country.

After doing business in Saint Paul, Minnesota, the capital, I headed straight for home. I left the business in Michigan and Indiana for a weekend in the near future when there was a meeting of the American Musicological Society at Michigan State University in East Lansing. I got home safely, just before the baby arrived. Kitty and I were back on our routine of night feeding the baby and washing diapers; we could not afford diaper service or disposable diapers. We did get some relief with the arrival of Mrs. Bernice Kinney, Kitty's mother, in Iowa City and the approach of warmer weather.

The thesis went from the outline stage to frequent meetings with my thesis advisor, Dr. Neal Glenn. My days in Iowa City were numbered, and the plan was for me to go back to Nashville in time to get on the payroll for summer school at TSU. I had heard from President Davis that I would be rehired at the Ph.D. minimum salary. We needed the money desperately, what with three youngsters living with us. I was so elated by the word from Nashville that I traded my trusty '53 Packard in for a new '57 Mercury. Then, realizing that Kitty would need transportation, I repurchased the Packard, and we became a two-car family. I used the Packard and left the new car for Kitty's use.

What happened was that I went back to the dealer and said I had a friend who was interested in the car and asked what he would sell it for. When he quoted me a price two hundred dollars lower than what he allowed in trade, I told him, "I am that friend, and I'll take the deal."

Kitty would remain for the summer school and would take care of the kids. With her mother there, she could attend classes. I knew that I would be back in Iowa City at various stages of the thesis project for conferences. We really couldn't move furniture until I found a place to move it to. When I left Iowa City I didn't realize how hard it would be to complete a thesis back home, but away from my family.

I was happy that my association with the tall corn country was coming to an end. I was even happier to get back to Nashville.

# CHAPTER 25

# NASHVILLE AS HOME

*T*he return to Nashville was a happy one, but I was full of apprehension. I had a deadline to meet: The thesis had to be finished and defended by the latter part of July. Not only that, I would have to send in the preliminary draft and, depending on the required revisions, have the final version ready in a matter of about two weeks.

There would be no time for gigs or for leisure. I got a room at my friend and TSU colleague's house on Villa Place in south Nashville, the home of Brenton and Janet Banks. I think of him even now as one of the finest musicians I have ever met. There was one drawback in this living arrangement: his house was a social center for the music faculty and others from TSU. Actually, it was a fine place to work during the day when everyone was at school, but the evenings were another matter. The evening social sessions almost torpedoed my efforts to finish the thesis on time. Most of my close friends in Nashville were in the group that met at Brenton's. They included the Franciscos (Maureen Stovall had married Anceo Francisco); voice teacher Eddie Goins; Chick Chavis and his new bride; Napoleon Johnson, dean of the School of Engineering, and his new bride, Thelma; W. Drury Cox, a drama professor; and assorted others. Most lived on Villa Place, which meant that a party could be on without warning or preparation. This was a very congenial group, and I found them difficult to resist as they welcomed me back to Nashville.

In spite of these pleasurable distractions, I was able to send Kitty the preliminary draft. She typed it and turned it in to my advisor's office in the nick of time. Naturally it had to be entirely rewritten, since this was the first project of this scope and length that I had ever attempted. I had about two weeks to do the job. No parties, no liquid refreshment breaks, no gigs—dawn to later-than-dusk writing did the trick. I turned in the final draft on time. Kitty engaged a professional typist, a guy who had a reputation as a thesis typist. I talked with him frequently by long distance. We agreed that he could correct or change anything that he knew would cause problems. It was the most cost-effective investment I ever made. His price was higher than the rest of the typists', but he was worth it. He typed the 200-page manuscript in two days and personally turned it in to the graduate school office. It's a shame that I can't recall his name, but I remember him gratefully as my insurance policy. Later, when I became the coordinator of graduate studies in music education, I advised any student writing a thesis to pay more and get an "executive" typist.

There followed a few days of relaxation mixed with anxiety. I still had to await the signal from my advisor, Dr. Neal Glenn, as to whether there was to be rejection (and frustration) or a date for my oral defense of the thesis. In less than a week, I got the word that the thesis had passed muster and the "defense" date was set for the next to the last possible day for inclusion in the summer graduation schedule. Soon I was steaming joyfully into Iowa City, eager to be with my family and anticipating the hopeful prospect of a permanent new base for all of us in Nashville.

Dr. Glenn assembled an examining committee made up of himself and three others: Himie Voxman, Albert T. Luper, and Tom Turner, whose field was music theory. I was permitted one additional choice of my own, so I selected Eldon Obrecht, a bassist and professor of applied music. The combined weight of knowledge represented by these gentlemen was frightening to consider. If so inclined, they could unglue me. The three-hour exam seemed like an eternity.

It is hard to realize this on the hot seat, but sometimes the members of the examining committee ask questions designed to impress their colleagues. Dr. Obrecht, the youngest of my inquisitors, asked me such a question. It was a blockbuster, and a cauldron of inner turmoil along with much sweat produced no semblance of an answer. The silence was beginning to be embarrassing when a familiar voice broke the tension. It was Mr. Luper, probably Iowa's toughest and most feared professor. He said, "I don't think the candidate should answer that question. We haven't resolved that question ourselves."

It wasn't exactly downhill from there, but thank God no more bombs of that tonnage were thrown. I don't mean that they lightened up on me, but at least they withheld the overkill ammunition. When the ordeal was finally over, they gave me the good news on the spot: I had passed.

With the members of my family and a few friends, we celebrated not only the "crossing" but the home presence of our newest family member, Joel. A few days later, I headed back to Nashville a happy man, looking forward to the future. Even though I was alone, I knew it would only be a short while before we would be reunited in Nashville, the city of our destiny.

President Walter Davis greeted me on my return to Tennessee State with a note. I had been rehired and promoted to full professor. Since I resigned my position in 1955 in order to cash in my retirement contribution, Dr. Davis was under no obligation to take me back. The Ph.D. minimum salary was $7,200 a year. Some of the guys who had graduated with me at Iowa wrote me notes asking me about the job prospects at TSU, which was understandable since many eventually took jobs at $4,500.

I set out immediately to find a house for rent. We had been cooped up for two years in an extremely limited space, and I felt that nothing but a fairly large house would do. I found one by the Cumberland River on Buena Vista Pike. It had four bedrooms and a three-car garage, which actually was a hangar for a small plane. There was one major drawback: it was a frame house so loosely constructed that we could feel wind direction changes inside the living room. But it was a house, and when I told Kitty about it, she was ecstatic. I tried to buy it, but could only get a 60 percent loan. I could not afford the down payment. That turned out to be a stroke of luck, since it would have taken the equivalent of the purchase price to insulate and tighten up the building.

Kitty came to Nashville with all three children after her summer session was over. Her mother returned to Baltimore from Iowa City, so we would have to deal with infant and child care ourselves. We finally found an elderly black woman who had done this for white people only, but we had a sociological problem dealing with her. Her list of what she would not do far exceeded the list of what she would do. I had to pick her up every morning and return her to her South Nashville home every evening. Ironically, I passed contingents of black women waiting for the bus to go to day-work in white neighborhoods. We treated the situation with dignity, care, and respect and muddled through our reintroduction to Nashville.

The music department had moved from the temporary buildings on the south side of the campus to the old "red" hall. The only
thing to be said for it was that we had more space. The walls were
thin, and we could hear everybody. The faculty was pretty congenial,
for the most part, and we developed some good social habits. Almost
everybody brought a bag lunch, and often we convened in my office.
We called this group the "lunch bunch." Very quickly, I was back in
my routine almost as if I had never left.

There had been some changes in our staff during my absence.
The marching band had achieved such national acclaim that Frank
Greer was authorized to hire two assistants to replace Anceo Fran-
cisco, who left suddenly to return to Oklahoma. Francisco took his
wife, Maureen Stovall, with him, and that broke up our string quartet.
It did a lot to indicate the value of Francisco that it took two guys to
replace him. But what a pair! Both Benjamin Butler and Edward
Louis Smith were rated at the top of their graduate classes at the
University of Michigan. Both were former TSU band members. Ed
Smith had been the first student in our graduate program back in
1952. He was also a remarkable trumpeter (jazz and classical), probably the best we ever had. Ben Butler was a remarkable clarinetist and
student as an undergraduate. I could never figure out how he did it.
The marching band practiced from four to seven hours a day during
football season, yet Butler never missed an academic assignment and
usually made the dean's list. If that was not enough, it seemed he
never missed a social assignment. Between football game shows and
the young ladies on campus, I wondered when he found the time to
study. Yet he was always an *A* student in my classes. I must add that
most of the music students would not characterize me as an easy prof.
Later, after Greer's retirement, Butler would prove to be an excellent
organizer and administrator. He went on to build a very competitive
program at Texas Southern in Houston.

In the early sixties, Butler bolstered our piano staff with four
brilliant pianists. We added Don Barrett, who got his master's from
Oberlin College in Ohio. He was what I would call a serious perfectionist. Carol Stone also contributed brilliance to that staff. Charlene
Harb McDonald came on to add more luster, as did Patsy Dugan.
When you consider that we already had E. C. Lewis, John Sharpe,
and Marie Brooks Strange, I'd say we could compete favorably with
any other college piano staff in the state. The community and the
general public didn't know this because we were more or less confined to the campus, not traveling as solo recitalists. Some did have

engagements with symphony orchestras, notably McDonald and Stone. All were respected, and their students attest to their effectiveness.

We even got some adjunct help from William ("Bill") Pursell, an accomplished pianist and composer. He would later play a part with me in integrating the Nashville jazz scene. Bill had a master's from Eastman and played jazz reminiscent of Oscar Peterson or even Art Tatum. Also, one of our own students came back to us as an instructor in piano. She was Charlotte Scott, who had developed a fine choir in Columbia, Tennessee, after graduate school at the University of Cincinnati. It was an exciting time for me; never had I been associated with so many excellent pianists.

In the early sixties, after the previous departure of our second violinist, Maureen Stovall, we lost our first violinist, Brenton Banks, to Los Angeles. It meant that the entire string instrument responsibilities would fall on me. Banks and Stovall had begun the string ensemble. The group was made up from the few people in the university who had participated in such a program in high school. There were never more than four or five of these. The rest came from some fine musicians who had been exposed to our string class. The string class was at most a one-year experience, so we had some one-year string players on the concert stage. The results were mixed: we were not "I Musici," but the tunes we played were recognizable.

Before Banks left for Los Angeles, he was doing a significant number of recording sessions. However, he found time for us to organize a string quartet. We couldn't call it the TSU faculty quartet because Banks got two other session musicians (both white) to play with us. We had Byron Bach on cello and Cecil Brower on second violin. I held down the viola spot. We called it the Nashville Quartet and played many of the gigs that the faculty would have played. We experimented and had a lot of fun rehearsing. Cecil had a tenor violine, which was larger and lower in range than a viola. I wrote several arrangements to make use of this new and distinctive sound. One of the arrangements was of Bach's "Art of Fugue." The tenor violine made it possible. I would like to relive those days because I learned a lot about ensemble playing from these virtuosi. Unfortunately, the total community knew very little of our efforts.

With Banks and Stovall gone, I plunged into the development of what I hoped would be a credible string ensemble. With help from some remarkable students, notably two bassists, Charles Dungey and Edward Moon, we would, on rare occasions, come close. We had one basic problem aside from the shortage of real string players: finding suitable rehearsal time. We were not an established group like the marching band or the choir, whose members knew in advance the rehearsal traditions and would fit themselves into the schedule. The history and prestige of those organizations demanded compliance by the student. Not only were we new but about half of our "real" string players came from areas outside of music. Some of our better players were from the School of Engineering. This is as it should have been, and I was glad to have them—even if it caused scheduling nightmares. We sometimes had key rehearsals without the viola section or the second violin section. Problems of balance prevailed, and we didn't know how we sounded until we got up on the concert stage. It peeved me that some of our colleagues who heard all our unbalanced rehearsals managed to skip all our occasionally triumphant concerts.

Eventually, I was able to add some personnel to the ensemble from outside the institution, picking up some young-looking, fine players from the Nashville Symphony or from other colleges. Everybody did it. Peabody College had a TSU trumpeter as their principal trumpet player without listing his college affiliation on the program.

Our aggregation played a mixed program, with the first half geared to classical music and the second geared to what I would call classical jazz. We would attempt some "top 40" things, but as strings were not sympathetic to the "top 40" sound, we held it to a minimum. We had to deal with the musical tastes of young black males and females, but I have always felt that taste, or lack of it, could be shaped by exposure to "good" music, whether it be classical or jazz. I have to admit that our string ensemble was not the most popular drawing card among black youth. I saw that the prevailing musical taste was in favor of "soul music," and worse, it was polarized against "European" music. I found that the symphonies, notably Mozart's G Minor, challenged our young players, but at the same time they reacted most enthusiastically to a good arrangement of a popular jazz tune. Our arrangement of the Beatles' "Eleanor Rigby" by a symphony colleague, Ken Krause, usually met with a good reception. In other words, we had to walk a fairly tight rope in order to gain acceptance in a predominantly black university. We met with a mixed bag of success, but our popularity was steadily increasing as we went along.

Tennessee State has a tradition of good to great bass players. Beginning with Jimmy Blanton, Duke Ellington's great foil of the forties, we had a line of bassists who eventually became the basis (no pun intended) of our developing string ensemble. I'm not pointing to myself as a great teacher because most of these people were good before they enrolled at State. We were the lucky recipients of some great talent. The symphony realized this in the seventies when three of the eight members of the bass section were Tennessee State students. They were Charles Dungey, Joe Phea, and Ed Moon. With such talent in school at the same time, we came up with the idea of forming a bass quartet. Ed Moon was the prime mover of the idea. Lady Luck shined on us, this time in the form of a lady. Deborah Parrish, a young math major, was our fourth bassist for the quartet. She was a bright young lady who, when I offered her a work-aid scholarship for the string ensemble, turned it down. She said, "State is a school for dummies."

I pointed out to her that since her family was living in public housing, it was unlikely she would be able to afford any other college. Luckily she enrolled, and as a math major she overcame her biased opinion of the caliber of Tennessee State students and faculty.

I think the early 1970s were my most satisfying years at State. I was offered the bass teaching job at several other area universities. That was ironic because by this time I was playing viola in the symphony and scaling down bass gigs for myself. Actually, I was looking at a younger generation of bass players, who were capable of doing everything—or more than I ever did—on bass.

With the ascendancy of "soul music" and "top 40" in the cultural life of black students on black college campuses, a person who played a string instrument in high school would ordinarily deny it. However, some who had a strong experience in high school were exceptions. We had such a person in Cheryl Pillow, who was our concert mistress for several years. Not only could she play violin well, but she was pretty and shapely. She was more a Dallas cowgirl prototype than one who was conversant with Mozart symphonies. One guy actually said to me, "She doesn't look like the violin type."

I told him, "Not all lady symphonic string players look like Gravel Gertie." Actually, most of our ensemble at any given time was female. There would usually be four or five guys standing outside the door of our rehearsal room waiting for our rehearsal to end. They weren't there for the music.

All was not peaches and cream, however. On one occasion, Cheryl, who had led us through all the rehearsals for our big spring concert, didn't show for the big event. She had gone back to the dormitory for a nap and didn't wake up until the concert was over. The show went on, but it was not as good as it could have been with her strong leadership. Fortunately, it never happened again, and since she was our top violinist, I had to forgive her.

I eventually got a violin student who was good enough to have won a scholarship to any of the leading string teaching institutions if she so desired, to schools that had conservatory-trained violinists for teachers. Jo Ann Sweeney posed a terrific problem for me in that I had to prepare for every lesson in order to keep her at a challenging level. I felt like Rimsky-Korsakov when he was designated to teach orchestration at the new Saint Petersburg Conservatory in Leningrad. He said he had to work like hell to stay one day ahead of his students. We tried pieces like Kreisler's "Praeludium and Allegro," which was loaded with such technical difficulties as double, triple, and quadruple stops. In short, I learned more about violin technique getting ready for Jo Ann than I had learned up to that point. Keep in mind that I had never had any serious, formal training on violin. I feel proud that we were able to present a creditable recital, one beyond the level that any previous TSU student had done.

Our curriculum at TSU called for me to be a specialist in violin, viola, cello, and bass—far more than I had mastered. (In fact, it's very unlikely that anybody could master all four instruments.) Having played the viola and the bass professionally, I would have to acknowledge that my weakest area was the cello, followed closely by the violin. Fortunately, we had very few advanced cello majors and not many more serious violin students. When we got them, I tried to face the situation honestly and arranged scholarships for them with specialist teachers around town. Both my department heads were furious about this, feeling I should handle the situation completely. However, I have always felt that what was in the best interest of the student should prevail. I didn't want to be responsible for holding anybody back or down to my limitation.

A few more faculty and students stand out strongly in my memory of those years. Sally Craighead is one of them. Without her enthusiasm, hard work, and public relations, the strong ensemble would not have survived. Sally played the viola as a second instrument and became a near-professional. She was a horn player in the band. I was especially pleased that she followed my route (brass major to strings) and eventually became a member of the Chattanooga Symphony. Rick Maness was our resident "loyal white person." He came to us from the school of business, and because he played bass on the road with Chuck Mangione, he was not always with us in concert. However, he supported us in every way he could. Rick brought us music arrangements from the professional world as well as some white students on campus who had string experience. His mature professionalism really helped us.

Another brilliant professional bassist was Jerome Hunter from Philadelphia. He reminded me of Charles Mingus in both appearance and playing style. Another loyal white person was Mike Doster, who was a bulwark in our ensemble and studied bass with me. I had a lot of fun teaching him. I would get on the piano and "comp" the chords of a few jazz classics while he tried various bass lines. He is now the regular bassist with B. B. King.

Our bass quartet was bottom heavy, and we tried to diffuse the situation by having some of them play cello. Ed Moon wound up playing a creditable second violin. We would have needed a couple dozen more upper strings (violin and viola) to balance the sound. Alas! It was never in the cards, so we went with what we had.

Our biggest concert when we had Dr. Thor Johnson, conductor of the Nashville Symphony, as the guest conductor and the university choir of around one hundred voices to do Mendelssohn's Second Symphony. That one work was the entire program. It was known as the "Hymn of Praise," although it actually was a cantata symphony. We only did selections from the symphony, and that took over an hour. I used the musicians' union trust fund to hire some extra string players, mostly violins, violas, and celli. We didn't need any basses. We did get primarily the younger looking players from the Nashville Symphony and took care that our own students maintained the majority of each section.

Dr. Lewis found the money to pay for one rehearsal. Dr. Johnson wrote a check for another rehearsal. The third joint rehearsal was donated in personal friendship by these union musicians. The results were truly impressive. The choir, prepared by Mr. Lusk, the regular director, was attention-getting. Thor Johnson was very pleased and gave us an intensive workout with what obviously was a work close to his heart. We had some tense moments in rehearsal as some of our younger players were intimidated by the technical skills of the symphony people. Some threatened to quit, saying we were out of their league. I had to draw on all of my people skills to convince and encourage them to hang in and learn. Everybody made it to the concert stage, and the total performance, in my opinion, was quite good. In a little speech at the end of the concert, Johnson said, "This shows what we all can do with a little help."

I felt somewhat vindicated in opposing the TSU credo of "We do it all ourselves and we don't need any help from whitey."

Somewhere in the blur of the early sixties the music department passed two milestones. We got our new building—complete with a recital hall and offices/studios for everybody. I have to thank the impressive success of the marching band for these new facilities. Very few of the legislators or board of regents visited the academic classes or heard the string ensemble. The marching band under the direction of F. T. Greer had achieved a national reputation, and the saying was, "We have to have a place for that fine band to rehearse." The entire department received greatly improved facilities, and I was not jealous but grateful as, I believe, was everybody else who had been with the department through our various "hideaway" locations.

The other milestone was our admittance to the National Association of Schools of Music, a prestigious association with rigid standards. I believe that Howard University in Washington, D.C., was the first black member at the time of our application. I showed Dr. Lewis some materials about the NASM, and we decided to go for it. We had nothing to lose, and we might even gain some recognition and respect in our own community. The university even appropriated some extra funds to meet the rigorous standards of the NASM. We were fortunate in having Dr. C. B. Hunt of Peabody College and a past president of the NASM as our advisor. He pointed us in the right direction and kept us apprised of political situations with the examiners.

Speaking of politics, it should be noted that the University of Tennessee at Knoxville and TSU were admitted to NASM at the same time. UTK had applied a couple of years before we did, and they had some problems with what were, in effect, two departments of music. It took the extra years to straighten out a battle royal. We were worried that the politics of that situation might defer our entry. However, since we were ready, we were admitted—and that happened to coincide with the admittance of UTK. Fortunately, all my apprehension was for nothing.

A curious thing happened to the department in the mid-sixties. Our respected department head resigned to become dean of the faculty at Alabama State. We found out later that E. C. Lewis had not actually resigned but had an arrangement with both institutions, Alabama and TSU.

I was approached with the idea of becoming the new department head. I may have been the choice of a majority of the music faculty, but when Dr. Malcolm Williams, dean of the School of Education, called us together and announced that F. T. Greer would be the new department head, I was relieved. I was more of an idea man than an administrator. Greer was perfect for the job and deserved it on the strength of his administration of one of the more successful band programs in the country. I love to teach and create and would have been most unhappy at the paper-shuffling games necessary at colleges.

I had only one regret—when Greer evaluated me as an "average" Ph.D. Average or not, I was glad not to be the department head.

# CHAPTER 26

# AND ALL THAT JAZZ

**A**midst all the departmental ferment following my return from Iowa, the gig scene flourished—if not in money, in connections with some extraordinary musicians. Andy Goodrich, a TSU graduate and one of the finest alto saxophone players I have heard, formed a jazz quartet. Brenton Banks, a faculty member and a superb musician, was our pianist and sometime violin soloist. I remember a gig where the piano was a minor third low. Instead of having everybody else play in a key a minor third lower, Brenton transposed his own playing a minor third higher. It meant that while we were playing in B-flat, Brenton played in D-flat, a key with more flats. I know very few musicians who could pull that off. We also had Morris Palmer, who may have been the finest jazz drummer east of the Mississippi and south of the Mason-Dixon line.

Morris was a driving metronome who inspired top play and interaction. He only tolerated the best and was uncompromising in his relationships with others who dared play with him. Everything had to be just right, and for his sometimes unsubtle reactions we referred to him as "cantankerous." Morris was our vocalist and could conceivably have made it as a singer. For me it was a privilege to play with these guys, and I had to outdo myself on several occasions to keep up. We were later joined by Louis Smith on trumpet, making us a quintet. Louis had just come back from New York and a stint with Horace Silver, an exponent of the post-bop progressive style of jazz. I believe our quartet/quintet should have been recorded. We were that good.

We didn't work very often, choosing instead to hold out for our price. It took time for us to be known. But we did come to be known and respected by Nashville area musicians, black and white, long before the general public caught on. Another factor was that jazz was fading as the popular music of the masses. The groups that played contemporary rock had taken over the young people and the various clubs. The shift was quite devastating for jazz musicians in this town, which was already saturated with country music. There were few places where we could work and be appreciated. There were no integrated groups in Nashville in the late fifties and early sixties. Blacks and whites jammed together but seldom played a pay gig together. The next few years would be dramatic in integration but would never get to what I would call a normal balance based on ability. Even now, the black groups tend to be all black and the white ones all white. I do occasionally see a token "other"—just enough to remind me that musicians as a class are usually more liberal than the general public.

The Goodrich quartet played mostly what I would call elite gigs. These were gigs for the jazz *aficionados* or the musically literate. Then one day I received a call that would change my life. Buddy Harman, a well-known white drummer, wanted to know if I would like to play at the Carousel in Printers Alley—with a white group that I didn't know. They turned out to be a fantastic group. Buddy Harman was the king of country music drummers. He was, at that time, the house drummer at the Grand Ole Opry, which was very near Printers Alley. As I found out, Buddy could swing with the best of the jazz drummers. He must have gotten my name from the musicians' union because I didn't know him. Hank Garland was the featured guitarist and band leader. A major-league jazz guitarist, he featured flying tempos and dazzling technique. To play with Hank, all his sidemen had to work on security and control. In other words, we couldn't let those sizzling tempos get away from us. Bill Pursell, our pianist, was up to it all the way. He had the technique of a classical pianist, brought from the Eastman School of Music and Peabody Conservatory.

Pursell was from California and had a liberal attitude on racial equality. This would become increasingly important in the development of our continuing friendship. At the time we were on the verge of the civil rights revolution, and it was important for me to have a close friend like Bill in this all-white situation. I had played with all-white groups in the North and Midwest, but never in the South. As a matter of fact, our quartet members were great in their attitude toward one another and their approach to the public. I was just one of the guys.

Printers Alley was what the name implies, an alley in downtown Nashville. The printers were no longer there, but the alley contained several nightclubs in its three-block run. Probably the most famous club was the Carousel, run by the well-known Jimmy Hyde. Nashville had no liquor-by-the-drink then, so all these clubs were illegal. They got around this by labeling every bottle of liquor with somebody's name. Theoretically, the customer was drinking his own bottle and paying only for service and storage. They sold me drinks poured from a bottle "belonging" to somebody I had never met. The prices were regular bar prices per drink. I also noticed that every Saturday night near midnight we were visited by a representative of Nashville's finest. Always it was a ranking officer, and the rank was geared to the prestige of the club. The Carousel never got less than a captain. I learned later that some of the other clubs were havens for gambling and bookmaking—not what the original printers had in mind. More about this unfolds when I relate my experience with the all-black Andy Goodrich quartet.

A sociological point should be noted in reference to a black performer in an all-white situation. We blacks are supposed to be sensational. We cringe when we hear the exhortation, "Get hot." Also, we are supposed to be tireless, that is, never a dull moment—which translates to no intermission. People would come into the Carousel during the intermission and walk over to me and ask, "When is the band going to start?"

I could be sitting at a table with Bill Pursell and Buddy Harman, but they would always approach me. Hank Garland would come to gig after his stint at the Grand Ole Opry and proceed to eat dinner, which always made us late starting. Again, I would be the focal point of questions about the quartet's actions. I would refer the questions to Hank, our leader. For some reason, very few interrupted Hank's dinner with the same question. Club owners had the notion that blacks would work longer and harder for less money. I noticed there was never a question of money or playing time when the group was headed by a white and consisted primarily of white players.

The Carousel was the headquarters for those myriads of frustrated country music sidemen who had an inclination for jazz. A lot of them sat in with us, and I was impressed that there were quite a few real jazz musicians. Some of these guys could really play, and I got the feeling that the Carousel was their outlet for some serious jazz expression.

There were, however, some flies in the ointment. One night

when the place was crowded, one of these country music musicians (complete with cowboy hat) yelled across the room, "Can y'all play the nigger blues?"

I was shocked and could not think what to do next. I finally got up and left the bandstand. The other members of the quartet were shocked, too, but finally Bill Pursell, our California pianist, grasped the situation and my hurt. He walked over to the culprit and explained to him the quartet's concern for their black colleague. The cat immediately came over to me and apologized. He said, "That's what we always called them."

I wasn't satisfied with that but decided to accept his apology. I returned to the bandstand with our country music friend, and he brought his guitar and sat in while we played a slow blues in B flat. That guy must have had some black blood or at least black experiences to play the way he played. We finished the gig with no further incidents.

Hank Garland's stint at the Carousel eventually came to an end. Also, his regular bassist, Chuck Sanders, had just returned from the service. This meant we both could resegregate. I worked several gigs with white groups after that, but none as a regular. I returned to my favorite group of guys. We went under several names, depending on who got the gig. We were equals, and there would have been a W. O. Smith quartet if I had gotten an engagement. That was not to be. Andy Goodrich got most of the gigs, and we were best known as the Andy Goodrich quartet. Brenton Banks and Louis Smith also landed a few and thus got top billing.

As a quintet we played the Nashville Jazz Festival and became established as the leading jazz group in town, black or white. We played primarily college gigs such as Vanderbilt, Peabody, and Sewanee. Thus, we came to be well recognized by young whites—but not by young blacks. We were prophets without honor at home. We did get a little bit of honor at a gig we played on Sunday afternoons at Brown's Hotel Dinner Club. This was really a restaurant on Jefferson Street across from Fisk University. Here we added Les Spann, a flutist and guitarist. Spann was with the Tennessee State marching band and could really play some up-to-date jazz on both guitar and flute. I remember advising him to go on to New York and get it out of his system. I think Spann was a senior, and as it turned out, that was probably bad advice.

A number of Nashville's leading black jazz artists sat in with us on those Sundays. Consequently, it turned out to be a big occasion for our dwindling jazz fans.

Some of the gigs we played were for Vanderbilt fraternities. One was in a fraternity house living room decked with sand and beach tables. This was supposed to be a beach party. The young ladies either had on bikinis or shorts and halters. The guys were walking around, usually carrying a quart of bourbon. There would be a quart on the piano for the band. This was lucky for me as everybody in the group had some development of ulcers, leaving me as the only guy who could touch the stuff. I solved the "finish the gig" law by allotting myself one drink an hour on the hour. Brenton Banks served as my monitor. He was adamant and saw to it that I didn't cheat. The record will show that I finished every gig in shape.

The Goodrich quartet became restless and frustrated with the few gigs we were getting in that heyday of pop music in the sixties. Where could we find jazz fans? The place that came to mind was Printers Alley. The only thing wrong with that area was that it was rigidly segregated. No black groups worked there. I had worked there with Hank Garland's group, and Morris Palmer, our drummer, had filled in for Buddy Harman on occasion. Morris told me later that the police had conspired with the club owners not to have any more mixed bands. We decided one night to go down to the Alley with instruments and see if we could give a free audition. Using this technique, we got to play in three or four clubs. What club owner could resist free music? We actually set up in the middle of the dance floor in one club because a band already had set up on the stage, and we got a feeler for a gig at that same club. I believe the band on the stand was closing that week. It was the Ebony Club, and it's ironic to think they were about to be christened with their first black group. We were armed with union cards from Local 257, and they actually helped us in negotiating the contract. The police lightened up since their main objection was to mixed groups. We had good crowds, and the white jazz musicians were there every night trying to sit in with us. Our reputation spread to the point that we were offered gigs by other clubs in and around the Alley. Actually, our first move after our contract expired was right next door to a club called the Black Poodle.

The Black Poodle was somewhat more posh than the Ebony. Prices were higher, and the crowd was smaller. There were no black customers except for some well-known black musicians who came there for the purpose of sitting in with us. For this gig we had ex-

*The Brenton Banks/Andy Goodrich quartet after a gig in Nashville's Printers' Alley in about 1960.* From left: *pianist Banks, drummer Morris Palmer, alto sax player Goodrich, and bassist W. O. Smith.*

panded to a quintet by adding Louis Smith, the outstanding trumpeter. We were then the Andy Goodrich Quintet since he got the gig. Every night was a romp. The standard of play was as good as Fifty-second Street in New York at its best. We experimented and introduced something new every weekend. We rarely mingled with the customers unless we received a specific invitation. The police knew us as the Black Poodle band and didn't bother us on the street. We were visited nightly by the town's leading white jazz musicians, including Hank Garland, Buddy Harman, Bill Pursell, Chet Atkins, Dick Cotten, and the truly amazing Tupper Saussy. There was never a dull moment, and on occasion we had to clear the stand so we could play our own arrangements unimpeded.

Some weekends we had a featured out-of-town singer like Paula Webster from Chicago. She had a frontline quality such that one hit record would make her nationally famous. Our intermission room had about ten phones in it, and the manager instructed us to use the one specifically marked "local." We guessed that the club was a front for gambling or bookmaking. That explained why with five pieces we were the largest band in the Alley. It also explained why we were so promptly paid even after a few bad nights of poor attendance. These episodes made me realize how lucky I was to be associated with musicians of this calibre. I would never miss New York or experience Los Angeles. I found what I wanted in Nashville.

I have mentioned the phenomenal Tupper Saussy: the name was enough to make you take notice. Tupper was a Vanderbilt student who had come from Florida and had been to The University of the South in Sewanee, Tennessee. He was well connected with the rich Belle Meade crowd and a very unlikely candidate for jazz piano. However, he was a good pianist, except for his lack of control and tonal memory. He had the technique and the style to play anything, but it would get out of hand. We, the rhythm section, had to follow him in his little out-of-control escapades. This wasn't so bad because he could be impressive like Art Tatum on occasion.

The quartet played Tupper's wedding party when he married Lola Hahn in Belle Meade. It was a Nashville society wedding, and the party was around the swimming pool on the estate. We drove about a block along a road lined with Japanese lanterns until we reached the beach house, which had male and female dressing rooms on the flanks and a bandstand in the middle. We set up station and began playing when we noticed that as the guests came in their evening finery they were dumped unceremoniously into the pool. After a few splashes of this nature, the Goodrich quintet prepared to defend their position. We won—nobody in our group got dumped—but I was glad to leave in one dry piece.

Tupper and his group of cronies would come by my house on Villa Place in South Nashville. They would drive up in their various sports cars bringing beer and chatting a little while on the porch. It was almost as if I weren't there: they would gossip and discuss some "black" subjects that were not ordinarily within my range to hear. It seemed that most of Tupper's group were graduates of Nashville's Montgomery Bell Academy, a distinguished southern prep school for whites. School integration was a hot topic. We were waxing along heavily on the topic when I suddenly said, "I wish you guys could help me get my son Jay a scholarship to MBA."

That did it. Within five minutes all the visitors were gone. There evidently was something about the southern mystique that I would never be a party to. Tupper went on to become an advertising executive and a symphony composer. I particularly remember his orchestral piece, "House Ghosts," commissioned by the Nashville Symphony. When last heard from, Tupper was in hiding from the Internal Revenue Service for some obscure disagreement over money. However, I see him at least once a year at some occasion where he unexpectedly turns up. I will not disclose the location out of loyalty to Tupper. I'd like to see him under less tenuous circumstances. Perhaps later.

Our next gig was at a club on the second floor of an auto dealer's office building at Fourteenth and Broadway, off the beaten track of clubs. It was special to a group of night people whom I had never seen before. The Louis Smith quintet was at another one of these "membership" watering holes. I could smell it—we would be raided! At the time, there were special groups of police anti-crime units such as Morgan's Raiders and Jett's Raiders. These motorcycle units terrorized primarily blacks in north and south Nashville.

My apprehension proved accurate shortly before midnight. Strangely enough, somebody must have been warned that Jett's Raiders were on the way because we were prepared when they roared in. We were debating whether to split the gig when the manager told us to stick around, "We'll be back in business in forty-five minutes."

The police confiscated all visible liquor bottles and arrested a barmaid, the bartender, the manager, and about eight customers. Everybody arrested was back in forty-five minutes as the courthouse was nearby. New whiskey appeared by the cab load, and business went on as usual. I don't know if there was a tacit agreement not to arrest the band, but I was greatly relieved. We played inspired music that night and became a favorite of the crowd. I have never heard Louis Smith, our leader for the occasion, play better.

Brenton Banks, our regular pianist, was beginning to crash the recording establishment on Music Row. We brought in Leonard Morton as his sometime replacement. Leonard, who would soon be the music coordinator of Metro schools, was a competent substitute. He could play everything we played with terrific drive and swing. Brother Morton would figure in a concert that was significant in our development. John Hunt, a local trumpeter who made good with Ray Charles, was phased in as a substitute for Louis Smith. Hunt had a peculiar style of his own, but he could play with dazzling techniques and drive.

Three evenings of modern jazz at the Circle Theatre constituted our highest recognition by the cultural elite of Nashville. We were recognized by the city's leading theatre group as the best in jazz.

*Kitty Smith* (center) *with band leader Cab Calloway and his wife at the Smith home in Nashville in the 1970s.*

The Circle Theatre really was a circle, with the stage in a smaller circle in the middle. I had never played in an indoor situation with people all around me. I remember a stadium or so, but nothing as intimate as this. We all tried to outdo ourselves, and the place was packed all three nights. Some of our pure jazz fans from the black community came over and alleviated our "homesickness."

With these three nights of concerts, we had reached the upper echelons of the Nashville cultural establishment. It is to be remembered also that all of us were past our youth and would be considered part of the cultural establishment. My feeling is that jazz is no longer a young man's game but a playground for us old men and women. Look at Dizzy Gillespie, Sarah Vaughan, and the Preservation Five—who all went into their seventies and eighties with verve and style. For us, those Circle Theatre concerts kept us alive.

Somewhere in the middle of the sixties somebody at Tennessee

State had the idea of really celebrating a homecoming. They wanted to bring back to the campus some of Tennessee State's jazz greats in one grand bash of a concert. They were successful in getting James Cleveland, the great jazz trombonist; Louis Smith, our former colleague now in Michigan; Sonny Turner, a former collegian trumpeter now in Chicago; and a Ray Charles trombonist graduate of TSU whose name escapes me. There were others, including Leonard Morton, who took over on piano for Brenton Banks. Leonard distinguished himself on this session as we hit a groove that prevailed all afternoon.

Actually, Andy Goodrich and Leonard quarterbacked the entire bash. The regular quartet was the foundation for the "jam" numbers. Morris Palmer, our drummer, would not allow an inferior drummer near his drum set. There were no bass players of reputation around, so I had to play the entire set without relief. This meant as many as twenty-five choruses of a fast number to accommodate all the horn players. Remember that all these guys were trying to impress home audiences; five or six choruses were practically required.

The great treat for us in this concert was the number of undergraduates who turned out. The affair was in the A Auditorium, and a standing-room-only crowd was on hand. That over half of the crowd were young jazz enthusiasts was heartening in that day of King Hard Rock. We were known all over town but not even recognized at TSU except by a few older jazz fans. E. C. Lewis, our department head, was one of these. He did us the great service of taping the entire proceedings, and some of those tapes sound unbelievable today. The atmosphere was explosive, with even the younger fans cheering on each soloist that they knew. Our problem was mainly what to play for this mixed audience. We were actually cheered when we left the stage at intermission and at the end. I kept hoping we would try it again. But, alas, it was never to be.

We had to accommodate some of our featured soloists, like Jimmy Cleveland, with his favorite show-off piece. This was no problem as the guys on stage were up to date in modern jazz. We featured such numbers as "Cherokee," which had become Andy Goodrich's "Embryo." My favorite was a real groove rendition of "Bye, Bye, Blackbird." Louis was fabulous on trumpet on this one. The rhythm section, if I may say so myself, was cooking like a nationally known and recorded section. I let myself go and plunged right into the music. I was oblivious of all but the beat and the music itself. Sonny Turner, our irrepressible Chicago trumpeter, introduced the "tag" to the program. The tag is an extension of the original out-phrase of a tune. Beethoven himself set the record with some 243 bars of music at the end of one of his symphonies. We had a lot of fun with these tags, with each soloist using his creativity to outdo the others. We finished the concert in a rising crescendo of excitement. Though I was physically drained, I felt less tired than spiritually renewed. At least we got some respect from home. The rest of white Nashville knew it already, but now some of our own folks knew it. That alone made this a key concert in our development scheme.

Toward the end of the sixties and possibly into the seventies, we settled back into our usual groove of a few gigs a month. The quartet played mostly in country clubs and area white colleges. A group of interracial jazz fans had organized a "friends of jazz" club that met in a loft on West End Avenue (or was it on Church Street?). These were important firsts for Nashville blacks and whites meeting downtown for an evening of conviviality. I attended some of the meetings and knew who were our friends and fans. They would sponsor a little session for some of the meetings, and these would be the most successful. Some of the residue from that original group of fans got together to establish the more formal Tennessee Jazz and Blues Society. Fred Cloud, director of the Metro Human Relations Commission in Nashville, was instrumental in both groups. Bruce Davidson and Brad McEwen were two newer guys with credentials in the recording industry and were the ramrods in the Society. No doubt I am overlooking many other key individuals, but at this late date this is the best I can do. What they did do was to bring jazz to the public mind. One of their first promotions was the Cannonball Adderley Quartet concert at War Memorial Auditorium. The Andy Goodrich Quintet was greatly flattered to be asked to cohost the concert. We got equal billing with Cannonball, which meant that we were considered a "draw" in our hometown.

The place was packed, and we had a true cross-section from Nashville. We had the rock-and-roll younger types all the way to the cultural elites of symphony and jazz. It was fabulous entertainment. Adderley and his troupe were able to bridge the gap with their somewhat commercial modern jazz all the way into some provocative and esoteric contemporary jazz.

We went on first, and the set was rather tentative as we had to work out the feel of the crowd. We were successful—the crowd cheered on their local protagonists, especially Andy, the saxophonist, in anticipation of competition by the outsider Cannonball. The Adderleys were great, especially in their dialogues introducing each tune. I was impressed with the mood they were able to set for each piece. The dialogues reminded me of witness day at a Primitive Baptist black church.

Trying to extend the sophisticated limits of traditional jazz, we played mostly jazz standards. Cannonball Adderley did that, too, but he added the dimension of popularization. It may sound simple, but listening to what he was doing revealed exploration and adventure.

Comments floating around during the concert mostly were of the "Gee, those old guys can play" variety. I was flattered and realized that all of us were at our midcentury mark or older. I may have been the oldest in the group. That we could produce energy enough to invigorate the crowd was truly amazing. And that wonderful crowd responded beautifully. It was to be our high mark in Nashville public presentations. We had everything from media coverage to street hype. We were known, recognized, and—even better—respected in our own community. What else is there but national recognition?

I foresaw that in this country music capital genuine recognition for jazz would always be limited. We got it on the streets and the institutions, but not in the commercial recording studio. With our personnel and local popularity, I thought we deserved it, but slowly disillusionment began to set in. I marvel at the freshness of all those New Orleans veteran jazz players. Maybe it's a state of mind. However, we had reached a pinnacle of development with this concert, better late than never. Morris Palmer, Andy Goodrich, Louis Smith, Brenton Banks, and I can talk about it and revel in the past. These concerts were a high-water mark for us. Our community gave, and we tried to give back the best that was in us.

# CHAPTER 27

# NASHVILLE SYMPHONY

One of the few fateful things to happen to me without a phone call was the invitation to join the Nashville Symphony. It happened one night in 1961 at the Carousel, the nightclub in the Alley, during an intermission of the Hank Garland quartet. I was their regular bassist. A gentleman whom I knew only from seeing his picture in the newspaper came up to me. It was Willis Page, the conductor of the Nashville Symphony. Maestro Page had evidently watched me during our last set. It turned out that he was a bass player himself. I guess he liked what he saw and heard. He asked me to come to the War Memorial Building on Saturday afternoon for a tryout.

I was flabbergasted because Brenton Banks had tried out on his own a year earlier and was informed that the orchestra board did not feel it was time to integrate. I noted that Brenton, who had a performance degree from the Cleveland Institute, was more prepared than I to make an audition. I almost chickened out of going into this unknown new world. I had played in college orchestras like NYU, Texas, and Iowa, but this was a professional orchestra, and individual performance standards were higher. I had a sleepless night, but the next day I took my bass down to the auditorium.

John Bright met me as I came into the space outside of the stage door. This was most fortunate. A Metro school teacher, he was the only familiar face that I was to encounter. John was the personnel manager. He alerted me to the audition procedure. I did not have a repertoire of difficult orchestral passages for bass as many of today's auditionists would have, and I had to wing it from whatever Maestro

Page put in front of me. John Bright told me what the orchestra was currently rehearsing and gave me the bass parts to preview. There was nothing there that I had previously played in college. One of the pieces was the "Rite of Spring" ballet by Stravinsky. This piece was really scary in its unconventional use of rhythm. It had unusual alternations of meter signature such as 9/16 and 7/8 time.

Maestro Page met me in his office at intermission. After a cordial greeting, he put the "Rite of Spring" music in front of me and asked me to play some designated passages. I was a fairly good reader, but not that good. I decided to let the sound of the whole orchestra that I remembered from the records guide me. I knew it was hopeless to try to read the music cold. What I did was pure jazz faking, but it came close to what was on the printed page. I was still shocked when Mr. Page asked me to make the next rehearsal and asked Bright to give me a contract.

I am forever grateful to John Bright for his sympathetic preparation and words of assurance, for thus began an eighteen-year association with the symphony that would eventually yield many unforeseen dividends.

That first rehearsal is a blur in my memory, but a few things stand out. First was the presence of another black musician on stage. He was sitting in the principal's chair of the second violins. He was Booker T. Rowe, a young graduate of Temple University in Philadelphia. He was an outstanding violinist, and we became companions in our distinction of being the only two blacks in the symphony. We left rehearsals and concerts together, usually winding up in my home for some food or other refreshment.

Booker was different in that he didn't drink and was younger than I. We had a sort of uncle/nephew relationship. He was more experienced in symphonic music, but I was more experienced with the southern community in which we worked and played. It panned out well for both of us. I was able to integrate him into our social community, and he was able to guide me through the intricacies of symphonic playing. His comments after a concert or rehearsal gave me insights and more commitment to serious orchestral playing. I was learning how to be an effective symphony sideman.

Booker and I were soon joined by James Hall, a Tennessee State undergrad who was a remarkable flutist. Within a few years, we would have as many as seven blacks—more, I believe, than any other major orchestra in the nation. In retrospect, the credit for starting this must go to Maestro Willis Page. I don't think Page was on a social mission but one of using all of Nashville's resources to convene the best orchestra available.

While the integration of the symphony was a big event to me, it was a nonevent to the community and especially to my Tennessee State University home. There was no publicity or news; nobody acted surprised. I wonder about the board who thought that the time was not ripe. The musicians and the conductor were great. I was with a warm and supportive group of people. Even the audiences took the black presence in stride, and most were friendly. I checked to see the extent of black audience participation. It wasn't much, but there were a few black supporters. They were mostly from Meharry and Fisk, one among them being Dr. John Work, the noted composer. There were other regulars; but, all in all, black support for the symphony was extremely small. Through the years I worked to increase this, as did the small elite group of faithful.

I got hardly any recognition from the administration, faculty, and students for what I considered to be an achievement. The exception on campus was the support of my colleagues in the music department and a few deans, notably Dean Williams of the School of Education. Eventually we had five TSU people in the symphony, more than any black institution anywhere. Of this, I was extremely proud.

One of the benefits of being in the symphony was the contact with Nashville's music establishment. I became acquainted with some of the movers and shakers of the community's music scene as well as a whole new collection of musicians. At Tennessee State, we kept ourselves isolated from the total music scene. Racism played a part in this—both ours and theirs. Actually both parties were ignorant of the other. That included me as well as our administration at TSU.

One immediate benefit of my symphony ties was my encounter with Sam Hollingsworth. He was the principal bassist with the symphony, the finest classical bassist I had heard up to that point. He could toss off all of the unplayable passages in symphonic literature, and he could hold steady time. He was the first musician in the symphony to invite me to his house. He was also the only player to challenge Maestro Page (a former major symphony bassist) about a conducting point as to how the bass section should play a passage in the Beethoven Ninth Symphony. The remarkable thing was that Sam was right. I will never forget him and am grateful for his counsel as principal bassist to an insecure novice.

I was fortunate in my allotment of principal section leaders. First after Sam Hollingsworth was George Hofer, who was a real leader. While George did not have Sam's reputation as a bassist, he was just what the bass section needed. He took the time to teach the less experienced section members. George even invited me to his house to give me some pointers on the difficult passages expected of us. On one rehearsal when an extremely difficult passage resulted in the whole section playing softly and hesitantly where we were supposed to be the soloists, George got on the case. He asked me, "What's the matter?"

I replied that I was trying to be unobtrusive. George blurted out, "Be more strusive."

I gave my all and attacked the passage with gusto. I was more "strusive," and so was the whole bass section, and we got away with it. I learned to be more aggressive with difficult passages. It was a gamble, but sometimes it can cover up your inadequacies.

Following Hofer was Ernie Szugyi, a solid rock as a leader. Ernie was a drill sergeant and brooked no nonsense from anybody. He was deadly serious about playing the music to perfection. We underlings of the bass section respected and appreciated his humor and firmness. When I shifted over to the viola section, Ovid Collins was the principal. He was one of the founders of the orchestra and had dedicated himself to its improvement. While he didn't say much to me, all I had to do was to watch him and listen. I found out what real viola playing was all about. I never would have survived an eighteen-year tour of duty with the symphony without these gentlemen's teaching and guidance.

It was a shock to me when the symphony board decided to terminate conductor Willis Page's contract. I attended his farewell party and did heavy damage to his bottle of Scotch. I hated to see him go, especially since he had brought me into the symphony. Our next conductor, Thor Johnson, was a heavyweight among symphony conductors. Dr. Johnson expected the same results as if we were the New York Philharmonic. His rehearsals were always tight and tense. He would give a member the evil eye on the slightest infraction, like a bow moving in the wrong direction.

Johnson was a master at taking us apart musically. We found out that he did not mean it personally but was only concerned with the music. He made us act like a major symphony. Johnson was also interested in developing younger players. As a result of his interest, we had a steady influx of capable kids from the youth symphony.

These kids developed into the backbone of the recording industry in Nashville as well as our present-day symphony. If they got through the Johnson school, these younger players were ready for anything.

He was also concerned with minority participation, both as players and audience. He treated a concert at all-black Pearl High School as if it were at Carnegie Hall. He had seven black symphony members in the peak year. Five of the players were from TSU, and the others were from the youth symphony. I believe there is only one black in the orchestra now; Dewayne Pigg, a locally developed oboeist, has stuck it out through many seasons. I think this pattern—from no blacks to seven to one—has to be a reflection of the racial attitudes of Willis Page, Thor Johnson, and subsequent conductors. Page and Johnson were conscious of the disparity and made an effort to correct it.

It is significant that the black players from the youth symphony had prior development in the Cremona Strings, a group founded and directed by Robert ("Bob") Holmes, a local Metro public school teacher. Kay Roberts, Patricia Green, and William Fitzpatrick were former Cremona Strings players. Bill Fitzpatrick was the principal of the second violin section during his tenure with the Nashville Symphony. Kay Roberts went on to distinguish herself as a violinist and conductor at Yale. Patty Green got into the Nashville recording scene. I consider myself lucky to have been on stage with them and with Dewayne Pigg and the others. Black symphony musicians are a rare breed. They are usually without honor or prestige in their own black community. I am hopeful that the day will come when they get the recognition they deserve from their own and also that the day will come when young black musicians will aspire to careers in symphonic music.

When Leontyne Price came to Nashville during Dr. Johnson's tenure, she was pleased at the number of black musicians on stage. She was so pleased that she commented on it to Dr. Johnson and to me. I guess she took me for the senior black.

Dr. Johnson used to call me into his office and inquire about any black compositions that I knew about. I told him of the availability of John Work's orchestral manuscripts, which I could get from Work's widow. I also told him about Duke Ellington's composition, "The Three Wise Men," which Mercer Ellington told me was one of Duke's last compositions and written specifically for symphony orchestra. Johnson always addressed me as "Doctor." He suggested that I try to get these works so that the Nashville Symphony could play them. In the case of the Ellington composition, it would be a world premiere. I got on the phone immediately and started trying to locate Mercer, Duke's son, and Ruth Ellington, Duke's sister. Meanwhile, I also got several John Work compositions from his widow. The symphony subsequently performed them. Probably the best was Work's musical impression of Haiti. Unfortunately, Dr. Johnson died before we could complete the Ellington project. That was one of the most traumatic periods in my life, visiting our great friend in the hospital and hoping that his cancer was not terminal. It was, and when Ed Moon and I attended the funeral, I found myself feeling that the black community of Nashville had lost a great friend, one who had worked and produced in our behalf.

The Nashville Symphony was, to me, a paragon of efficiency of operation. In the black community, we often saw ourselves as screw-ups functioning on CPT (colored people's time). In the orchestra, we saw and respected white efficiency and punctuality. However, the whole myth was blown one Saturday afternoon when someone had given conflicting signals about that Saturday's rehearsal. Half of us showed up at our regular base, the War Memorial Auditorium. The other half went to the musician's union rehearsal facility about a mile and a half away. I was with the War Memorial group when we realized that we were in the wrong place. I also realized that a rehearsal costs the symphony about twenty-five dollars a minute. After about half an hour, we all rushed over to the union hall. We found the other half of the symphony standing around outside the building. Somebody had forgotten to get the key from the appropriate union official. We all agonized as we waited for our courier to come back with the key. That took another half hour. I calculated that the symphony board had spent about fifteen hundred dollars for this snafu. I realized then that whites are human and that blacks are not the only ones who can come through with mess-ups. It made me feel better, although I would have died inside if by some circumstance I had been late for a rehearsal or concert. I was relieved in this instance that I had not been the one to mess up. Fortunately, it never happened to me. I went through eighteen years without a lateness or an absence. I was free to be punctual through disciplining myself not to let anything interfere with this program. Lateness and absences are a state of mind.

Before one of the series concerts, I received a letter from Gene Gutche, an Iowa composer. I didn't know him, but he must have gotten my name from the university's list of music doctorates. He was coming to Nashville to attend the world premiere of his symphonic poem about the north woods. The piece was a good one, and I'll say it was different, contemporary or even post-modern. I was supposed to be his host while he was in Nashville. He was living in Minnesota, so immediately I wanted to show him the contrasts in lifestyles. We couldn't really get together until after the concert. At the concert, his piece went well, and he was asked to stand by the conductor to receive the applause, which was generous. I felt a one-upmanship on my colleagues in the orchestra for having the responsibility of hosting this young American composer.

After the concert, I took him to my favorite barbecue spot at Twelfth and South Street. This was a true ghetto joint, one frequented by very few whites. We were there in our full dress suits. In this poor neighborhood, we stood out like a light in a bushel. It probably would have been all right for me alone—at least I felt reasonably safe—but my guest was uneasy. The neighborhood toughs noticed not only our formal clothes but my Packard. Even the female manager of the place pointed out a gathering of young men across the street. She suggested that we leave immediately while we still had a chance to get to the car untouched. I am sure this was a different experience for my white Minnesota friend. Although the pork barbecue was excellent, we gathered up the remains and made a beeline for the car. We made it as the group of toughs was crossing the street toward us and sped away to my house only a few blocks off without incident. We finished our barbecue and relaxed with coffee and drinks. I'm sure my new friend was as impressed with southern hospitality as he was with the reception of his composition. I never saw him again, but I did get a letter of thanks.

One Saturday afternoon I walked into the War Memorial Auditorium with a viola instead of a bass. This change was at the request of Dr. Johnson. Johnson was a violinist himself and a very persuasive man; I couldn't tell him no, especially if he had decided what my future in the symphony was to be. I was scared as I got on the rehearsal stage. I had played viola in college symphony orchestras, but this was the big league. I couldn't fake it here. After nine years on bass, I was about to begin another nine years on viola.

For those who have reservations about my viola playing, I can attest to playing and passing three auditions in front of the orchestra committee and the conductor. While I was never placed in the first two stands, I did get as high as the outside man on the third stand. For me, these were challenging but fun years. I had many stand partners in those nine years, including John Bright, who had ushered me into the symphony, and Ovid Collins, our principal violist, and nineteen-year-old Bobby Becker, the youngest principal in the orchestra. There was also Gary Von Osdale, a session musician and part-time orchestra musician, and there were others as well. I found the viola section very much like the bass section. We were all for each other's improvement and the betterment of our symphony.

My years with the orchestra are clustered in my memory under the various conductors for whom I played. First of all there was Willis Page, who got me into the symphony. Page was a very emotional conductor. Our newspaper critic called him orgiastic; the critic, Louis Nicholas, evidently did not like Page. I would call his conducting enthusiastic; he certainly got involved with the music. Page was the best children's concert conductor I ever encountered. He went about it like a big kid, and the children loved it. Relatively calm and even-handed in rehearsal but dynamic in concert, he left us feeling we dared not fail him. We in the orchestra were used to that intensity, and we tried to give him everything he wanted in concert. I think most of us felt we knew Page as well as he knew us. And I thought the results were consistently good. In essence, Page was a musician's musician, and to our bass section he was a bass player's bassist.

Second to arrive in my tenure was Thor Johnson. I was to be with him the longest, and he was my favorite. Dr. Johnson was almost fanatically meticulous. What we played in concert had better be what we rehearsed, the way we rehearsed it, or there would be hell to pay. Johnson and I had a special relationship. He was keenly interested in and liked to talk about black artists, black manuscripts, and, even more generally, the social-cultural dimensions of the black community. He was especially fond of Duke Ellington and was thrilled to know of my connection. For reasons that I never understood, the symphony board took the junior symphony away from him, and Dr. Johnson was absolutely devastated by that decision. I could feel his pain every time he talked about it. After all, he had developed several outstanding youngsters who had gone on to become valuable members of the senior orchestra.

I mentioned earlier that Dr. Johnson paid out of his pocket for extra rehearsals at TSU in order to present the best for a black audience. He also paid tuition at Blair Academy of Music for some talented black musicians. He even made it possible for some deserving musicians to have decent instruments. Most of these were violas

*Conductor Thor Johnson rehearsing the Nashville Symphony in about 1967. W. O. Smith is second from the right among the five bassists in the rear.*

owned by Johnson himself. Although I never felt myself to be in his inner circle of friends, I did feel myself privileged to have gotten as close as I did to such an outstanding conductor and human being. I know of one case in which the recipient of Dr. Johnson's largesse did not show up for the lesson. I was so mad that I walked over to the dormitory and arranged to get her out of bed.

With the death of Dr. Johnson, the symphony board arranged a series of auditions for the job of director. Among the applicants was Kay Roberts, one of our own. She had come through the junior orchestra to the senior symphony and had won everybody's respect. I was bursting with pride when she ascended the podium and did a masterful job of leading our group. Unfortunately, she was not selected for the post.

John Nelson, who was to be the director of the Indianapolis orchestra, was selected. His tenure was brief but different. A closet opera singer, he had a fine operatic voice that sounded to me as good as some of our operatic guest soloists. Our rehearsals even without our guest singers were almost like the opera itself. Conductor Nelson would sing each part with such fervor and understanding that at times the actual performance by guest singers was anticlimactic. My memory records the tenure of John Nelson as uneventful except for his beautiful singing.

Next in line for the directorship of the symphony was Michael Charry, who was of Russian descent. I tried to get closer to him by loaning him books about the Russian people. One of the books was *The Russians* by Hedrick Smith. It didn't work. Charry returned the books with thanks but no other comment. Again, memory records my experience with conductor Charry as uneventful.

After nearly two decades of symphonic discipline, I found that I no longer wanted to be a part of the scene. I had paid my dues with punctuality and private rehearsals. Eighteen years were enough to be a symbol to young blacks that classical music was a valid form, not merely white man's music. So it was with reluctance and fine memories that I chose not to try to retain my seat in the orchestra after the 1978–79 season. I was beginning to feel the encroachment of age. My actual retirement from TSU was only three years away. I am eternally grateful for the orchestral experience because it changed my life completely for the better.

# CHAPTER 28

# TENNESSEE STATE UNIVERSITY

*L*ooking back on thirty years at Tennessee State University, I am haunted by the words of Dr. Herbert F. Mells, the man who hired me: "You will die here."

He meant that I would spend the rest of my career here in Nashville. Considering my past record of two years here and two years there, TSU did turn out to be a radical departure from my established style, and it was mostly a happy and lucky time for me. Without foreseeing any premature and sudden departure, I concede that Dr. Mells was right on target.

There were some wavering moments, though—like the time in the 1960s when I applied for a teaching position at Temple University in my former home of Philadelphia. I was emotionally ready to leave TSU, but my department head, Ed Lewis, scotched that effort in a meeting with Dr. David Stone, dean of the Temple University School of Music. Dr. Lewis told Dr. Stone how valuable I was to TSU's program, almost an indispensable man. This was great praise and recognition, but it was also the kiss of death. I received no more communication from Dr. Stone, whose previous notes had sounded interested in hiring me. Two more inquiries came later—one from NYU and the other from the University of Iowa—but I did not pursue these because by that time I had made up my mind not to disrupt the family with a move to another area.

I was also determined not to let the disruptive elements at TSU bother me; I would get along no matter what. I am happy it turned out the way it did, in view of the events that were evolving and that turned into the fulfillment of a dream. What has happened to me here couldn't have happened in Philadelphia, New York, or Iowa City. Therefore, I am grateful to TSU, and Nashville, and the symphony. Obviously, I made the right choice.

The beginning of my tenure at TSU was a major culture shock, to say the least. Consider, for example, a ritual called the legislative banquet. I thought it was the plantation and *Uncle Tom's Cabin* revisited. Our faculty string quartet was asked to provide the music for the members of the state legislature while they ate. The dean of arts and sciences was the official greeter. Other faculty members parked cars. The head of the art department was the head waitress. President Walter Davis did not sit at the table with the legislators but walked around supervising. Our faculty string quartet was invited to eat, but it had to be in the kitchen. We refused the offer, and frankly I was shocked and vowed never to participate in this kind of thing again.

I came away with a low opinion of President Davis, thinking of him as a modern-day academic Uncle Tom. Now, taking into consideration his successors, I have revised my opinion of both Dr. Davis and Uncle Tom. I see now that they both did what they had to do for the betterment of their communities. They were limited to the means available and legal. Funds for the physical plant and for most of the programs were raised in a pre-civil rights atmosphere. Compared with his successors, Dr. Davis was a giant, but in all fairness he had more time and more internal control. There were, of course, budget restraints, but nobody tied the hands of anyone who had a good idea and could bring it off. This meant lots of encouragement but no money. The budget restraints were tighter after Dr. Davis's death, and the status of the university changed to just another regent's school, rather than a special college for blacks. I forgive Dr. Davis for the embarrassing experience of the legislative banquet since I now see that he did what he could, when he could. Even with some shenanigans about faculty pay I would give him pretty good grades for his administration of TSU.

In my thirty years, the student body was a mixed bag. Because of our admissions policy, our students ranged all the way from morons to geniuses. By law we had to admit all Tennessee high-school graduates. That meant that we had students with a fifth-grade reading level mixed in with average and superior college-level students. Later on we got some white students, and that would change the dynamics of the classroom. Most of the white students were there because of the integration scholarships, so they were screened a little more carefully. I remember two white ladies who were Metro school teachers. They actually intimidated the undergraduate class with their competence. I was angry that none of our better black students would rise to compete. I talked about it in class when our white students were not around, but it was futile. As time went on and we became used to whites in the classroom, the atmosphere gravitated toward normalcy. There was less resentment of whites and less fear that they were trying to take over our school.

Two students I'll never forget were Roosevelt Hill and Vernon Beard. These guys had my number. Both were excellent students and were on the dean's list. They anticipated correctly almost everything that I put on an exam or quiz. It was uncanny; I was never able to surprise them. It was almost as if they could read my mind like an open book. They never made lower than 92 on any exam that I gave. I was both pleased and chagrined and probably did some of my best teaching because of the challenge they offered. These guys were so sure of me that they coached the rest of the class in sessions held a few minutes before my arrival in the classroom. As a result, the whole class prospered. Their class actually read the textbook; I was challenged and delighted. Teaching a class in which everybody knew what the professor was talking about was a rare experience in any undergraduate school—and still is. I was fortunate and privileged to have known two such enterprising scholars as Roosevelt Hill and Vernon Beard.

In thirty years of active duty at TSU, I had two friends who were really the best. The first was Raymond H. Kemp, the embattled athletic director of the university. We met through our wives, who both worked in the public relations office. Waiting for our wives to finish work, we had conversations about anything and everything, but mostly TSU. Ray had revived men's track and had coached Ralph Boston to national and Olympic recognition. Because of some unsavory campus politics, Ray was not permitted to go to the Olympics in Rome and coach his protégé. He was very bitter about this and eventually left TSU to return home to Pittsburgh. Kemp had played with the Pittsburgh Steelers as one of the first black players in the NFL. When I knew him, he was in his sixties and looked as if he could still play. He was about six feet tall and packed about 240 pounds of nonfat weight. So when he came to my house on Sunday morning and said, "Okay, Smith, we're going to church this morning," who was I to refuse? He kept a half-pint of bourbon for me when I visited, though he didn't drink or smoke. We had father-and-son outdoor barbecues and other similar activities involving our sons. I never met anybody like him and was pleased to have him as a friend.

The other special friend was Harry S. Blanton, who was in the school of education. The difference between Blanton and Ray Kemp was that Blanton could and would drink. We would have a drinking session at his or my home until about midnight. Then we would call each other about 7:30 A.M. the next day to check on the effects of the alcohol. There was some concern, but we both respected each other's ability to drink responsibly, drive home safely, and perform on the job. Blanton was as much younger than I as Ray Kemp was older. Still, I feel that we made a great duo. We were kindred spirits, and in our conversation we analyzed TSU's administration and politics. As a native Tennessean and the first black Ph.D. in education at the University of Tennessee, Blanton knew a lot more than I did about TSU's administration and politics. Our families became close, and our wives both had the same name, Catherine. When I bought a new 1965 Datsun, I took it by Blanton's house to show it off. While we were having a couple of drinks, his daughter laughingly informed me that I had a flat tire. Blanton, an ex-footballer himself, fixed the flat. I was indeed hurt when he left Nashville to become part of the administration at Florida A&M in Tallahassee. He has not been replaced. I missed his level-headed judgment and experience in academic matters.

I shamelessly pursued Coach John Merritt to make him one of my friends. He was my type of guy. Anybody who smokes cigars and offers me one can't be all bad. I did get him to come to my house for a Wednesday Night Club meeting. Since he didn't drink alcoholic beverages, I had a special decanter of apple juice reserved for his use. He had a good time but left early. I could not connect with him again, and his early death followed—much to my regret, for I felt that we could have been great friends.

W. Dury Cox, the drama professor, was with me practically all during my Tennessee State tenure. We lived on the same street, Villa Place, and we sometimes depended on each other for transportation. Cox had charge of the stage in the A Auditorium. His cooperation was mandatory for the programs given on that stage. He was very gracious, if a bit gruff, and gave us useful advice about staging our various programs. He was always good for a drink of bourbon whenever I stopped by his house.

Alonzo Stephens, a professor of history, was the third person outside of the music department that I tried to get close to. Steve had had some jazz experience singing with big bands during the thirties. We talked the same language in regard to jazz. He was the editor of the faculty journal and made me an associate editor. I didn't thank him for that, but it made me think about contributing an article. The journal ran afoul of the budget cuts at TSU, and its life was short. These were some of my friends outside of the music department. They were important to my development in connecting me to the totality of the university. There was more to it than just music.

One of my more disappointing experiences at TSU came after my colleagues in the School of Education named me as a member of the lyceum committee and later as a member of the faculty senate. The lyceum committee was charged with improving the cultural life of the university through artistic programs. The idea was fine except that we had a limited budget. We had about six thousand dollars a year in a time when a first-class artist would cost at least forty-five hundred dollars. Not only that, but we had student representation on the committee. My main problem was with the students. They wanted acts like the Temptations or the Supremes. We would fight over this as I suggested the Nashville Symphony or some concert pianist. I was annoyed with the students because of their preferences for commercial music. They never even mentioned jazz or a jazz artist. I tried to explain that we were here to expand their cultural horizons. Fortunately we were able to outvote the students and present four representative cultural experiences a year.

The faculty senate was much worse for me. I feel that the less said about it, the better. The senate had no power and was pooh-poohed by the administration. It was a waste of time to spend those afternoons arguing about matters that we could not do anything about. I hated every minute of it, feeling that it was just a sham. I always felt that I knew best how to waste my own time. In that regard I've always had talent, experience, and resourcefulness. I was gleeful when that term was over. I had contributed nothing, so I don't blame the people who tried. All I got out of it was being called "senator." I suppose it was an honor.

After the death of President Davis, we had a motley crew of chiefs. Dr. Andrew Torrence came in and immediately expanded our already enlarged administration. Where we had functioned with one vice-president, we wound up with about seven—probably more than Michigan State, which had an enrollment about six times ours. For example, where we had a business manager who handled our financial affairs, we added a vice-president for financial affairs. We kept the business manager, who did all of the work. We had two high-salaried people doing the work formerly done by one person. I said at the time, "Too many chiefs, not enough Indians."

Even a later president, Fred Humphries, admitted that we were "long on administration." It pained me to go to one of these vice-presidents' offices and see several secretaries with time to kill, while our music department had only one secretary for thirteen people. With that many vice-presidents, who runs the store? There should probably be an executive vice-president for academic affairs who would take the role of the dean of the college. He or she should be in charge, since the main mission of the university is education. All other vice-presidents are in service areas.

In my mind, the president who did the least damage was Dr. Roy Peterson. He was apparently unpopular on campus. He did not participate in the black nationalism designed to keep TSU as an over-whelmingly black school. I had retired from TSU during his tenure, but from what I could read in the newspaper, he was never given a chance. Dr. Fred Humphries, who preceded Peterson, was what I considered to be neutral with leanings toward black nationalism. The main thing I remember him for was his attempt to bring Sarah Vaughan to the campus. This involved me as an agent and permitted me to make long distance calls to Sarah Vaughan. While the project came to naught, it gave me the great thrill of talking person to person with the "divine one."

Presidents Otis Floyd and George Cox are too new for me to comment on. I knew Cox as a fellow professor, but I knew nothing about President Floyd except news accounts.

Tennessee State University was, and still is, an under-valued institution in the Nashville community. Fisk University gets more re-spect from the community because of its heritage. None of this is based on performance, because TSU has performed. We have gradu-ated a significant number of students who have gone on to make con-tributions to society. Coach Kemp used to say that "Vanderbilt got more credit trying to run than TSU got running." This was definitely true when I first came here in 1952, but things got better as time went on. Today TSU gets more attention from the media. We did get grudg-ing credit for our athletic prowess and to a lesser degree our marching band; we got mostly put-downs for our academic or intellectual abil-ities. Most of these criticisms were based on ignorance of our recorded and provable accomplishments. We had achieved accreditation by the various pertinent accrediting agencies. These agencies had taken the trouble to look past the public's conception of the school and probe for our value attributes. Memphis State University and the University of Tennessee at Knoxville have the mainstream business community behind them in support. In Nashville that support is given in order down from Vanderbilt to Tennessee State at the bottom.

Racism is not the total explanation for TSU's problems and its perception by the community. I think the university has contributed to the difficulties by its lack of a public relations policy and its reluctance to participate in the mainstream in partnership with the white community. Upwards of two thousand students commute to Murfreesboro and Middle Tennessee State University, thereby strengthening their enrollment. What if the locations were reversed, with MTSU in Nashville? I believe there would be fewer problems and total community support. At least MTSU would not be on the bottom in terms of mainstream business support, and MTSU would gain in enrollment because there would be none of that white reluctance to attend.

In the black community's eyes, Tennessee State's music department suffered in comparison to Fisk. Fisk has a long and honorable tradition dating back to the original Jubilee Singers. We at TSU recognized and respected that fact. However, the public perception put us at a disadvantage in spite of our record of achievement. Our music department is now roughly twice the size of Fisk's. We turn out more graduates and eventual Ph.D.s. We have more of an instrumental program, capped by the marvelous marching band. Both TSU and Fisk are members of the prestigious and elite National Association of Schools of Music. I want to take nothing from Fisk, because they are good at what they do. I only ask that TSU be perceived objectively rather than by subjective and somewhat biased criteria. There is room for both schools, and a mission for both.

Preoccupation and worry about the future seem to go with the territory of every historically black college and university. What if TSU were to become a regional/urban university open to all instead of being the state's predominantly black college? I think the advantages outweigh the drawbacks.

The first line of defense for the mostly black scenario is that it presents more opportunities for blacks in proportion to their numbers. TSU had about eight thousand students in 1991, and close to two-thirds of them were black. The same ratio prevails among the faculty and administration. One of the principal worries is the need to protect black jobs. None of that would have to be changed if the university went the regional/urban route with all ethnic groups involved in the student population, the faculty, and the administration. The school could conceivably develop to ten thousand or even twenty thousand students. Assuming that the largest group of students would be black, such expansion would actually provide more opportunities for blacks than exist now.

TSU can always remain a black heritage university, and probably the largest group of students, faculty, and administration will always be black. Most of the buildings could be named for important black personalities, as they are now. We could still play our traditional black rivals in football and basketball. But I envision that without an overwhelming black presence, TSU would attract many of those whites who commute to MTSU. The university would be perceived as a total community asset. Then we could get the mainstream business backing that Memphis State now enjoys. With increased community support and millions of dollars from the Nashville business community, the school could grow into one of the strongest universities in the state. We could offer a first-class education at state college prices to all who would enter. I believe a white president might help achieve this and change our image in the Nashville community, just as a black president at MTSU has done.

In this day of desegregation, a "black" school or a "white" school is an anachronism. We have an excellent urban location and a large population base. Actually, the only thing blacks would lose would be our personal claim to TSU. Let us share that claim and make TSU a better university for all, black and white.

# CHAPTER 29

# LOOSE ENDS

S ome of my experiences in Nashville and far afield will always rank as singular adventures in my mind. It's pleasant to recall them, and to write them down here. These are a few of the choice anecdotes.

### The Wednesday Night Club
It began sometime in the early 1960s with a handful of us meeting informally and almost accidentally on Wednesday evenings. The same three or four guys showed up at about the same time at somebody's house, almost as if it had been prearranged. We were all black and had some connection with Tennessee State University or radio station WVOL, so you could say this was strictly a north Nashville phenomenon.

Driving around on a Wednesday evening, I would stop by W. C. Lathon's or Ben Butler's house just to see if they were home, and then we'd have a few drinks. Generally I would find another guy there, and within a few minutes a couple more guys. The conversation would go on until about nine o'clock, when the host would bring out some food—usually inexpensive and plain, like hot dogs or a pot of beans. The second bottle of whatever the host was drinking would be on its way out when the meeting was about to break up around 10:00 P.M. We had no roster, no officers, and no mission except to discuss topics relevant to TSU, Nashville, Vietnam, or civil rights.

Besides me, there were four or five other stalwarts. W. C. Lathon was a high school choral director and a beautiful singer. Ben

*Members of the Wednesday Night Club at a moving party for Frank Sutherland* (right) *in 1982. Those present* (from left): *Del Sawyer, Bill Barnes, Willie Caruth, Bernie Schweid, John Egerton, Walter Searcy, W. O. Smith, John Hatcher, Bob Harrison, and Sutherland.*

Butler was the assistant band director at TSU. Noble Blackwell was the station manager at WVOL. Buddy Taylor was the football team trainer. A guy who went by the name of Princetta was a jazz drummer and had no college connection. Later we got Jerry Crosby, a former University of Michigan football player with a doctorate in education, and Chuck Mitchell, a WVOL announcer. This was our nucleus. Others were in and out, but with no lasting impression.

We met about once a month, usually on a Wednesday because most of us were tied up on weekends. No dues were taken or records kept. Announcements were all by phone, so no written records exist. The meetings got pretty dynamic, and we solved all weighty problems with wisdom and ease. Bobby Kennedy was our candidate for president, and Malcolm X was our guiding star. I was the unofficial chairman, more like a coordinator without power.

By the late sixties, we had begun to break up. W. C. Lathon left Nashville to become assistant dean of the University of Louisville School of Music. Ben Butler left to become band director at Texas Southern University in Houston. Jerry Crosby became an administrator in the Louisville school system. Noble Blackwell went to Philadelphia to manage WCAU-TV. The group just evaporated, and to my regret we didn't have enough left for a decent quorum.

A few years later, in the early 1970s, I had a conversation about the earlier group with my friend John Egerton, a Nashville author. He pumped me for information about the original Wednesday Night Club. We decided to reorganize the group along interracial lines. We talked to Walter Searcy, an articulate young political character from the black community; Bernie Schweid, a liberal and respected bookstore owner; Willie Caruth of the Metro Action Commission; and my musician friend Bill Pursell. There may have been some others. Anyway, we caucused, as they said in those days, to produce a lineup of suitable candidates for membership. Little is remembered of those early meetings. We had about a dozen communicants, evenly divided between black and white. Some of the meetings were intense and stimulating. This was an excellent forum in which to clear up a lot of the ignorance that existed between the races. We discussed busing, integrated schools, and the whole range of civil rights issues with objectivity. Even in the heat of battle no black was called "nigger," nor was any white called "honkie." We did flirt with the line of demarcation in our kidding of one another. Here I think humor wiped out the ridiculousness of prejudice. Here also we could be honest, frank, and, above all, objective.

To me it was a valuable lesson about people. Most of our guys were intellectually inclined. We were fortunate in getting some of them into the fold before they became well known. I am thinking of Steve Cobb, who went on to become a very valuable state legislator; Warren Moore, who became the executive director of the Tennessee Human Rights Commission; Del Sawyer, dean of the Blair School of Music at Vanderbilt; Frank Sutherland, now editor of *The Tennessean*; and Al Birch, now a Tennessee appeals court judge. Several ministers joined the group. The Reverend Bill Barnes, the pastor of an integrated church, Edgehill United Methodist, was an early member. So was John Hatcher, a chaplain at Vanderbilt. Two other men of the cloth, Inman Otey and Hogan Yancey, followed. The Reverend Kelly Miller Smith was a later member; he died of cancer shortly after we welcomed him into the club.

It was ironic that we had a preponderance of Vanderbilt people, considering the fact that the original Wednesday Night Club was primarily Tennessee State University people. Most of the people we approached from TSU were not interested. Bill Pursell and Steve Cobb did teach part-time at TSU, so along with me that gave us some connection. Among our newest members we have one Asian, Win Myint, who also teaches at TSU. With this mix of people, we have generally had lively rap sessions.

The beauty of the Wednesday Night Club is in its diversity. We have mostly Democrats, but also a few Republicans. We have Catholics, Protestants, Jews, and even one Buddhist. We have lawyers, musicians, ministers, educators, and public officials, not to mention our resident author, John Egerton. Our resident composer is Bill Pursell.

On several evenings I brought up the idea of "Music City, USA" providing some outlet for our musically talented low-income kids. We batted the idea around for a few meetings until Del Sawyer and Frank Sutherland decided to take the ball and run with it. More about that later.

### Radio Programs

Along about 1961, I mentioned to Noble Blackwell, the station manager at WVOL radio and a member of the original Wednesday night group, the possibility of my doing a symphony program on the station. I proposed an hour and a half of classical music on Sunday afternoon. This was accepted by the white owner of the station, so we began production of a program called "Symphony Hall." We soon spread out to other members of the chain of stations of which WVOL was a part, notably WLOU in Louisville, Kentucky, and WCIN in Cincinnati. What is amazing is that these are rock-and-roll, rhythm-and-blues stations. We had monthly programs printed up as flyers touting our sponsors. Fortunately, there were enough of them to sustain the program.

Danny Owens, the assistant band director at Tennessee State, was my advisor during all of this. He had previous radio experience in Charlotte, North Carolina, and had a jazz program on WVOL immediately after mine at four o'clock. Danny gave me the professionalism needed to make the program credible. There were others who helped me, among them gospel music expert Morgan Babb and a great announcer, Chuck Mitchell. We got some good reviews and even an award from the Nashville Broadcasters Association. After eight years, a new station manager decided that classical music was at cross-purposes with WVOL's stated rhythm-and-blues format, and we went off the air.

With the demise of "Symphony Hall," I became restless and tried to come up with ideas that would support a new program. I had the thought of doing something with the works of black composers of classical music. In the early seventies little was available on commercial recordings. For that reason alone, I got a sense of mission. The extensive repertoire of classical music has been enriched by the creative efforts of black composers. For various sociological and related reasons, however, the majority of black composers—some of them internationally renowned—were relatively unknown even among their own people. I had done some research on the subject and kept notes, and I also had purchased what was available in recordings. I went first to WVOL, but they evidently had had enough of classical music after years of "Symphony Hall." Then I turned to WPLN, Nashville's public radio station. Alvin Bolt, the station manager, liked the idea. I got a minimum stipend and had to rely mostly on my own record collection and what could be taped from local colleagues at Fisk and TSU. We were able to put together a thirteen-week series of one-hour programs. Bolt insisted that I have all thirteen programs organized and timed before the first one hit the air. The advantage of this was that we could print a brochure advertising the series and listing everything we were going to play.

The series, called "Black Composers and Their Music," included several compositions by John W. Work, the noted Fisk University composer, and several by T. J. Anderson, who was my colleague at TSU. I also featured Duke Ellington with his extended compositions, such as "Harlem Suite." They were symphonic in scope, with the only difference being that he used his own jazz orchestra instead of a symphony orchestra. He even did that with his "Golden Broom and Green Apple," using the Cincinnati Symphony as his vehicle. Chuck Mitchell was my announcer. He had been at WVOL but had transferred to WPLN just prior to the airing of my program. I give him full credit for his professional advice. He made it a better program.

### Three Significant Gigs

The Andy Goodrich/Brenton Banks quartet got a call from one of our young fans, Harry Cash, who was also the program manager at WSM-TV. He commissioned Brenton to do a series of arrangements and the quartet to record them. It was to be a set of promos for the TV station. Cash had also hired the King Sisters, a famous female jazz quartet, as featured singers on these promos. Banks created some really swinging arrangements, and it was a pleasure to hear some real jazz on commercial television. We had a ball recording those promos. The King Sisters were very gracious and professional. We even had a party for them at Brenton Banks' house, and they gave us all autographed photos of themselves.

At the recording sessions at Columbia Records on Music Row, I was appalled to see that the only other black person in the building carried a broom. In spite of that, all in all, it was one of the most satisfying experiences of my musical career.

In 1966 Kitty and I bought a house on Kirkwood Lane in Nashville, about two miles south of the heart of downtown. We were the only black family in a square-mile area. For Sale signs went up all over the place, and we even made the newspaper. Kitty protested, "They don't even know us," in a reply to *The Tennessean*. Things stabilized after a few months, and we settled down into what would become a mixed neighborhood.

Shortly after we moved I received a phone call to grab my bass and rush over to a new recording studio on Gale Lane near Belmont Boulevard. No further information was given. This turned out to be producer Shelby Singleton's new studio, and it was only about eight blocks from my house. To my surprise, I learned that the session would be about country music; even more remarkable, it would be with a group from Israel. I had never been on a country music session or gig before. However, I felt that if some of these country music cats could play jazz, then I ought to be able to play country. I was in fairly good spirits when the Jewish cowboys came into the studio. They were wearing ten-gallon hats and cowboy boots. I learned that their regular bass player did not clear immigration at the airport and that I was the nearest bass player to the studio.

The main shock was that no one in the group spoke English. One of the engineers knew some Hebrew and Yiddish and was our main communication link. Just telling me the name of the tune did no good as I was not familiar with country music. If time permitted, the piano player played for me the tune they were about to record. Since there were usually three or four takes on each tune, I was familiar with it by the third take. A couple of times they just started right up with no preparation. I didn't even know the key until the second or third bar; and I couldn't understand their sign language. I did understand the music, though. Fortunately, the words were unnecessary for my performance—but just imagine country music in Hebrew.

They were good and well organized. They had two guitarists, a drummer, and a pianist, along with three singers. My understanding was that these records would not be released in the U.S. but only in the Middle East. I wondered if the good Jews and Arabs, when they heard these records, would know that a black guy from Nashville was on bass. It was a strange experience, but I made it through with a minimum of errors. My few words of North Philadelphia Yiddish did not help. The cowboys were all smiling at the end of the session, so I guess I did them no harm.

Sometime in the midseventies, I got a call from a young man who was in the student government at Fisk. He asked me to bring a five-piece group to play for a dance at the Henderson A. Johnson Gymnasium. We agreed on the time and the money, so I immediately lined up the necessary musicians. Being a group leader was a rare experience for me. I had an impressive group of pure jazz musicians. Our regular quartet of Andy Goodrich on sax, Brenton Banks at the piano, Morris Palmer on drums, and me on bass was joined by Louis Smith on trumpet. This was an all-star group, which I was sure the Fisk students would appreciate. We arrived on time and found the dance floor already crowded with students. There was a phonograph in the middle of the makeshift bandstand, and they were playing all of the hits of the day—records by the Temptations, Gladys Knight and the Pips, James Brown, Wilson Pickett, and the like.

As soon as we turned off the phonograph and started playing, everybody left the dance floor and proceeded to the stands on the side. This was embarrassing to me because it put us in the position of playing a concert rather than a dance. As soon as we finished a set, somebody would turn on the phonograph. It was like a signal for everyone to return to the dance floor. They danced until we came back for the next set. Then, as if by signal, they disappeared to the stands. At the intermission, the phonograph went on for real. The crowd was obviously not interested in jazz, particularly as dance music.

With the members of the band, I approached the bandstand somewhat timidly after the intermission. I realized that I would have to turn the phonograph off. Sensing the mood of the crowd, I hesitated. I checked with the kid who was in charge and asked him to turn it off. He said, "They seem to be enjoying it, so why don't I pay you off and y'all can go home?" It was now about 10:30 P.M. on an eight to twelve gig. I accepted, knowing that my sidemen would have no objections. The kid in charge paid me in cash, and I immediately paid off the men. The gig was over.

I was hurt, especially when I considered that we had brought the best available jazz to Fisk. I really shouldn't have been surprised because I had a house full of teenagers at home. These were the records they played and lived by. I was so embarrassed that I tried to sneak out. We went to the exit nearest the bandstand and got outside without going through the crowd. I didn't want them to know that we were gone, but I was relieved to get out. I saw the handwriting on the wall for jazz and jazz musicians. The thought came to me that this was the last gig, or at least the beginning of the end. Since I was with the symphony at the time, my loss was more spiritual than financial.

For the Banks/Goodrich quartet, it was downhill all the way after that, until its final demise with the departure of Banks and Goodrich for more fertile climates. I had to come to grips with the new conditions. Knowing that there was no place for me, I went into other endeavors. This was truly my last gig.

### Travels in the Caribbean and Latin America

Early on, Kitty and I embarked on a family travel plan to show our kids that there is a bigger world out there, with real people and different cultures from Nashville. We began with the Bahamas, alternating with Canada in the summer. All of us learned a lot, but Kitty and I learned most about managing teens and preteens on long trips in one midsized car.

In the midseventies I saw an item in a campus newsletter dealing with the Phelps-Stokes Fund. They had funded a student-teacher exchange with Mexico and were looking for faculty members as well, especially those with a research project. I immediately formulated a project based on black music and its origins in Africa and Latin America. The maximum stipend was a thousand dollars, and I knew that would not take me to Africa, so I concentrated on the Caribbean. Specifically, I requested eight days in Kingston, Jamaica, five days in Panama City, and eleven days in Cali, Colombia. I had selected Cali because of its large mulatto population. I hoped that these mixed blacks would remember their African heritage. I was lucky enough to receive the grant, and Kitty and I decided that I would take our youngest son, Joel, along with me.

Joel and I arrived at the Kingston airport with a new friend we had met on the plane, a University of Connecticut football player who was going home to visit his parents. He arranged for us to ride in the family Volkswagen van to town to find a hotel room. They suggested the Roseneath, an inexpensive, clean little hotel near the downtown.

It was black-owned. The major setback for us was the U.S. dollar, which was artificially pegged below the Jamaican dollar. That made just about everything cost more than at home. For example, a lunch at Kentucky Fried Chicken cost us about twice as much as it did in Nashville. One exception to this inflation was the fish-fry stands along the ocean. We could get a freshly caught fish, just fried, for about seventy-five cents. At our hotel I ordered the most expensive breakfast on the menu: American-style sausage and eggs. What I got were two little Vienna sausages with about two tablespoons of scrambled egg. I put the whole breakfast on one corner of the plate and protested to the waiter. All I got was an insult: "Jamaicans don't eat as grossly as the Americans." We never ate there again.

I spent several days at the Jamaica School of Music on Hope Road. I could take a local bus out there and have only a one-block walk to the school. The director, a young lady from Australia, filled me in on all of the school's problems. She was impressed with my college teaching experience as well as my doctorate. I was introduced to most of the faculty. This was a gold mine of information on Jamaican and other Caribbean music. I met Melba Liston this way. She was a Count Basie trombonist and had a good reputation among U.S. jazz performers as a progressive arranger. At the Jamaica school she was the director of the jazz curriculum, which was very popular with the students.

Melba was also popular with the area's most prestigious and capable musicians. She did the arrangements for the major record sessions on the island. Kingston was similar to Nashville as a recording center for the entire Caribbean, especially in reggae and its many derivative musical styles. Melba invited Joel and me to dinner at her house, where we met quite a few Jamaican musical personalities. I was so pleased with the information and contacts from the school that I promised to leave them my own musical library on my demise. Fortunately, that hasn't happened yet, but the promise will be kept. It's in my will.

We went on an excursion up Blue Mountain with some local musicians to meet some recording stars who lived there. We were offered a cigar-sized *ganga* stick (marijuana), which I declined in favor of some available Scotch whisky. Joel took one puff of the *ganga* and almost turned green. He declined any further tokes, and we were able to depart gracefully.

I finished out the week with daily visits to the musicians' union. I was able to interview the secretary, who not only filled me in on the current situation but took me to several record sessions. It was like Nashville, except that the studios were smaller and the equipment seemed older and less modern. No matter—the results were invariably good. I was informed that some of these recordings were to be marketed in New York.

After attending some reggae concerts at the Devon House, we packed to leave for Panama. I left without realizing that I had met a future daughter-in-law and the mother of my two fine grandsons. Actually, Joel met her first, at a supermarket. He got out of our van and introduced himself. The attractive young lady, Sandy Lewis, eventually came to the U.S. I met her in Baltimore and drove her to Nashville and Tennessee State University. She did not marry Joel, though, but his older brother, Jay. But that was in the future. Not anticipating any of this, Joel and I left Jamaica on a British Airways flight to the "crossroads of the world," Panama City.

The first thing we noticed was the electrified insect net around the airport building. It was brilliantly lit and teeming with zillions of insects in various stages of expiring. I had never seen this before and was later impressed with the scarcity of insects in the city. Also it was not as hot as I had anticipated for July. Recalling some of the tropical movies I had seen, I had expected a steam bath.

Panama City itself was also a surprise. It was a relatively modern city without skyscrapers but with some high-rise hotels. We booked our hotel room at a courtesy counter in the airport, and the taxi ride into town was fascinating. We took a *colectivo* and shared the ride with some Spanish-speaking customers. The driver was black and spoke fluent Spanish to others while speaking British English to us. He could break off in the middle of a Spanish sentence and address us in impeccable English. I was to find out that this was customary among black Panamanians.

Our hotel, the Gran Lux, was delightful, and we hated to leave after our five scheduled days. The black community had advance notice of our coming, and a reporter for the black newspaper showed up the next morning for an interview and pictures. He said that the interview and pictures would also appear in their New York edition. The friendly reporter also set me up in meetings with the most influential black musicians. One name stuck with me, that of Arnold Walters, the director of the Panama National Choir; he invited us to dinner at his house. We also met with the director of the Panama National Band, who lived in Colón at the other end of the canal, and with one of Panama's leading musicians, a young black composer. Before we met any of these people, however, an event transpired on our first afternoon there that literally shook us up.

It all began with a loud explosive sound like a shot from a twenty-one-inch cannon. The whole building jumped about six inches sideways; Joel was on the balcony at the table while I was in the room reading. Then the entire building shook almost rhythmically for what seemed a long time but actually was no more than a minute. It was enough time for my bottle of Scotch on the dresser to dance the five feet from one end to the other. The bottle did not fall on the floor, but Joel was not as fortunate; his drink fell to the street from our fifth-floor room. We checked the street from the balcony as soon as it was over; no one was in sight. No one answered the phone downstairs, so we just sweated it out for the next hour. Our newspaper friend came by later and said that it was not an earthquake but a major tremor. He said they got these often and that it wouldn't even be mentioned in the newspaper. The only thing the people at the front desk said when we got to them was, "When it happens again, do not ride on the elevators." Later, when we went to dinner at the Walters home, nobody mentioned it.

Walters gave me some of their past programs, which contained all kinds of music from Brahms to contemporary Caribbean and late show tunes from the U.S. Later, we were talking about race when he mentioned the phrase "grandmother in the closet," referring to the conductor of the Panama Philharmonic, who had a Jewish last name but, unknown to most, a black grandmother. I thought that was a rather revealing bit of information.

The next morning we left for Colón on the other side of the canal. We went by train, a truly fascinating ride that went alongside the canal. While we could not see the various locks with the locomotives pulling the ships, we could see the ships in the connecting lakes. We could also see the contrast between the American zone and the Panamanian outside. The American side was clean and green, just like a suburban middle-class town; the Panamanian side, while not dirty, displayed poverty in a tropical setting. Colón was as bad a slum as I have ever seen. We were warned not to go down any street beyond the railroad station. We felt that being black in this case was an advantage, so we set out on foot to explore the town and find our man, the director of the Panama National Band.

We found him without incident and had a very satisfactory interview. He gave me some band music scores and past programs. On our way back to the train station, we stopped at a neighborhood bar for some beer. This place was tough—sawdust on the floor and full of seedy characters. As soon as they found that we were U.S. blacks, they bought a couple of rounds of beer. They even guided us to the train station. We arrived at the hotel and packed for our departure in the morning. We had only five days in Panama, but I felt we did an awful lot.

Cali, Colombia, with about two million people, is a huge city to be as little-known to outsiders as it is. A year earlier I had never heard of Cali, but through reading I imagined it to be just the place for my investigation of black international music.

In Colombia, the higher people climb up the social ladder, the whiter it gets. Bogotá, which I had visited previously with Kitty, was at the top of the mountain and was practically an all-white/*mestizo* city. Cartagena was on the coast practically at sea level and had a much darker population than Bogotá. Cali was about halfway up and thus had a blend of whites, *mestizos,* blacks, and mulattos, which fascinated me. (Tennessee gets whiter as you leave the Mississippi River going east toward the mountains, and from near Crossville to the Tri-Cities area it's mostly white. It seems that there were very few plantations in the mountains.) Cali is a beautiful city with its semi-tropical ambience and Spanish architecture. We had eleven days there, but regretfully not much contact or musical experience. It was enjoyable, but not productive by way of interviews, music, or concerts. I had simply miscalculated, so we just relaxed and acted like tourists.

In spite of the general failure of my mission there, I did return to Cali with my wife a few years later. By then my Spanish had improved, and I had a delightful opportunity to show Kitty what a beautiful city and setting it was.

In the spring of 1979, I noticed a column in the paper that said the U.S. State Department had opened a temporary window to Cuba. I seized on it because Cuba's shortwave radio station featured black music. Because it was a Communist country, one could not go individually but only as a part of a group. Then, in *The New York Times* I found my group, an aggregation of former Cuban nationalists and others preparing to attend Carifesta III, the Caribbean arts festival. I got my passport in order with special permission from the state department to attend. I drove to Saint Petersburg, Florida, and took a plane, an old two-propeller job that shook all the way to Havana. When our party arrived, we had to wait in the airport for about four hours as the Cuban workers were loath to unload anything from the U.S. But the wait was not so bad—we were entertained by various groups arriving from other countries. The Bahamas *gombay* group gave an impromptu and irrepressible performance to start things off.

Finally we settled into the Riviera Hotel, and I immediately felt the impact of socialism. We could not go anywhere as individuals but only as part of a guided group. I eventually found ways around this and ventured out to practice some "street sociology."

Carifesta III was a gathering of performers from some thirty nations in and around the Caribbean, including the Bahamas, Trinidad, Barbados, Jamaica, Guatemala, Mexico, Panama, Nicaragua, Guyana, Venezuela, Colombia, and the U.S. There were more than two thousand artists. Musicians, dancers, poets, painters, photographers, and others were all involved.

It was a political event as well as an artistic one. The Somoza government in Nicaragua had just been overthrown, and the appearance of the Sandinista musical groups was dramatic. The cultures of the various countries were on display; so too were the cultural ministers, who had to give speeches, each speech longer than the preceding one. Also, Carifesta '79 was dedicated to five persons important to Caribbean, Latin American, and U.S. black history. They were Toussaint L'Ouverture, Simón Bolivar, Benito Juarez, José Marti, and Marcus Garvey. I got quite a bit from my street sociology. Whatever problems there might be in Cuba, Havana appeared to be one of the most integrated societies I had ever seen. There was none of the subtle polarization that I had seen in North America, Europe, and, to a lesser extent, South America.

Carifesta III presented a problem of choice. At any one time there could be three dance festivals at three different locations, four theatrical presentations, two sets of chamber recitals, concerts, and more. Some of the events were in stadiums, theatres, or public squares, and others were simply staged at large intersections. The variety of music was majestic. I remember a small "Basie" type band from Panama; a modern jazz group from St. Lucia; a "salsa" group from Cuba; a calypso group from Trinidad; a Trinidad steel band that played music from rock to Rachmaninoff. They even had the Folklorico Ballet of Mexico. The stream of black culture seemed to undergird most of the music I heard, reinforcing my theory that black music crossed the Atlantic during the westward push to the Caribbean and North America centuries ago. The music ran into cross-currents wherever it landed. The Brazilian version is spiced with Portuguese. The Caribbean is flavored with Spanish and Northern European and

North American. When I spent some time in Africa, I could hear the strains that produced the rhumba, salsa, and ultimately jazz.

What I was not prepared for was the evident relationship in all of this music. Carifesta III gave me the opportunity to hear the Western results juxtaposed in a short time/space interval. It was educational as well as entertaining; I'd like to do it again.

### Travels in Africa

Sanchez Harley, a former student of mine, came by my office and offered me a strange proposition. He was forming an instrumental group to go to Africa in the summer of 1977. Even though it was a rock-oriented group, I grabbed the chance to go. It turned out to be Alain Bongo's attempt at emulating James Brown, the popular rhythm-and-blues entertainer. Since Alain Bongo was the son of the president of Gabon, we had the financial and political backing of that country. Our full itinerary would be developed as we went along, but mostly it would include the French-speaking countries of West Africa. We were to receive $350 a week and all expenses. We played in Libreville, Gabon; Abidjan, Ivory Coast; Dakar, Senegal; and Lome, Togo—and then returned to Libreville. In a group of young musicians mostly in their twenties, I was the oldest by at least 35 years, but I never missed a rehearsal or performance. I was the nominal head of the string section, although Kay Roberts was the *de facto* head because of her competence. We had about a dozen strings, some from TSU and others from the Nashville Symphony. There were at least thirty musicians in all, counting the conga drums and other percussion. After almost a week in New York, we flew to Paris where we rehearsed for about a week. The thing that impressed me the most was not Notre Dame Cathedral, the Louvre, or anything like that, but a McDonald's restaurant on the Champs Élysées! Finally, we boarded a Gabon government 747 jet, and we were on our way to Libreville, the capital.

Never having been to Africa before, I had no idea what to expect. It certainly was not like a Tarzan movie. What I saw was a city, maybe not up to the most sophisticated U.S. standards but like some rural cities. Libreville reminded me of Hagerstown, Maryland, but with a beachfront added. A four-lane, limited-access highway went along the beach to the end of the city, but it was practically useless for getting anywhere in town. I think it was there just for show purposes. It seemed that people were nobody unless they had a Mercedes; Renaults and an occasional Peugeot were the working-class cars. We stayed at the Okoume Palace, a luxury hotel in an intercontinental chain. All meals were free, and we could get a bottle of French wine with dinner. The wine tasted like flavored dishwater to me. I got in the habit of taking the bottles and promptly giving them to our chamber-maids. They would thank me by saying, "Merci, vous êtes mon Papa." It was disconcerting until I found out that Africans revere old age. I couldn't maintain a conversation in French with my Berlitz phrase book, but I could take care of my rudimentary needs. For-tunately most of the managers who were white spoke several lan-guages, including English. The thing that irked me the most was that these managers were constantly saying that the Africans wouldn't work. I had heard that back home about blacks, of course, so I asked what was their economic stake in the deal. That question was never answered to my satisfaction.

This was a good time to be in Libreville, because an Organiza-tion of African Unity (OAU) meeting was in progress. At least once an hour there was a motorcade with military escort and national flags on the front of the principal vehicle. That would be the head of one of the African countries in transit to some official spot. I looked forward to seeing Idi Amin, who was at the height of his notoriety. I saw him coming down the steps in the rotunda of the auditorium; he was one big African dude.

As we approached the newly built auditorium, the road was lined with performing groups. The singer/dancer section was on one side of the road with the drummers directly across the road. They all had on colorful uniforms, and each represented a different locality. The music was pure African and was fascinating to me. I could feel an affinity with it. It was rhythmically charged, and I could sense that each group was trying to outdo the others, like the jazz bands of my youth. It was also a photo opportunity with its riot of color.

There were two kinds of African music: traditional and high life. What we heard on the road was traditional. High life was more contemporary, close to American jazz of the early twentieth century, and could be heard primarily on radio or the very scarce television. In both types of music I could hear the kinship to American jazz and rhythm-and-blues. I didn't have a tape recorder but did buy some very expensive phono records. It was thrilling to hear all of this in its natural setting.

The first concert we played was in a medium-sized stadium. Other groups preceded us, and we had a chance to hear contemporary popular music by various singers, groups, and combos. They were good, and I began to wonder how we would go over with the crowd. We also got a demonstration of the *"Fleur d'Afrique."* It was a hot and humid night; and as each group finished its act, the musicians came up into the stands, wringing wet with perspiration. Nobody seemed to mind, and we did our best to congratulate each group for a fine performance. We went on last and blew the roof off with our new arrangement of "Rocky Top," which is a pretty rousing piece. I think we got away with it; the crowd applauded lustily when we finished—maybe because this was the Alain Bongo Band. We featured a lot of James Brown's hits. The president's son was not a prince, but that's what we called him. The Prince did not bounce around like James Brown, but I think he had better vocal quality. He could really do a slow, romantic ballad.

We played a gig in the newly built national auditorium, to which there was a parade of national heads of state. They were all there, but I was only interested in Idi Amin, who was constantly making the news with either his brutality or his stupidity. There were some kings, some presidents, and some prime ministers.

Our contribution to the music program was well received. After about three weeks in Libreville, we moved on to Abidjan, Ivory Coast.

Abidjan was the most modern city we would see in Africa. It had everything from four-lane highways to concentrations of high-rise buildings. The hotel we were in had, of all things, the only ice-skating rink in Africa. I was reminded of Syracuse, New York, more than my conception of what Africa was supposed to be like. I'm sure the thatched-roof huts were around somewhere, but we didn't see them. I did see modern apartment complexes, supermarkets, and malls that would not be out of place in any big city in the U.S. Still, the first thing I noticed on arrival was men beating their clothes on the rocks (more like beating the rocks with their clothes) in the brooks and small rivers in town. These must have been strong, well-constructed clothes. I never saw any women doing this.

We appeared on Abidjan television without our instruments to advertise our upcoming concert. Besides having a terrific view from our rooms on the seventeenth floor, our hotel had a casino. One of our musicians made a two-hundred-dollar killing one night, and we were out in force the next night. I played only the slot machines and got about fifteen dollars ahead when I decided to cash out. The cashier tried to keep me in the game, but I explained to him, "I am small potatoes." I took my few francs and called it a night. Our musician friend who started all this lost her two hundred dollars the next night.

After one concert we were summoned to the top tower of the hotel where we were to be received by President Houphouet-Boigny of the Ivory Coast. We had no idea what to expect. We partook of the *hors d'ouevres* and the free drinks until the president and his party arrived. Then we assembled in the main room to be presented. One by one we stood in line and approached the president's dais. He then presented each male member an ivory statuette and each female member a beautiful African dress. Better yet, the president presented our business manager with a generous honorarium for the group. I took my share downtown the next day and had the bank make out a check payable only to me and to my bank in Nashville. I didn't trust myself to walk around in a foreign country with a lot of cash in my pocket. It was a good thing, too; one of our group lost his windfall the day I went to the bank.

Next we went to Lomé, Togo, another nation in the French bloc. I was always amazed that Africans spoke French in business and their own African language at home or amongst themselves. That meant that the Africans in business were at least bilingual. Some even spoke English as well. Lomé was a smaller town and came closer to my preconception of a truly African city. It was colorful and had huts almost everywhere. Downtown resembled an extended bazaar more than a business area. The streets were teeming with people, and sidewalks were rare. It was there that I noticed the occasional barebreasted woman. After a half-hour of this, I got so that I didn't notice anymore.

We were there for about a week. Our concerts were in an auditorium that was not downtown. We had our usual full house, and I am sure they understood very little of the English language, but they clapped and demonstrated that they understood the rhythm. Overall, the programs were successful, and I was surprised that our audiences were evidently fans of James Brown. I heard less music on the street or radio here than elsewhere in Africa.

Our next stop, Dakar, Senegal, was a beautiful city. Most of the men wore the robes and headdress of the Muslims. The women wore explosive colors. Otherwise, this could have been Richmond, Virginia, without the interstate highways. It did have a beach, and looking at the Atlantic Ocean pounding on it, I became aware of a difference. I was in the East looking West. This was not Miami.

*Cellist Terril Arnst and bassist W. O. Smith on tour with the Alain Bongo band in Dakar, Senegal, 1977.*

Rather, it was a medium-sized modern city with sidewalks, a viable downtown with high-rise buildings and several cultural amenities. One of those cultural amenities was the theatre that we played in, basically a state or national theatre. It was the home of the national ballet and other such groups. After we played our first concert there, I became aware of the purest black people that I've ever seen. When they turned on the lights at intermission, I saw a sea of pure unadulterated ebony. No brown skins, no mulattos, and no whites made it like nothing I've seen in the U.S., the Caribbean, or South America. I marveled at the spectacle.

Our James Brown format went over well there, and we had that modern auditorium to practice in daily. We would leave the rehearsals and go on our own to explore downtown Dakar. In the process we passed several souvenir factories where rows of men and women turned out the masks, statuettes, decorated clothes, and pottery. We could see them in a back room. I understand that they exported these knick-knacks to all of the West African countries, and they in turn passed them off as native to that individual country. In spite of that information, I bought some trinkets for Kitty and the kids.

Between concerts and rehearsals we had a day off. My room-mate, Vando Rogers, and I decided to go to Goree Island. Several other members of our party joined us. We worked up a cab load to the docks where the ferry took off. Goree Island was a main shipping point for slaves bound for the New World. I had to see that; I had to see where my ancestors left home. We went out on a rickety ferry and approached the island about three-quarters of a mile from our depart-ing dock. The ferry landed near a restaurant that we made our head-quarters. After a beer, we walked down the road to the slaves' building, which was really an administrative building and fort. The road exemplified the tropics with its lush greenery and fabulous trees.

Inside the building I saw the shackles and manacles on the floor. Also, there was a room about four feet high, which was called *La Salle des Enfants*. That got to me, and I became imaginative about the situation. The thing that drove me over the edge was the little back door that opened to the ocean. There was a long, forbidding walk down the big rocks to the ocean. I could visualize the procession of men, women, and children making this trip. They did not know why—or what their fate would be. I broke down as I went back out on the street. I wept uncontrollably at first, but I finally got it under control and went to join my party at the restaurant.

A tropical rainstorm came up suddenly, and we ate while we waited out the storm. When I returned to the docks of Dakar, I saw Granville Sawyers, the president of Texas Southern University, and his wife waiting for the next boat out. The chances of running into someone you know like that must be a million to one, but it didn't lift my spirits. I went back to the hotel feeling sick in my heart and soul. That image of the African slave building still lingers in my mind.

CHAPTER 30

# THE MUSIC SCHOOL

**F**or as long as I have been in love with and in debt to the wonderful world of musicians and their music—which is to say, for going on three-quarters of a century now—I have always felt that I have received much more than I have given. And for almost that long, I have dreamed of finding a way to put some of it back. Seeing so many youngsters with a deep desire to learn and excel but with no resources to develop their budding skills, I invariably picture myself as a kid on the streets of Philadelphia. Some generous people and some lucky breaks pointed me in the right direction. My dream of having a school of musical opportunity for kids like these was born out of my own experience. Ironically, it has turned out to be one more example of my getting more than I gave.

This glorious adventure began somewhat ingloriously with my trying to figure out the fingering patterns of an Albert system clarinet. I was in the third grade, and my school only had a roving music teacher in strings. That left me to find out how to play a tune on that clarinet by myself. I worked out the basic scale of the instrument, but not all of the sharps and flats. I had no instruction book or guide. I worked hard enough to become a member of the United Negro Improvement Association Children's Marching Band. I got no help there either, not even from my young peers. They had no idea about the Albert system clarinet. It was trial and error—mostly error—all the way, but at least I was able to make a few sounds on the danged thing.

My first encounter with instruction was with a teacher named Fred Tindley, the son of our church minister; he taught all instru-

295

ments. He taught me violin and my sister piano. Looking back, I realize with amazement that he had no experience on either. He was a trumpet player. In all fairness to Mr. Tindley, he did leave me with a sense of musicianship and the principles of reading and counting simple music. While my public school instruction did lead me into the all-city orchestra, it was not much better. The most I got was orientation sessions on new instruments, including tuba and bass (I think I have already mentioned how an instant bass section was created from the less competent violinists). In their defense, public school teachers did not have time even to think of private lessons for up to a hundred students. Considering their other responsibilities, the miracle is that they managed to help us as much as they did.

Later, when I was a volunteer teacher at the Bedford-Stuyvesant community center, I began to realize how much help even a little instruction can be. My mission was to develop a creditable jazz orchestra out of this mixed bag of teenagers. They were all public school youngsters who were given an instrument and a mandate to "go forth and learn." They might have gotten an instruction book, but no lessons—at least not until I arrived. Our rehearsals were held up many times while I tried to show some kid how to make F sharp on a saxophone or how to manipulate a slide trombone. Not being an expert myself, many times I had to look it up. I asked each student to bring his method book to rehearsal, so some of the boys got to be pretty good—even self-sufficient—at looking things up. Some of them were talented. What might they do, I wondered, if they had a chance to take private lessons? That was the beginning of my dream.

I saw some of the same problem at Seward Park High School, and this, combined with my personal experience as a student, pushed the idea to the forefront of my mind. After examining and analyzing the situation, I concluded that the problem was simply that we had many talented low-income kids, but our system of knowledge transfer in music was not set up to reach and help them.

Skip ahead to the late seventies: Occasionally, I brought up this topic with my companions in the Wednesday Night Club. Two members of the group—Del Sawyer, dean of the Blair School of Music, and Frank Sutherland, editor-to-be of Nashville's largest newspaper, *The Tennessean*—showed particular interest. In our discussions, we agreed that "Music City, USA" ought to be able to handle this problem. Sawyer always stopped me by asking, "Do you have a framework for this?"

I didn't have an answer then, but I began to try to envision a solution. I wrote down the outlines of a program of private lessons for gifted but financially needy youngsters. My thought was that the program would be based at TSU. What I had was actually a proposal for a possible grant. My department head, E. C. Lewis, enthusiastically endorsed the idea. He sent me with his blessings to the development office.

Basically, the idea called for using graduate students as instructors in a special school on the TSU campus. Instruments and method books would also be provided. I figured that with our falling enrollment in music, this could help future recruitment. Kitty had typed up a rough copy of my proposal, which included a fee for the director and a small staff. When the director of development first told me that I would have to bring him a finished copy of the proposal, I pointed out that we had only one secretary for thirteen music faculty members. Then he said that the university would have complete financial control and would also choose the director. These seemed like major obstacles to me. I went away discouraged.

In one of my conversations with Thor Johnson, the conductor of the Nashville Symphony, I mentioned my idea and was surprised when he asked me to bring the proposal by his office. As soon as he read it, he said, "Let's do it." We changed the base from TSU to the symphony. His office typed up professional copies, and we mailed the proposal to the National Endowment for the Arts. At Johnson's suggestion, we sent a copy to Dr. O. A. Anderson, who was a black member of the NEA board and selection committee. We never heard from him at all, and the NEA rejected the proposal.

I had completely given up on the idea when in about 1982 I received an invitation to attend a meeting of the Music Consortium of Nashville, an umbrella organization made up of representatives of the city's leading music establishments like the school music programs, the symphony, the Jazz and Blues Society, the media (sound and print), and others. I was flabbergasted when my idea came up for discussion. The consortium then formed a committee to study further and pursue the project. Members of that committee included Del Sawyer of Blair; Leonard Morton, director of music in the Nashville public schools; Don Butler, president of the Gospel Music Association; Anne Brown, head of the Metro Arts Commission; and me. The project was put on the agenda for subsequent meetings. I began to take heart when I saw that this was an action committee. Sawyer was a formidable and relentless chairman, almost frightening in his ability to get things done. I'm glad he was on my side. Before I knew it, we were no longer saying *if,* but *when.*

For about a year before we opened in October 1984, we all worked with frenzied activity. The Reverend Fred Cloud, a member of our committee, got us the official charter for the proposed school. Then the committee reorganized and redirected its commitment, not to the consortium but to the new school itself. Thus we became an independent committee. Sawyer undertook the task of trying to find the right chairman to form a board of directors. After several months, we got a good break when Don Butler suggested that Buddy Killen could be that person. Subsequently, Butler took Sawyer and Killen to lunch to talk about it.

William D. Killen, better known as Buddy, was one of the most influential power sources in the city, the driving force behind Tree Publishing Company. Luckily for us, he liked the idea and became a tower of strength as the chairman of our board of directors. In less than a year's time, Killen and Sawyer spearheaded the push that maneuvered the dream into a reality.

We got a consultant, Dean Kenneth Wendrich of Bowling Green State University in Ohio, to come to Nashville and advise us. He had been the director of the Neighborhood Music School in New Haven, Connecticut. Wendrich's advice and strategies saved us years of time and helped us avoid many pitfalls. Although we had considered many applicants for the directorship, we were impressed with Dr. Wendrich's experience and know-how. Dean Sawyer called him late one night and asked him to consider the job; and he accepted, even at a reduction in salary from his Ohio job.

Next we needed money, and we got a big lift when the musicians union local in Nashville voted us a fifteen-hundred-dollar grant toward a fund-raising concert. Fred Cloud not only helped us with the union but also enlisted the aid of the Jazz and Blues Society as sponsors. Musically, the concert was a smash. We had Beegie Adair and her group, along with a revised edition of the original Andy Goodrich Quartet (Andy on sax, Lewis Smith on trumpet, Morris Palmer on drums, and Charles Dungey playing bass in my stead). The donation for admission was twenty dollars, and we managed to clear about three thousand dollars toward implementing the music school project.

We had come a long way since the time in about 1982 when Del Sawyer and Frank Sutherland took the proposal to the Music Consortium of Nashville. Now in the summer of 1984, we had an executive director, a board of directors with a dynamic chairman, and

*W. O. Smith* (front) *with board president Buddy Killen* (left) *and director Ken Wendrich raising the first sign of the W. O. Smith Community Music School on Edgehill Avenue, Nashville, 1984.*

the beginnings of sound funding for a budget. Buddy Killen, our chairman, next directed us to find a building. We located a house near Music Row but also near public housing. We purchased the three-story, red brick building at 1416 Edgehill Avenue, and Buddy Killen dubbed it the "little red schoolhouse." When we opened for business in October 1984, the board had worked out the operating policies. First, we decided to charge fifty cents a lesson to the students, who would range in age from four to eighteen. We wanted the students to have some monetary stake in their music education. Second, we decided that the faculty would be made up entirely of unpaid volunteers. There was considerable worry that we wouldn't be able to maintain an adequate supply of talented instructors, but that fear has not been borne out. On the contrary, our teachers have been one of our greatest assets.

We borrowed ten thousand dollars to buy instruments for needy students. Here again, we were lucky; the generosity of the Nashville community has supplied us with many donated instruments. In fact, all of our seven studio rooms are equipped with usable donated pianos. One manufacturing company in Los Angeles sent us a new complete drum set. Retired musicians have sent us surplus instruments from trumpets to drum sets. We were well related to the community, and the community responded magnificently.

Our volunteer teachers have come from all facets of the Nashville music community. They came from the symphony, the recording studios on Music Row, the area colleges, the public schools, and the network of retired professional musicians. No history or accounting of the Nashville Community Music School would be complete without a tribute to them. They *are* the school. Most of the people listed here have been with us since the beginning and are still with us. Others came a little later. They have given hundreds of hours of their time and have taken their "pay" in the satisfaction of seeing their students succeed. We have changing personnel from year to year, so I regret that everybody cannot be mentioned here. They all deserve the recognition, and we are grateful.

The full-time staff consists of just two people: Ken Wendrich, the executive director, and Juanita Dean, who is all-everything. They have both been on board since day one, keeping things running smoothly at the heart of our organization. And here is a cameo introduction of about a dozen of our teachers at random, just to give you a hint of the quality:

*David Bess:* A big, jolly human being, witty and fun to be around, he loves to teach, and you can see it in his students. He has taught clarinet and guitar.

*Tim Hubler:* A consummate musician with impeccable taste, Tim does more than give private lessons; he also uses his pianistic skills to accompany our students and groups, and he solos on some programs.

*Charles Wyatt:* A colleague and friend since my days in the symphony, where he was and is the principal flutist, he has not only given us prestige, but also has brought his wife, Cindy, into our family of teachers.

*E. Perry Crump:* A remarkable octogenarian, who has been with us from the beginning, is a physician, artist, and musician (he played with Count Basie in Kansas City). He is also a champion tennis player. His youthful spirit inspires our kids. Dr. Crump teaches clarinet.

*John Bright:* A bulwark of our program, since his retirement from the Blair School of Music and the public schools, he has adopted us, giving generously of his teaching and operational know-how. A former symphony member, he teaches violin and viola.

*BMI executive Frances Preston* (right) *at a presentation ceremony with music school leaders* (from left) *Ken Wendrich, Jim Ed Norman, and W. O. Smith, 1987.* [Photo: Don Putnam]

*Phillipa Thompson:* A musician and teacher to her very bone marrow, she is a jazz enthusiast who plays her saxophone in several good organizations around town. A no-nonsense person who gets good results.

*Byron Bach:* A former symphony and sessions (recording) cellist, Byron is an old friend who played with me in the symphony and the Nashville String Quartet. He is a strong teacher who has produced some of our leading young cellists.

*David Vanderkooi:* A brilliant cellist who joined us early in our program, he gave us the prestige of his lofty reputation as a constant recitalist in Nashville. He went out of his way to help us when we needed it.

*Carol Gorodetsky:* A former principal violinist with the Nashville Symphony, she has risen from the youth symphony to the front ranks of the orchestra. A beautiful person in appearance and in heart, she has given our students care and concern as well as musical skill.

*Majorie Campbelle:* A retired Metro school teacher who has been with us since our opening, she specializes in young people's choirs and preschool music fundamentals programs. I have known Mrs. Campbelle for almost forty years. She symbolizes the heart of our project.

*Margaret Dugard:* A Metro teacher who specializes in the newer techniques of teaching young people music (for instance, the Orff method). She is Mrs. Campbelle's daughter and works with our preschoolers.

The credentials and experience of these people and their many colleagues make this one of the top teaching staffs in the Mid-South.

They have gone far to establish our prestige and success. We owe them a lot, and so does the Nashville community.

Our board of directors makes the program possible through its responsibility of raising money. It has been an exhilarating experience for me to be associated with so many gifted people who know how to get things done. Board meetings in the start-up years were an education. Dean Del Sawyer was our first leader, and Buddy Killen was our trail boss; without them we would have gone nowhere. A tower of strength was Jim Ed Norman, president of Warner Brothers in Nashville. Jim Ed took care of many of our needs, including parties for our volunteers. For the record, both Buddy Killen and Jim Ed Norman have been known to play electric bass. That pleases me greatly in view of my own career on acoustic bass. Bill Hudson used his own public relations agency to our advantage. He didn't miss a trick or photo opportunity; we were well known in the community before the first year was out. I never before saw such teamwork between a board of directors and the director of a school. I should mention, too, the savvy advice we got from Don Butler. It was his counsel that set our fee at fifty cents a lesson. There were others who helped formulate policy, people like Eleanor Willis, Peggy Steine, Bruce Hinton (president of MCA Records), and Frank Chalfant. There were and are others, past and present, who have given us the benefit of their time, counsel, and money. We are so grateful to all of them, and I regret that I can't list all of their names. All must accept credit for pushing this project ahead of anticipated schedule.

Since our aim is to reach economically disadvantaged students, we used the school reduced-price lunch program as our guide. If a youngster is on the program, he or she is automatically eligible for admission to our school. Our policy is to work hand in hand with the public school program and teachers. We believe in the one-to-one approach, but we don't start this until the youngster has reached the fourth grade. First, rhythm and fundamentals classes prepare youngsters for the initiation into private lessons. We don't want to waste the time of the professionals who are volunteering their services. We hope that by the time the youngsters get to private lessons, we have set up a profitable exchange of mentor experience and knowledge of the youngster's enthusiasm. A child from an unsuccessful background can often gain dramatically from dealing with a successful person. Something should rub off. It's not necessary to be on a music career track to benefit from focused practice sessions, setting and achieving goals, or presenting a personal achievement to the public. We believe

*Ken Wendrich and W. O. Smith at the W. O. Smith Nashville Community Music School, 1987.* [Photo: Skip Shaw]

that the self-discipline involved in the process can help any developing person, whether or not he or she goes on to pursue a career in music. Music was my ticket out of the ghetto, and my hope is that music can help the youngsters we touch to realize their own ambitions. They will have gained if they can use the self-discipline to become doctors, law-yers, business persons, scientists, or anything honorable and legal.

Throughout our seven years of operation we have had an aver-age of 250 students and 45 teachers a year. Our executive director, Ken Wendrich, says we have three levels of students: first the gifted, the music career track students, the ones we hope to point toward profes-sional careers; then the ones who will keep music as a supplementary interest in their lives; and third, a group who we hope will benefit incidentally from the process. As Wendrich points out, "We don't measure our achievement in typical terms of success. We know we're doing good work in some way through every one of our students."

I wish there were a way to follow every one of our students to show the total impact of our program. I can do that now, in a small way, by citing the experiences of two of our most successful students. They are Joe Chappel, a viola student, and Lisa Williamson, a cellist. Both of these Community Music School students wound up with scholarships in music, first in the prep program at Blair and then at Oberlin College in Ohio.

I once said in a speech that I hoped to live long enough to deliver some of our graduates to the major music establishments in the United States. I made that speech in 1984, and by 1989 it had become a reality. I literally delivered Lisa Williamson to Oberlin, driv-ing her there from Nashville when she enrolled. It was an intensely proud and emotional moment for me. The fact that one of our level-one students made it to one of America's premier music schools was proof of our investment in her and of her investment in us. It was no surprise to me that Joe Chappel went the same route a year later. I didn't get the chance to deliver him as I was in the hospital at the time, but I was equally proud and emotional about his success.

The case of Lisa Williamson is especially meaningful to me. She got everything in her development that I did not get in mine. As for me, I used to be wracked with envy every time I went to a sym-phony rehearsal or concert. I would hear all these fine young players tossing off the most difficult musical passages with ease and con-fidence. They were all graduates of the Blair School of Music, Indiana University, Juilliard, or other great schools. I had to put a lot of my technique together by observing and imitating them. My eighteen years in the symphony gave me enough time to be competitive, but under stress of survival. I did manage to get there, but it took me a lot longer to unlearn bad habits and faulty techniques. That is why I am so happy for Lisa. She has worked hard and deserves everything that has come her way. At age fifteen, she was at a point that I didn't reach until I was nearly sixty. I only hope that the Nashville Community Music School can do this for many other kids who otherwise wouldn't have a chance.

Music was my key to a good life. Time after time, it opened doors for me—to school, to work, to friendships and professional associations. I give thanks to Nashville, a warm, loving, and concerned community, for making my dream a reality.

# ENCORE

On Thursday morning, May 30, 1991, at Baptist Hospital in Nashville, William Oscar Smith lost the final round of an eight-month struggle against cancer. Just one month before he passed away, he completed the last chapter of this book. It gave him great satisfaction and pleasure to know that he had seen the project through to the end.

In his introduction to *Sideman,* written a month before the onset of his illness, Smitty summarized his life in these words: "It has been a long and interesting gig for me, and I have played with abandon, giving myself to the music and to the life it opened up to me. I embrace it all, body and soul."

He did, he truly did. And the melody lingers on.

# INDEX

References in *italic* are to illustrations